FLAUBERT'S STRAIGHT AND SUSPECT SAINTS

PURDUE UNIVERSITY MONOGRAPHS
IN ROMANCE LANGUAGES

William M. Whitby, Editor Emeritus

Howard Mancing, General Editor

Enrique Caracciolo-Trejo and Djelal Kadir, Editors for Spanish

Allen G. Wood, Editor for French

Volume 36

Aimée Israel-Pelletier

Flaubert's Straight and Suspect Saints

AIMÉE ISRAEL-PELLETIER

FLAUBERT'S STRAIGHT AND SUSPECT SAINTS

THE UNITY OF *TROIS CONTES*

JOHN BENJAMINS PUBLISHING COMPANY
Amsterdam/Philadelphia

1991

Cover illustration: *Salomé*, 1870, Alexandre Georges Henri Regnault.
The Metropolitan Museum of Art, Gift of George F. Baker, 1916 (16.95).

Library of Congress Cataloging in Publication Data

Israel-Pelletier, Aimée.
   Flaubert's straight and suspect saints : the unity of "Trois contes" / Aimée Israel-Pel-
letier.
       p.   cm. -- (Purdue University monographs in Romance languages, ISSN 0165-
8743; v. 36)
Includes bibliographical references and index.
1. Flaubert, Gustave, 1821-1880. Trois contes. 2. Flaubert, Gustave, 1821-1880 --
Technique. 3. Narration (Rhetoric). I. Title. II. Series.
PQ2246.T73I87   1991
843'.8 -- dc 20   91-30579
ISBN 90 272 1757 2 (Eur.) / ISBN 1-55619-300-9 (US) (alk. paper) (hardbd.)
ISBN 90 272 1758 0 (Eur.) / ISBN 1-55619-301-7 (US) (alk. paper) (paperbd.)   CIP

To my parents, Pauline and Saul Israel

La tâche que j'entreprends sera exécutée par un autre. J'aurai mis sur la voie quelqu'un de mieux doué et de plus *né*. Vouloir donner à la prose le rythme du vers (en la laissant prose et très prose) et écrire la vie ordinaire comme on écrit l'histoire ou l'épopée (sans dénaturer le sujet) est peut-être une absurdité... Mais c'est peut-être aussi une grande tentative et très originale!

—Flaubert

L'utopie est familière à l'écrivain, parce que l'écrivain est un donateur de sens: sa tâche (ou sa jouissance) est de donner des sens, des noms, et il ne peut le faire que s'il y a paradigme, déclic du *oui/non,* alternance de deux valeurs; pour lui, le monde est une médaille, une monnaie, une double surface de lecture, dont sa propre réalité occupe le revers et l'utopie l'avers.

—Barthes

Table of Contents

Acknowledgments .... *xi*

Introduction: Meaning and Character in Flaubert 1

1. The *Trois contes* 17

2. The Women of Pont-l'Evêque: A Subversive Sorority 25

3. Murdering the Father: Re-writing the Legend
    of Saint Julien l'Hospitalier 59

4. Reading the Landscape of Desire and Writing 89

Conclusion: Straight and Suspect Texts: A Poetics of Transgression 109

Notes 131

Bibliography and Selected Works on *Trois contes* 151

Index 163

Acknowledgments

I wish to thank the University of Rochester and Director Robert Freeman of the Eastman School of Music for awarding me a Mellon grant which enabled me to complete parts of this book.

I am very grateful to John Baldo, Robert Chumbley, Ruth Gross, Hans Kellner, and John McGowan, who read the manuscript and contributed valuable advice. I would also like to acknowledge my debt to English Showalter, who supported and encouraged my work during the difficult early years.

Chapter 3 has already appeared in slightly different form under the title "Desire and Writing: An Allegorical Reading of Flaubert's *Hérodias,*" in the *Selected Proceedings 32nd Mountain Interstate Foreign Language Conference,* ed. Gregorio C. Martin (Winston-Salem: Wake Forest U, 1984) 153-58. I wish to express my thanks for permission to use it here.

Special thanks go to Philippe Pelletier for his always sensible advice and for his friendship, and to my daughter Pauline for the joy and love she inspires in me. I also want to thank Mary Erickson, Cheryl Reitano, and Cindy Sturcken for the care and attention they gave Pauline during the writing of this book.

Introduction
Meaning and Character in Flaubert

It is a curious fact that despite the number of articles devoted to the individual stories which make up the *Trois contes*, only a handful treat the work as a unity. Nearly all tend to view the three stories as condensed versions of the larger works which preceded them; thus, *Un Cœur simple* is compared to *Madame Bovary,* while *Saint Julien* and *Hérodias* are related to *La Tentation* and *Salammbô*, respectively. The *Trois contes*, I will argue, occupies a distinct place in the Flaubertian corpus. The last completed work, it represents a dramatic change of attitude on the part of Flaubert toward his characters and toward the status of fiction and illusion in life and in art.

As nowhere else in Flaubert's work, the three stories end on an unambiguously positive note. Félicité, Julien, and Iaokanann are visionary characters whose desires and fantasies seriously threaten to undermine and disrupt the traditional order of things. The three characters, each in his or her own manner, succeed in overcoming the limitations imposed on them by an oppressive and corrupt society. They achieve this by a deliberate and systematic subversion of the established order. This is unique in Flaubert's work. Although the characters themselves and the world they inhabit do not differ significantly from the characters and the landscape we find in Flaubert's earlier novels, their desires and aspirations are not frustrated by society or undermined by Flaubert as are, for instance, Emma's desires and Frédéric's illusions. Rather, the characters are saved in a glorious manner and serve as an example and a source of inspiration to others. Thus, for example, even though at the end of *La Tentation*, Saint Antoine is rewarded by the vision of Christ in the "disk of the sun," he is nonetheless doomed to repeat the scenario of his frustrations till the end. Not so with Julien. He is lifted up to Heaven in the arms of Christ himself, with whom he becomes literally one and the same. Moreover, whereas at the end of *Madame Bovary,* Homais is triumphant, his counterpart in *Un Cœur simple*, Bourais, is revealed to be an immoral man, a scoundrel publicly ridiculed and banished from the town.

In the *Trois contes,* Flaubert not only allows his characters to win in the end but makes it possible for them to live their lives working steadfastly toward that end. He refrains from exposing to irony their efforts and illusions as he does with characters like Emma, Frédéric, and Saint Antoine. In previous works from *Madame Bovary* to *La Tentation*, Flaubert takes pleasure in undermining his characters' (and fiction's) confidence in novelistic versions of life. The characters' capacities to produce fictions and live through them are invariably undercut by Flaubert's intent to prove the insufficiencies of illusion in the face of reality. The characters fail in the end both because the world seems unresponsive to their desires and, more seriously, because Flaubert dismisses their aspirations, making it clear to the reader that their uniqueness and superiority can be reduced to the level of that of their adversaries. Emma is, finally, as mediocre as Homais and Charles; and Saint Antoine, though not mediocre, is caught in self-generated visions which are not justified by anything that can be found in the world. In the *Trois contes*, on the contrary, Flaubert presents illusion and imagination as successful modes of psychic adjustment, as positive means of accommodating desire and influencing the world. Illusion is presented as an effective way for the characters to challenge the laws and conventions of a system which alienates them. The private language of illusion sustains the characters in their struggle against the system. In addition, it proves to be equally successful at undermining the system itself and influencing others to do the same. All this, naturally, will need to be defended, and I will do so in the subsequent chapters.

The last completed work of Flaubert, the *Trois contes* is ironically both an ending and a turning point. It is as if from *Madame Bovary* to *La Tentation*, Flaubert was unable, perhaps unwilling, to accept his main characters' capacity to believe in fictions about the world. Before the *Trois contes,* characters who represent the bourgeois order are given a great deal of weight in his work. Their unimaginative fictions about the world (fictions of power, of propriety, and of progress) are, in a certain sense, legitimized by the attention Flaubert lavishes upon them. They are also more seriously legitimized by his inability to imagine socially integrated characters as other than victorious. In the *Trois contes*, Flaubert might be said to have discovered something about the role of fiction in life and to have come to terms with his antagonism toward characters who stand out from the rest. Instead of undermining their desires, Flaubert accepts, even valorizes, their faculty to fictionalize scenes of bliss, union, revolution, and violence in a way he had not previously done.

Given Flaubert's customary identification with his characters, it is not unlikely that he used the *Trois contes* to play out a scenario whereby writing novels, like the illusions of his characters, becomes an imaginative and successful response to the world. Flaubert wrote the *Trois contes* during an especially difficult time in his life; *Bouvard et Pécuchet* presented enormous problems of execution; Flaubert was experiencing financial problems; and he seemed to despair more than ever before about the political and moral climate around him. At this time, too, he was close to friends and fellow writers like George Sand, Zola, Daudet, and others who believed fervently that literature had an obligation to address social problems and that, moreover, it had the power to influence and change some of those problems. These writers were responding in a practical way to a different social situation from that faced by an earlier generation of writers. Baudelaire and the Flaubert of *Madame Bovary, L'Education sentimentale, La Tentation,* and other early works, were still defining themselves in terms of Romanticism. But in the 1870s and 1880s, post-Romantic themes like the emptiness of life, the quasi-religious conviction of the "nothingness" of the world, and the defense of the superiority and autonomy of art and the artist had become, at least for many novelists, difficult inspirations to sustain in the face of mounting social discontent and political defeat and embarrassment. Thus, these novelists were moved to write on behalf of workers, peasants, and others on the fringes of the ruling classes; they were moved to give voice to the grievances of these groups in a language that was not available to the socially and intellectually disadvantaged. I am not suggesting that Flaubert was inspired to address social concerns in the *Trois contes*. I do not believe that he was. I am suggesting, however, that disappointed by the course his work and his life in general had taken and surrounded as he was by a sense of purpose and optimism regarding the role of fiction as an agent of change, in the *Trois contes* Flaubert might have been predisposed to fantasize and dramatize the possibility that fiction and illusion can have an effect on the world. The fantasy that illusion can exercise a real and effective force, that it can disrupt and disarm the established system, informs the *Trois contes* and possibly *Bouvard et Pécuchet* as well.

But quite apart from the valorization of illusion and quite apart from what seems to be a rethinking of the role of fiction in art and life, the *Trois contes* presents a valuable opportunity for looking at how Flaubert might have imagined the process of writing, how he might have envisaged and worked through problems of representation, style, and allegiance to his literary antecedents. Written at a time when he was having serious doubts about his capacity to write, the three stories bear the marks of an attempt to work out problems with language and representation. The three stories can be read as allegories of the writing process; each highlights a problem in representation and dramatizes some of the aesthetic and psychological constraints placed on the writing self at the moment of writing.

We tend to think of Flaubert as belonging in some ways to modern literature, a sort of Mallarmé of the novel. Flaubert is perceived, and rightly so, as the precursor of the *nouveau roman,* the chief inspiration for a preoccupation with language and the writing process, and as the original dismantler of fixed reference. But a precursor's work is not without ambivalence. There lie his interest and his value. Unquestionably, Flaubert marks a turning point in the history of the novel, a point at which two notions, one, the notion of the adequacy of language to express being and, two, the notion of the self as a stable reference point, were beginning to be undermined. The case for his modernity, however, has been exaggerated. This is perhaps not entirely unsalutary given the value Flaubert himself placed on exaggeration. He claimed that exaggeration was a sign of genius and an expression of the desire for perfection: "Et qu'est-ce que c'est que l'idéal, si ce n'est ce grossissement-là?"[1] Nonetheless, Flaubert's perception of the relationship between language and being, and his conception of character in fiction, are by no means issues he had addressed in a consistent manner. Rather, these problems of representation manifest themselves as a vague malaise regarding the insufficiencies of language for expressing the complexities of desire and thought. Flaubert's aesthetics is informed by radically different concerns from those found in the works of modernist writers such as Robbe-Grillet, Beckett, and Butor, writers to whom he has been often compared. Flaubert's work is most intriguing to me not for how it illustrates the modernist's concerns, but for the way it tries to resolve these concerns, often by skirting the issues.

Recent criticism, even when it has argued for the meaning-fulness of Flaubert's texts, has tended to undermine the notions of psychological depth and authorial intention. It seems at times when reading Roland Barthes, Jonathan Culler, Gérard Genette, or Jean Ricardou, some of the thinkers who continue to influence the way we read and teach Flaubert, that to speak of the meaning of a narrative or of the psychology of a character in Flaubert is to commit a serious conceptual mistake. The critics I have just mentioned, however, are careful not to claim that in Flaubert subject matter is absent, narrative technique is drastically disrupted, or characters are not psychologically grounded. They only assert that his work "resists and problematizes" (Culler) or "devalues" (Genette) attempts at discussing it in these terms. Flaubert's aim, Culler suggests, is to demoralize and frustrate his readers in their efforts to make sense of the work. For Genette, Flaubert's texts subvert narrative expectations, elude meaning; novelistic details have no symbolic or even explanatory potential but are empty tokens of meaningfulness placed deliberately to distract the reader and paralyze the narrative. Exceptions granted, character and psychology are dismissed by most critics in readings of Flaubert in favor of discussing language and, especially, the resistance to meaning in his work.

Without minimizing Flaubert's modernity, the present study tries to bring into perspective different and, at times, contradictory impulses at work in his conception of language and character. I want to show, through the study of the *Trois contes*, that Flaubert is a writer at the crossroads of two opposing aesthetics. On the one hand, there are values which can be roughly identified with the classical tradition's confidence in language's signifying capacity, its concern for style, for clarity of meaning, plausibility, symmetry, adequation of form to content, emphasis on the text's coherence, reliance on "strong" centers of consciousness as ways to inform us about the world, and the value of communicating and entertaining ("plaire et enseigner"). On the other hand, there are the modernist indifference to subject matter, a devaluation of the notions of coherence and depth, an undermining of character psychology and authorial intention, some strong reservations concerning language's signifying function, a sense that reading cannot teach us anything about ourselves or about the world, and an emphasis on the activity of writing as an end in itself. It is obvious to me that Flaubert's work as well as his explicit references to aesthetics aligns more cogently with classical rather than modernist aesthetics. But my aim in this book is not to deradicalize or to simplify Flaubert by insisting on his affinities with a literary past. Nor do I want to dismiss the modernist crisis of language and representation as it surely begins to manifest itself in Flaubert's work. I do, however, want to draw special attention to the way Flaubert tried to deal with this crisis, the way he tried to make sense of a vague loss of confidence in language's ability to represent ideas and desire. The *Trois contes* is an exemplary work for such a task mainly because in this work we find Flaubert himself, more consistently than anywhere else before, trying to understand what moves him to write, how he writes, and what distinguishes him as a writer of his time.

In the process of trying to address these questions, both in the *Trois contes* and elsewhere, Flaubert may indeed have underestimated the depth of his problem with writing. Throughout his correspondence, for example, he shows a tendency to simplify both his goal and that of classical writers by defining the ideal style as one in which language serves as a perfect reflector of thought. Flaubert's diagnosis of the problem of representation as trying to say too much with too little, "trop de choses à dire et pas assez de forme," cannot account entirely for his difficulties with language and writing. But this is not the point for me. Flaubert tried to resolve what he vaguely perceived as a problematic or uncomfortable fit between language and being by looking for ways to expand the expressive potential of language through "style," by focusing on the possibilities of prose through narrative and stylistic techniques. The *Trois contes*, here again, is an excellent illustration of a successful attempt to expand prose. For instance, by constructing narratives that accommodate equally well two different and conflicting levels of meaning, a straight and an ironic reading, Flaubert does indeed expand the space of representation; for one thing, he opens the text to complex, contradictory, and yet equally legitimate, interpretations.

This enlargement of the narrative space is inspired by Flaubert's recurrent desire to enrich prose, to make it more meaning-ful. Flaubert's discovery that in literature all is a matter of perspective ("Il n'y a pas de vrai! Il n'y a que des manières de voir" [8: 370]) leads him to diagnose the problem of prose as resulting from too limited a perspective on the world. This is why, in a sense, he defines poetry principally as a way of seeing the world. "La poésie n'est qu'une manière de percevoir les objets extérieurs" (3: 149). For Flaubert, the advantage poetry has over prose is that its meaning is suggested rather than stated; and suggestion, by its very nature, is an expansion of the space of expression. The vague sentiment that words are somehow in a troubled relationship to thought and being does not elicit in Flaubert a sense of ontological uncertainty. Rather, and here is his significant contribution to the novel, it translates into a practical and ambitious plan to make language more expressive, more responsive to what he perceived (and strongly believed) to be the complexity of human experience and the richness of thought. To this extent, Proust and Sarraute are his most immediate and faithful successors. Flaubert's valorization of prose and style does not suggest, as is often argued, that he undermined meaning in the scheme of values. The characters' psychology and interpretation are of central concern in Flaubert's work as a whole. As a reader, it was characters and characters' psychology that he admired and enjoyed in the works of Balzac and Zola, and correspondingly, it was what he especially disliked about Hugo's novels. The post-Romantic notion of the meaninglessness of life may have marked Flaubert's early works, but it is not reflected in the *Trois contes*.[2] For Flaubert, ideas are never lacking. What he perceives as insufficient, on the other hand, are the forms in which to cast these ideas, "la plastique." The richness of desire and ideas and the notion that language is an inadequate and suspect form of expression have always been at the core of the Flaubertian conception of character.

Flaubert's often repeated goal of enlarging the space of representation by enriching prose is one we also find expressed in art in the nineteenth century. Impressionism, a contemporary movement, sought to create effects of light and air as a way of breaking up the plane of representation. It tried, as did Flaubert in the novel and Rimbaud in poetry, to open the frame of representation to connotations that could not be represented in the earlier idiom. Hence the difficulties. Because in trying to resolve these difficulties, artists and writers, invariably, had to address problems of execution, it is often assumed that they valorized their media (paint and language) at the expense of subject matter. But, for most, the subject matter of reality was still of primary concern. It was, at least initially, as they perceived it, the reason for seeking new forms. Flaubert's narrative space is not a space where language folds back on itself in a self-reflexive gesture, as in Mallarmé for example. Though questions of language are dramatized in Flaubert, they are not the main subject of concern in the novels. Flaubert's interest remains very much the representation of mental states, of desire, and of reality. Flaubert's novelistic space is not an empty and meaning-less space, but one which aims to deepen and enrich language so that it can more fully express desire and represent the world.

Flaubert's own estimate of his place in literature is rather conservative, as we would expect. He considered his work as fully within the "tradition." He was convinced that his aesthetics had more in common with classical writers, both the Ancients and the French, than with his contemporaries: "Ah! que je voudrais être savant! et que je ferais un beau livre sous ce titre: *De l'interpretation de l'antiquité*! Car je suis sûr d'être dans la tradition; ce que j'y mets de plus, c'est le sentiment moderne" (3: 137). There is in Flaubert a nostalgia for the "golden age" of literature. As he saw it, writers of the past experienced no problems in trying to represent ideas because they understood the laws which govern expression. They also knew the value of style both as a way of seducing the reader and of communicating meaning ("plaire et enseigner"); and, unlike Flaubert himself, they were writing to a public who appreciated their works. This idealization and simplification of the past is one of many indications, some more explicit, as in the letters, that Flaubert felt overwhelmed by the task he had undertaken to make prose as rich as poetry. To develop the possibilities of prose, Flaubert read and reread the classics, looking for inspiration and instruction, looking especially for the way that language served to express ideas, "la pensée." Hence, his preoccupation with the "mot juste," with sonority, with "harmony" between words and sentences. Though he admired Ancient and French classical writers, Flaubert esteemed them mainly, as the *Correspondance* shows, for their command of art. He refers far less to their knowledge of human nature, for instance. He believed that people and institutions were more diverse and more complicated in the nineteenth century than in earlier times. Classical writers appealed to him principally because they valued style; some, like La Bruyère, were obsessed by it.

Style, which remained Flaubert's constant preoccupation throughout his career, was hardly commented on by contemporary critics except to point out its oddities. Even Flaubert's closest friends, Bouilhet, Colet, Sand, Turgenev, writers themselves, thought him too exacting when it came to stylistic concerns. However, throughout his career Flaubert believed that the future of the novel lay in a more ambitious exploitation of prose. Prose, Flaubert was certain, had the potential for developing a rich and subtle language that could rival and, ultimately, replace the language of poetry. Poetry was the form of the past, and prose, that of the future. Flaubert's concern that the language of fiction be written and read with the same attention as the language of poetry is central to his aesthetics; and it is a significant cause of his many difficulties with writing. He shares this concern with several writers of his generation. Poetic prose to Flaubert, like prose poetry to Baudelaire, Rimbaud, and Mallarmé, for example, is a hybrid genre valued for the way it combines breadth of meaning with economy of expression. "Quel est celui de nous qui n'a pas, dans ses jours d'ambition, rêvé le miracle d'une prose poétique," wrote Baudelaire in the preface to the *Petits poèmes en prose*.[3]

On the whole, before Marcel Proust, readers who discussed Flaubert's style in earnest were apt to consider Flaubert's syntactical peculiarities, his "odd grammar," as instances of error or of poor writing.[4] For Albert Thibaudet, the great analyst of desire was not "un écrivain de race"; Flaubert was not a born writer; he had to work very hard to achieve the effects he wanted and his style showed it. His style was ponderous, his grammar sloppy. Flaubert's preoccupation with language, his syntactic peculiarities, those very features that his contemporaries dismissed, wrongly, as negligence in writing, are perceived today as the hallmarks of Flaubert's modernity, as signs that the novel, under his pen, moved into a problematical sphere where it no longer served as a "statement about anything in particular" but became, instead, concerned with its own activity as a linguistic artifact. Thus, Jonathan Culler can write that in Flaubert "awkwardness becomes a feeble sign of the written,"[5] that in his style "discontinuity, fragmentation, awkwardness, flatness, are modes of ironic distancing which produce a space of uncertainty."Culler concludes that "it is quite understandable, then, that those who praise Flaubert as stylist should find themselves in the awkward and indeed paradoxical position of praising what they feel at times to be clumsy writing."[6]

But Flaubert's "odd" style is, as Proust suggested, deliberately awkward; it had to accommodate certain aesthetic exigencies. Proust's discussion of Flaubert's style remains the most enlightening to date. "Awkwardness," Proust recognized, is an effect of Flaubert's conception. It reflects a certain perspective on the world and a certain effort to bring this new vision to the surface. Flaubert does not seek to be awkward, quite the opposite. Moreover, given the time and attention he spent revising his work, he could not have failed to detect a style he, at any rate, would have considered awkward. Flaubert considered fragmentation and the lack of unity as a serious flaw in a work of art. He always aimed for unity and suffered when he could not find the "fil du collier." He criticized Michelet's *La Bible de l' humanité* for just such a reason: "Ce qu'il y a d'atroce dans ce . . . livre, c'est le procédé fragmentaire";[7] elsewhere he cried out, "L'unité, l'unité, tout est là!" (1: 375).

Whether or not one thinks Flaubert's style odd, what is unique about it in the novel is the way it demands that the reader read carefully for allusions. Flaubert's style highlights the semiotic or symbolic and meaningful potential of novelistic detail. It calls attention to the material qualities of language, to sound, to rhythm, to balance and harmony, to repetition. The attention placed on these material qualities, unusual in the novel, sometimes slows down or perturbs the logic of the signifying chain. As a result, the text might strike the reader as odd. This interruption of normal processing of information which might strike us as odd in the novel would not strike us as such in poetry, and we are less likely to refer to a poem's style as odd. We expect that a poem will take liberties with our expectations. However one may characterize Flaubert's style, it is the result of an attempt to make language as suggestive as possible, as subtle as poetry. Form and content, style and sensibility, are two faces of the same aesthetic coin. Neither term could carry more value than the other, style being, as Flaubert pointed out, an absolute way of seeing the world. Thus, Flaubert's obsessive attention to stylistic details such as harmony between the parts, the right word, the appropriate rhythm, the elimination of assonances and repetitions, and the absence of the authorial voice, is calculated to generate meaning, be it singular or plural, be it, in the case of the *Trois contes,* either straight or suspect, or both. Flaubert's prose, like poetry, suggests (that is, it seeks to mean) by a deliberate and complex manipulation of language; "d'où tout le temps que j'y mets," he writes Louise Colet (3: 20). As important as language is in Flaubert's aesthetics, it does not have primacy over meaning. By insisting and demonstrating that the language and procedures of prose can be as rich as the language and procedures of poetry, Flaubert elevates the writing of novels from its pedestrian status to that of an art form. This has to be considered Flaubert's principal contribution to the novel.

When inspired by structuralist and post-structuralist criticism, Flaubertian critics of the past two decades have worked on the assumption that to value language and to multiply the possibilities of meaning, as Flaubert likes to do, is to undermine meaning. But to multiply possibilities of meaning is theoretically to undermine meaning only if we think of meaning as absolute and univocal. One need not imagine that because meaning is not perceived as absolute, all interpretations are then acceptable and inconclusive, as Stanley Fish has rightly argued. Ironically, Flaubert's predilection for overdetermining his narratives, for offering more than one possible interpretation of events and characters in a given work, provides the strongest argument for the devaluation of meaning in his work. How, for example, can a narrative be both straight and ironic? But narrative overdetermination in Flaubert aims primarily to frustrate easy reading pleasures, those conventionally circumscribed interpretations which display a lack of sensitivity to the demands and nuances of the all-important aesthetic dimension. Overdetermination thwarts responses to the work that tend to fix and limit its meaning, to destroy its suggestiveness.

In the best nineteenth-century tradition of artistic elitism, Flaubert's narratives are meant to confuse and, consequently, exclude only a particular type of reader, namely the reader who, in haste or blindness, is apt to reduce literature *solely* to what it means rather than to how it means. To give attention to how a text means, one must, among other things, look closely at the structure, language, and images of the text and interpret stylistic gestures and details in the same way one would in approaching a poetic text. Meaning is not an individual creation of the reader. It is the product of an effort to put together aspects contained in the text according to a system of conventions which are assimilated from reading other texts both by Flaubert and by other writers before him. Thus, though overdetermination may discourage some readers from searching for any meaning at all, the reader is always invited by Flaubert to search in depth and between the words and lines for the vision that animates a given text. Flaubert does not fight against meaning but against *easy access*. Michel Butor is absolutely right when he suggests that Flaubert "fait partie de ces auteurs qui préfèrent que l'on ne voie pas trop vite comment les choses sont faites, qui s'expliquent, mais en partie, pour que les structures agissent plus fortement dans l'ombre, prennent certains lecteurs par surprise."[8] Flaubert's preference for a style that demands that the reader pause to construct the meaning of a text, a style that requires that the reader take time to read closely ("lentement"), helps to explain Flaubert's frustrations with the theater, a genre which had always attracted him but in which he was never successful. The language of the theater must be accessible to the public immediately, not after some thought; ideas must be easily communicated or the play will not have an immediate effect on its audience. Theatrical language is frustrating to Flaubert because it lacks depth and materiality; its meaning is too transparent. It bubbles and fizzes like seltzer water at the surface: "Le style théâtral commence à m'agacer. Ces petites phrases courtes, ce pétillement continu m'irrite à la manière de l'eau de Seltz" (7: 78).

Flaubert's narratives, both in the *Trois contes* and elsewhere, are most intriguing when they artfully propose alternative and at times conflicting solutions to sensitive interpretive issues, when they offer the reader more than one possibility of interpretation. But the *Trois contes* remains the best example for illustrating Flaubert's strategies for making meaning the focus of the reader's experience of the work: Is Julien a saint or a sinner? Is Félicité really as simple as she seems? Why is Herod fascinated by Iaokanann? How do we interpret the inspired endings of the three stories? Are the characters victorious over those who undermine their aspirations, or are they victims of society, destiny, or stupidity and greed? More generally, do the narratives allow the reader to speak with a reasonable degree of "certainty" about their meaning? I think that it is not only possible to recover meaning in the *Trois contes,* but that, moreover, meaning itself is thematized in the tales. The *Trois contes* poses some important questions regarding the meaning of texts: Who, for example, authorizes the meaning of a document (the dogma in *Un Cœur simple*, the prophecies in *Saint Julien*, the phrase "Pour qu'il grandisse, il faut que je diminue" in *Hérodias*)? Can meaning slip from the hands of those who have the authority to define it into the hands of the individual who is asked to accept it as truth, dogma, law? Can the authority to fix meaning pass from author to reader, for instance? How and at what price does meaning slip from one source to the other? And finally, what motivates the desire for meaning? The search for meaning is self-consciously dramatized in the stories as the necessary condition of the characters' existence and of their survival in the world. Furthermore, Flaubert creates in the *Trois contes* a work which clearly calls, dares, the reader to take up the challenge of interpreting the stories, of, precisely, fixing their meaning. To refuse to do so, as I argue in the chapter on *Hérodias*, is to act like Herod, to opt for aesthetic contemplation over responsibility, to choose death over life; it is also, perhaps, to choose the common or straight reading of the text over the singular or subversive one.

Félicité, Julien, and Herod are, all three, characters who are called upon to interpret words and texts that organize their lives and exercise power over them. These characters are, in other words, readers and figures for the reader. (To the extent that reading is a metaphor for writing, they also stand for a certain aspect of Flaubert himself.) The reader can see himself or herself doubly reflected in the images of each of the three characters. On the one hand, the reader is represented in the figure of the common reader of the straight text, the naïve (Félicité), the passive (Julien), and the confused (Herod). On the other hand, the reader might see himself or herself in the figures of the three saints, not the legendary saints, to be sure, but the saints whose stories Flaubert has written (interpreted himself from other texts) in the *Trois contes*. The three stories of the *Trois contes* are some of the most richly suggestive in Flaubert, and the reader is called upon to participate in the formulation of this meaning.

Flaubert believed that a "good" work of art, like truth and beauty, is characterized by internal order, harmony, and unity. He considered that this unity is hidden for some but evident to others. Without structural and stylistic coherence, he was adamant, a work of art had no merit. Flaubert's critical perspective falls into what Wolfgang Iser has termed the "classical norm of interpretation." This view holds that meaning is at the service of a mimetic truth; it manifests itself in the text as a harmonized totality of balance, order, and completeness.[9] Despite the diversity of its parts, despite complexity and contradictions, the whole constitutes a stable and homogeneous view. The writer, Flaubert felt, having internalized the principle of unity in a given situation or in a given work through his experience in life, and armed with a method of operation, can reproduce that principle in his own work. The writer is a reader of the world; the goal of style is to be the perfect vessel or most faithful representation of desire and of thought. Throughout his career, Flaubert never doubted or undermined this goal. He expected experience and art to confirm his belief that a perfect fit between what is written (provided it is well written) and what it refers to is possible. He was joyful when, for example, having written a scene or used a particular word, he found it repeated in a "real" context: "J'ai eu, aujourd'hui, un grand succès," he writes.

> J'ai trouvé ce matin, dans le *Journal de Rouen*, une phrase du maire faisant un discours, laquelle phrase j'avais, la veille, écrite *textuellement* dans la Bovary (dans un discours de préfet, à des comices agricoles). Non seulement c'était la même idée, les mêmes mots, mais les mêmes *assonances* de style. Je ne cache pas que ce sont de ces choses qui me font plaisir. Quand la littérature arrive à la précision de résultat d'une science exacte, c'est roide. (3: 285)

Flaubert expresses the same excitement in a similar situation. Having discovered that his interpretation of a question in botany was confirmed by his expert friend, Flaubert, in a letter to Caroline, exclaims: "*J'avais raison!* ... j'avais raison parce que l'esthétique est le Vrai, et qu'à un certain degré intellectuel (quand on a de la méthode) on ne se trompe pas. La réalité ne se plie point à l'idéal, mais le confirme. . . . Ah! ah! je triomphe! Ça, c'est un succès! et qui me flatte" (9: 33). This confirmation of the writer's interpretation holds equally true for the reader as well, not the "premier venu" perhaps, but the reader who can perceive the unifying element. Flaubert's critical stance relies not on the assumption that unity is in the interpreter's mind only, but that it is in the text, insofar as the text is derived directly from the structure of the "real world." "Tout ce qu'on invente est vrai" (3: 291), Flaubert suggests, provided that what one has invented has internal coherence, that is to say, provided it obeys universal laws.

In summary, I read the *Trois contes* as an ironic text, insofar as this characterization implies a duality between two superimposed semantic levels where one level puts into question the other but where neither one is more legitimate than the other. I argue that the three stories can be read as straight accounts of just what it is they appear to be about as well as suspect narratives, more subtle and subversive accounts of the power of the characters' desires to reshape the self and subvert "the order of things."

The unity of the *Trois contes* is a factor of Flaubert's change of attitude toward his characters and toward the role of illusion. Flaubert dramatizes through his characters not the tragedy and shortcomings of illusion but its power to shape and transform the self and the world. He creates characters who are victorious in the end over those who represent the dominant order in society. This is unique in Flaubert's work and marks a radical change of perspective. At the same time, Flaubert dramatizes his encounters with language and with the writing process. It is as if by allowing himself to create a new scenario for his characters, Flaubert discovered a way of rethinking language and writing, of rethinking his own illusions (or disillusionment) with regards to fiction. My work focuses on the characters' desires as well as on the writing self, on a kind of autobiography of the writing process.

In Chapter 1, I discuss the circumstances under which the *Trois contes* was undertaken and suggest that the work might offer us a new perspective on how to interpret *Bouvard et Pécuchet*.

Chapter 2 deals with *Un Cœur simple*. I argue that the story of Félicité as a selfless and naïve victim is but the superficial side of a more complex subtext. This subtext is a text authored by Félicité herself with the complicity of the women of Pont-l'Evêque. My approach, here, is feminist and psychoanalytic. This chapter does not focus on Flaubert's aesthetics nor does it develop the allegory of writing, as do the next two chapters. However, I deal with these concerns in the conclusion.

Chapter 3 turns to *Saint Julien l'Hospitalier*. Julien's struggle to differentiate himself from his father and his father's world reflects, on the one level, Flaubert's ambivalent feelings of inadequacy regarding his own vocation and celebrity when set against the backdrop of those aspects of his father. On another level, Julien's crisis reflects Flaubert's attitude toward classicism and what he perceived to be its affinities with his own art. Flaubert's acknowledged vacillation between "lyricism" and "realism," dramatized in *Saint Julien,* is a sign of his attempt to come to terms with his originality, his relationship to the "great" literatures of the past. The opposition "lyricism" and "realism" which Flaubert himself makes is a false one, while the concern he has of writing "du Balzac châteaubrianisé" hides a larger and more troubling concern, namely the fear of deviating from the principles of classical literature, in which he strongly and unswervingly believed. I establish a connection between Julien's father and classicism and suggest that Flaubert draws up a case for an alternative to, or an alternate form of, writing, using the mother as a model.

Hérodias is Flaubert's most abstract text. In Chapter 4, I show that it can be read as an allegory of the writing process, a narrative of the way desire (the idea, or whatever else one might call it) is shaped, transformed in the very act of writing. My own interpretation takes on an abstract dimension as I try to unravel linguistic categories from the description of the landscape. This leads me to argue for a relationship between Salomé's dance and the activity of writing, between Iaokanann's (or John the Baptist's) head and the linguistic sign, between Iaokanann's voice and Flaubert's "gueuloir," between words and the body of Flaubert.

In the conclusion, I argue for the unity of the work and for its unique place in Flaubert's corpus. In writing the *Trois contes*, Flaubert discovered a way to reconcile within himself classical principles of representation with the less than ideal realities of language. By working through his characters, he built scenarios in which he was able to imagine a kind of language capable of reflecting and, paradoxically, of transfiguring reality. In other words, he found a way to conceive of and to believe in a language that could translate desire and illusion into action. This may have been no more than a fantasy on Flaubert's part; yet, it allowed him to return to *Bouvard et Pécuchet* with a sense of optimism concerning the future of illusion in life and in art.

1

The *Trois contes*

> Voici donc ce que j'ai résolu. J'ai dans la tête trois romans, trois
> contes de genres tout différents et demandant une manière toute
> particulière d'être écrits. C'est assez pour pouvoir me prouver à
> moi-même si j'ai du talent, oui ou non.
>
> J'y mettrai tout ce que je puis y mettre de style, de passion,
> d'esprit, et après nous verrons.
>
> —Flaubert, *Correspondance*

This passage does not, as far as we know, refer to the *Trois contes*.[1] It is
from a letter written by Flaubert in 1842 from Paris, where he was studying
law, and was addressed to his lycée teacher, Gourgaud-Dugazon. However, it
most strikingly describes both the concept which informs the *Trois contes* and
Flaubert's state of mind prior to writing this work. Moreover, it calls to mind
in a peculiar way the letter Flaubert wrote more than 30 years later in which
he expressed his intention to begin work on the *Trois contes:*

> Quant à la littérature, je ne crois plus en moi; je me trouve vide, ce qui est
> découverte peu consolante. *Bouvard et Pécuchet* étaient trop difficiles, j'y
> renonce; je cherche un autre roman, sans rien découvrir. En attendant, je
> vais me mettre à écrire *La légende de Saint Julien l'Hospitalier*
> uniquement pour m'occuper à quelque chose, pour voir si je peux faire
> encore une phrase, ce dont je doute. Ce sera très court; une trentaine de
> pages peut-être. Puis, si je n'ai rien trouvé et que j'aille mieux, je
> reprendrai *Bouvard et Pécuchet*. (7: 267)

Flaubert did not take up *Bouvard et Pécuchet* until he had written two more
stories, "de genres tout différents," to accompany *Saint Julien*. Flaubert's
letter of 1875 seems more knowing, far less giddy and optimistic, about the

prospects of finding out whether, indeed, he could still write. Both letters, however, suggest that from early on in his career Flaubert had identified three different subjects and styles of novelistic interest. In both instances, he seemed to have considered these three themes test cases for judging his abilities and his future as a writer.

The period preceding the composition of the *Trois contes* was a trying one for Flaubert. Professionally, he was deeply disappointed by the failure of his play *Le Candidat*—which he thought good. Moreover, his work on *Bouvard et Pécuchet* was seriously undermining his self-confidence as a writer. At this point, the conception of the work was not entirely clear to him and he knew that he would have to work five to six years to complete it. Slow and painful progress on this "impossible book" convinced him to write a work that would be easier to handle, a work which apart from being a source of income could prove to him that he could still write. This decision brought relief not only to Flaubert himself but to friends like Turgenev and Sand, who could see how complicated Flaubert's conception for the work was and could not have much enthusiasm for it. When he wrote George Sand to announce his plans to drop *Bouvard et Pécuchet,* she wrote him back: "Tu as fait un progrès, tu as renoncé à un sujet de travail qui n'aurait pas eu de succès. Fais quelque chose de plus terre à terre et qui aille à tout le monde."[2] Certainly, *Un Cœur simple* fits Sand's prescription. This is perhaps true of *Saint Julien l'Hospitalier* as well; hagiographies with their medieval settings were likely to appeal to the novel's general readership. It is not the case for *Hérodias,* however, for reasons of style.

In addition to professional disappointment and self-doubt, Flaubert was experiencing serious financial problems. These resulted in the loss of the property left to him by his mother. He came close to losing Croisset, and this gave him the deepest anxieties. The loss of property for Flaubert had always signified moral as well as financial disintegration. He was effectively bankrupt and was never to recover financially. Only in the last year of his life did he express optimism that de Commanville's speculations were turning for the better. Flaubert, who had never before concerned himself with money and least of all associated it with his vocation, began to talk seriously about his work as a potential source of income. He sought to have *La Tentation* translated into Russian and was disappointed that the Russian censors rejected it. As it turned out, although the French edition was nonetheless available and could be bought, few were interested in it.[3] Later, Flaubert pressed a busy and somewhat reluctant Turgenev to translate and publish the *Trois contes* even before it was published in France, "la pénurie où je me trouve me fait désirer cela *fortement*" (7: 370). He did not seem concerned about the quality of the translation and accepted for *Hérodias* a translator who did not come especially recommended. I am not suggesting that Flaubert wrote the *Trois contes* primarily for financial reasons. However, his financial problems coupled with doubts about his ability to write had to have encouraged him to think of writing a work that would appeal to a larger audience, a work that would appeal to the "few" for whom he had always written as well as to the rest; namely, to those readers who were mostly drawn by a "good story" and an interesting landscape for dreaming. Perhaps, too, Flaubert's feelings of self-doubt and failure caused him to consider more seriously than before George Sand's reproach concerning his "cynicism." In short, it might just be that Flaubert was more willing at this point in his career to take her advice, and the advice others were giving him directly and indirectly, not to write about failures but to allow for a sense of optimism in his conception of fictional characters. As I pointed out in the introduction, it might just be that Flaubert felt that his attitude toward his characters and the role of illusion was responsible for the dead end where he found himself with *Bouvard et Pécuchet*. What is certain is that in the *Trois contes* Flaubert does not undermine his characters' illusions and aspirations as he did in previous works.

The *Correspondance* is a poignant testament of the difficult time Flaubert was undergoing in the period preceding the composition of the *Trois contes*. He expresses his despair to George Sand in the following: "Je me perds dans mes souvenirs d'enfance comme un vieillard... Je n'attends plus rien de la vie qu'une suite de feuilles de papier à barbouiller de noir. Il me semble que je traverse une solitude sans fin, pour aller je ne sais où. Et c'est moi qui suis tout à la fois le désert, le voyageur et le chameau (7: 234-35). In another letter, he tells her of his regrets at having failed at a most basic level: "Jamais je ne me suis senti plus abandonné, plus vide et plus meurtri. Ce que vous me dites (dans votre dernière lettre) de vos chères petites m'a remué jusqu'au fond de l'âme. Pourquoi n'ai-je pas cela? J'étais né avec toutes les tendresses, pourtant! Mais on ne fait pas sa destinée, on la subit. J'ai été lâche dans ma jeunesse, *j'ai eu peur de la vie!* Tout se paye" (7: 122). Flaubert was sincere in this complaint. He was not merely writing what he knew Sand wanted to hear; he expressed the same regret to others as well during this period.[4]

These letters are typical of Flaubert's state of mind during this period. Writing, however, lifts his spirits slowly and by the time he is engaged in writing the second story, *Un Cœur simple,* he is enthusiastic and optimistic. If we go by his correspondence, this feeling does not leave him until his death three to four years later. Writing the *Trois contes* made Flaubert feel especially confident about himself again. "Jamais je n'ai été curieux de voir l'ensemble d'une de mes œuvres comme cette fois-ci" (7: 325), he writes to Caroline; and to Zola: "Jamais je ne me suis senti plus d'aplomb" (7: 325). He was feeling good physically, too. He reports to Madame Genettes: "Je travaille comme un frénétique. Pourquoi? Je n'en sais rien! Mais vraiment j'ai le diable dans le corps. Je ne me couche plus qu'au soleil levant et je *gueule* dans le silence du cabinet à me casser la poitrine, laquelle ne s'en trouve que mieux" (7: 331). "Faut-il te dire mon opinion?" he writes Caroline. "Je crois que (sans le savoir) j'avais été malade profondément et secrètement depuis la mort de notre pauvre vieille [Flaubert's mother died on 6 April 1872]. Si je me trompe, d'où vient cette espèce d'éclaircissement qui s'est fait en moi, depuis quelque temps! C'est comme si des brouillards se dissipaient. Physiquement, je me sens rajeuni" (7: 338-39). He begins to enjoy nature in a way he had not before. This might be due to the fact that for *Un Cœur simple* Flaubert's "research" led him to revisit some of the beautiful Norman landscapes of his childhood. But, more significantly, this return to nature serves to explain in part why we find in *Hérodias* so strong a condemnation of art in favor of nature and the "natural." With an exuberance typical of him, he writes Caroline: "Tu n'imagines pas comme je deviens 'amant de la nature.' Je regarde le ciel, les arbres et la verdure avec un plaisir que je n'ai jamais eu. Je voudrais être vache pour manger de l'herbe" (7: 383-84). Clearly, writing the *Trois contes* served a therapeutic effect. It also allowed Flaubert to return to *Bouvard et Pécuchet* refreshed and, perhaps, too, with some new ideas.

I have pointed out in the introduction that from the time of its publication to this day, the *Trois contes* has been regarded as a kind of anthology of Flaubert's range of subject matter and style. There has been a tendency to view each story as a diminutive version of the larger work. To some, like Brunetière, the work remains a sign of imaginative sterility that compares poorly with the earlier works. It is in his words "certainement ce qu'il avait encore donné de plus faible." He expresses surprise to see "un écrivain qui finit par où les autres commencent, ayant jadis commencé par où les autres finissent. . . ."[5] Characteristically, Maurice Bruézière writes in the "notice" of the Classique Larousse edition of 1953 that Flaubert adds nothing new in the *Trois contes:* "*Un cœur simple* n'est guère que la réduction à l'échelon domestique de *Madame Bovary,* et *Hérodias* n'est pas beaucoup plus qu'une transposition en miniature de *Salammbô.* Quant à *la Légende de saint Julien l'Hospitalier,* elle demeure surtout comme un très brilliant exercice de style, un morceau de bravoure un peu gratuite." It is clear that both Brunetière and Bruézière chose to focus on the similarities between Flaubert's "major" works and the *Trois contes*—similarities which are obvious. Flaubert himself was very much aware of this. In the case of *Hérodias*, he writes: "J'ai peur de retomber dans les effets produits par *Salammbô*, car mes personnages sont de la même race et c'est un peu le même milieu. J'espère pourtant que ce reproche, qu'on ne manquera pas de me faire, sera injuste" (7: 350). For many critics, however, the *Trois contes* is rightly considered the distillation of Flaubert's art, its purest and most economical expression. John Fletcher, for instance, points out: "The *Trois contes* together represent the master's virtuoso performance."[6] Marc Bertrand suggests that the stories "constituent la confession déguisée d'une maturité artistique inquiète mais persévérante."[7] Harry Levin calls the *Trois contes* Flaubert's "one unqualified success."[8]

Since the work first appeared, the question of the unity of the *Trois contes* has been debated. Thibaudet, for example, sees the work as "un ensemble harmonieux, classiquement composé."[9] Margaret Tillet and Jacques Suffel also consider the three stories as a harmonious whole and as a demonstration of Flaubert's stylistic virtuosity.[10] Michael Issacharoff argues in *L'Espace et la nouvelle* that the three stories represent a unified vision that can best be understood if we read them in the context of one another. Issacharoff considers *Hérodias* the key for the exposition of a central network of symbols uniting the work. "La structure de base qui semble régler tout le système des trois récits est celui du dedans/dehors," he suggests; "le réseau des symboles dérive essentiellement de cela."[11] For Per Nykrog the three stories are the dramatic representation of the Trinity: the Holy Spirit in *Un Cœur simple,* Christ in *Saint Julien,* and God the Father in *Hérodias.*[12] Marc Bertrand argues that what unifies the *Trois contes* is that each story demonstrates the tension between "parole singulière" and "parole commune"; in other words, the individual's search for meaning is always met with resistance from the outside world. Bertrand suggests that this resistance is temporarily resolved at the end of each story.[13] Robert Chumbley does not stress the unity of the *Trois contes,* per se, but develops a reading that shows a clear growth in abstraction from the quasi-realistic setting of nineteenth-century France in *Un Cœur simple* to the "pure archeology of form" in *Hérodias.*[14] Similarly, John O'Connor's study suggests that the geometrical matrix, the important figure of the double cone, underlies the *Trois contes.*[15] Still many other critics point to the obvious theme of sainthood as underlying the unity of the stories. Victor Brombert, for example, suggests that "overtly or implicitly, the subject of sainthood is at the heart of the *Trois contes*."[16] It is undeniable that saints and mystics had always concerned, even obsessed Flaubert. Moreover, he thought of his own literary vocation in terms of suffering and salvation. The *Trois contes* is most superficially and most profoundly involved with depicting sainthood—Félicité's no less than the two other "legitimate" saints, a fact that Flaubert makes more explicit in the drafts.[17] For Félicité is surely a modern saint. She is a pious woman who, after years of selfless devotion and after many acts of kindness to the community and to enemies of France alike (the Prussian soldiers and even Old Colmiche, for instance), ends her life in a mystical reunion with the Holy Spirit. Flaubert has indeed given the accounts of three saints. Yet, Raymonde Debray-Genette and others undermine sainthood as a unifying element in the work because the theme is not unique to the *Trois contes*, as we see in her following response to the question of unity at the Colloque de Cerisy:

> . . . on veut absolument que le recueil ait une unité. Or nous savons que Flaubert, tout simplement, en a écrit assez pour que cela puisse faire un volume. Il n'y a pas plus d'unité dans les *Trois contes* qu'il n'y en a entre les *Trois contes* et *Madame Bovary* ou les œuvres de jeunesse.
>
> ....
>
> Ce thème de la sainteté a été pris pour unité . . . le thème de la sainteté est dans toute l'œuvre de Flaubert, c'est à travers tout le texte qu'il faut l'étudier.[18]

John Fletcher suggests that "the issue is, probably, unimportant." Yet he goes on to say that "what matters is that the book was conceived as a unity in that the stories were written one after the other."[19] My own view was stated in the introduction and I will develop it more fully in the conclusion. But, in short, I see a unity to the *Trois contes;* and this unity is a factor of Flaubert's positive change of attitude toward his characters and toward the role of illusion in life. More specifically, the three stories form a unified whole which, from *Un Cœur simple* to *Hérodias,* makes the subversive intent of the characters progressively more explicit; in the end, in *Hérodias,* the reader's suspicions of the characters' and Flaubert's subversive intentions are confirmed.

After he had completed the *Trois contes,* Flaubert returned with enthusiasm to *Bouvard et Pécuchet.* He even planned to write a decidedly optimistic account of the battle of Thermopylae—which, "unlike his other works," in the words of Margaret Lowe, "would at last have been a story about accepted heroes."[20] It is outside the scope of this study to evaluate the possible influence of the *Trois contes* on *Bouvard et Pécuchet.* I think, however, that an analysis of the manuscripts and drafts of *Bouvard et Pécuchet* would reveal invaluable insights into their relationship. The final texts we have on both works, however, will be sufficient to make a few observations. I have claimed, and I will defend this view in the subsequent chapters, that in spite of an apparent superficiality, the characters in *Trois contes* are solid centers of consciousness. They are reflectors of a point of view, Flaubert's undoubtedly, which considers illusion not solely a private affair but the arena in which the individual challenges the established order and, in this case, wins. Illusion becomes the means of a putting into question and a dismantling of concepts essential to that system. It is in this light that *Bouvard et Pécuchet* might be understood. Bouvard and Pécuchet may have started their adventure into the "bibliothèque" of Western thought as a couple of docile and somewhat dispassionate investigators. However, at the end of the first volume they become openly hostile. They develop a critical spirit; they are torn by doubt and tortured by the "stupidity" of those around them. They become more and more subversive of social values; they argue for the emancipation of women, for a revolution in education, and other antiestablishment notions. They multiply the public's antagonism against them until, in the end, they are arrested for inciting people to revolt.

A look at the correspondence shows that Flaubert meant for the two characters to evolve in the direction of more awareness and a more critical perspective. One can only regret that Flaubert did not live long enough to work on the second volume. It would have surely shed more light not only on the "Copy," which the two men decide to spend the rest of their days writing, but also on the way we understand the first volume. If at the end of the first volume, Bouvard and Pécuchet seem no longer to believe in what they read, frustrated and angry with the world, how do they deal with that hostility—the underlying subject of the *Trois contes?* What do they do in the "Copy"? Do they, for example, attempt to integrate and shape their past experiences and experiments and, in doing so, comment (indirectly) on these experiences for the readers to draw their own conclusions? My guess is that *Bouvard et Pécuchet* started as a dispassionate critique of encyclopedic knowledge and possibly as a critique of poor methodology; the characters were conceived as passive, uncritical, and mildly pathetic. In mid stream, however, perhaps after Flaubert had completed the *Trois contes,* the two characters took on subversive qualities. Apart from the change in the characters, mentioned above, the last chapters mark a change of tone; the style becomes more lively, the narrative more heated.

The *Trois contes* interrupted the writing of *Bouvard et Pécuchet.* Indeed, as I show in my readings, it shares one important feature with that work. Both, like the *Dictionnaire,* which was to be part of the second volume, are conceived as a superior joke, a "blague," to be played on society. In the *Dictionnaire,* Flaubert wanted to give the public the impression that the work was written with the purpose of bringing people back to tradition and to order while, in fact, it was intended to mock tradition, to disrupt the order of things and spread confusion in the minds of people. I suspect that, as with the *Trois contes,* the second volume of *Bouvard et Pécuchet* would have suggested that subversive intent more playfully than does the rather tedious first volume. The second volume was not conceived, literally, as a copy, a duplication; rather, judging from the few notes we have, as a potential *commentary* on the first volume. Had it been completed, I suspect that the second volume, like the *Trois contes,* would have offered the reader a double narrative, a straight text and a suspect subtext, with the latter serving to express the characters' and the writer's radical designs against civilization.

2

The Women of Pont-l'Evêque: A Subversive Sorority

Quant à l'oiseau que l'on dessine, le perroquet empaillé que l'auteur serait obligé de tenir à la main, ferait pouffer de rire la salle et suffirait à lui seul pour faire tomber un chef-d'œuvre. Comment se fait-il que tu n'aies pas vu cela?
—Flaubert to Louise Colet,
advising her against displaying a stuffed
parrot onstage for her play *L'Institutrice*,
Correspondance

Félicité is not a psychological blank page. She has desires that are not lacking in complexity, fantasies that are unsettling and subversive. Typically, Flaubert manages the character with a great deal of subtlety; he laces his characterization with an irony which, though not directed at discrediting her, moves us to question her "simplicity" and expose the radical nature of its, of his, conception.[1] Yet the tendency has been to read *Un Cœur simple* at face value, as the story of an exploitation, the exploitation of a selfless, kind, hard-working, mystical, and, on the whole, unintelligent woman—a reading that is surely justifiable but one that I shall, nonetheless, address and challenge on the grounds that it oversimplifies the character and concurs too readily with those who, in *Un Cœur simple*, have an interest in silencing and undermining her kind.[2]

My aim in the following chapter is not to reconcile the straight and the suspect narratives nor is it to establish a dialogue between the two; I do not believe that this is possible or, for that matter, desirable. My study will try to bring to the fore the unsettling and subversive nature of Félicité's character. If in the process I appear to have undermined the straight and conventional interpretation, it is mainly because this posture of exclusion has proved to be the most effective way to bring to light the not so obvious subtext.

> Nous sommes simples . . . mais nous voyons aux champs où nous vivons de jour et de nuit, des choses que vous ne voyez pas et que vous ne connaîtrez jamais.
> —said by Jeanne in George Sand's *Jeanne*

Though in the final text hardly a trace of superstition can be sensed in Flaubert's characterization of Félicité, his original conception was to present her as a hopelessly superstitious woman. As can be noted from a study of the drafts, Félicité's character undergoes some subtle and some not so subtle changes in the course of writing.[3] In the early drafts, for example, Félicité is presented as a more dense and less sympathetic character than she is in the final text. There is something about superstition that does not quite fit Félicité's character as it evolves. Superstition, in its limited sense, is blind faith in received ideas; it is an irrational belief founded on fear or on ignorance. Félicité's ignorance, however, does not occasion that type of belief; moreover, her faith is far from blind. Rather, her "ignorance," or her simplicity, is a form of wisdom which allows her to circumvent and work both inside and outside the system that tries to alienate and confuse her. "Ignorance" frees her from conceptual constraints intrinsic to the system, concepts which might limit her imagination and thwart her desires if she were to "understand" them, or, more correctly, if she were to act as if she understood them. This posture of ignorance and simplicity gives her room to interpret, or misinterpret, accepted notions as it suits her, giving people and objects her own meaning. It is this imaginative Félicité that Flaubert juxtaposes to the likes of the pedantic and fraudulent Bourais.

Félicité may indeed be simple in one or all of the following senses: ignorant, ordinary, naïve, natural, or pure. But her simplicity is not itself entirely unaffected; it is not, in other words, innocent, as any reading that takes her point of view with a degree of seriousness could discern—granted that to ask a culture-bound reader to assume Félicité's point of view is to ask for a major act of accommodation. What does it mean to say, then, that Félicité is at once guileless and calculating? The suggestion is that Félicité's simplicity is the manifestation of a superior intuition, a complex intentionality; it is a form of enlightened wisdom, that is to say, a wisdom that comes from a higher position, as from God (or Flaubert). This wisdom, however, I should like to underline from the onset, does *not* represent someone else's point of view, say the narrator's. It does not derive from a source outside Félicité; it is not a consciousness apart. Like Julien, whose parricide seems at once to be directed by some force outside his control and yet appears to be the deliberate enactment of his desire to kill his parents, Félicité behaves in a manner that seems both uncannily conscious and unaware of its subversive operations. Thus, we have a sense that the actions of both characters are deliberate and purposeful although the evidence to show intention is deliberately made vague and indeterminate by Flaubert. This is done for the sake of certain stylistic exigencies, because Flaubert's technique for presenting information relies on and values suggestion and implication over declamation and direct and univocal meaning.

Simplicity as a complex and superior wisdom or strategy is built into Flaubert's conception of Félicité as the desire for parricide is into his conception of Julien. Thus, by virtue of a superior strategy, which must be seen as of a piece with her, Félicité's simplicity is the very means of her triumph over those who undermine her desires and her imagination. Michal Peled Ginsburg, in her excellent work on Flaubert, has made a point of explaining this application of the term *strategy*. She writes: "By talking about 'strategies,' we imply a distinction between means and end; we imply that there is an aim that precedes and determines the means, a certain intentionality that dictates a choice of means, and so on."[4] But whereas Ginsburg's Derrideanism moves her away from ascribing any responsibility or intentionality to a source "beyond representation," I do not deny the possibility that Flaubert deliberately composed *Un Cœur simple* and *Saint Julien l'Hospitalier* to show the reader two sides of each narrative, the straight and the suspect, at once.

Un Cœur simple is a story about power, about who has it, how it is used by those who have it, and how those who, like Félicité, find themselves without it manage to subvert it. The story is, in short, one of a woman who outmaneuvers the system that exploits her.

The narrator of *Un Cœur simple* must occupy a singularly difficult position in order to convey the impression that the character of Félicité is autonomous, that her superior wisdom, like her ignorance, does not spring from the narrator, while allowing the reader to enter the consciousness of a basically inarticulate character. At once detached and mobile, that position is, at times, hard to define. It could be open or on the contrary diffuse. At times, far from being impartial, the narrator seems to stand behind as the ideological focus of the story, as a representative of the dominant bourgeois order, and a native of the region. This is the case in the scene of the atlas when the narrator, assuming Bourais's posture, remarks that Félicité was so stupid that she very likely expected to see a picture of Victor's face on the map. On the other hand, the narrator functions as the voice that gives expression to Félicité's inner thoughts and feelings and, at such times, can be said to embody her.[5] Thus, even though the narrator tries to impart an air of detachment toward Félicité, leaving her on her own, so to speak, and, contrarily, makes a number of cutting observations at her expense and places her in situations where she is dealt one cruel blow after another, the reader has no problem in recognizing that, for the most part, the narrator can be relied on to reveal Félicité's inner thoughts and that a discreet compassion binds them together.[6] Thus, the narrator, neither supporting nor undermining Félicité's intentions, acts as the vehicle through which she expresses her potentially disruptive and essentially critical point of view of the social order.

A study of the drafts indicates that Flaubert carefully eliminated details that would have provided easy access into Félicité's feelings and motivations.[7] This is a narrative strategy typical of Flaubert in the *Trois contes* and elsewhere. In the drafts of *Un Cœur simple,* for example, Félicité is angry at the way Paul handles the liquidation of his mother's estate; she goes so far as to curse him. She also expresses anger and indignation when she sees the "For Sale" sign at the Aubain's house. Another example is the scene in which Félicité sits by the river to wash clothes after she has learned of Victor's death. In the final version, we can only assume that she is on the verge of crying and that she is associating the tall grass in the water with Victor's dead body (thinking, wrongly, that Victor had drowned). Yet, in the drafts, Flaubert makes this association clear; "La vue de l'eau par une liaison d'idée la fait pleurer" and "vue des chevelures de noyés/son cœur éclate."[8] In the drafts, too, we have a better sense than in the final text of why Théodore likes her (she is different from the rest, she has the demeanor of "une dame") and why she, in turn, likes him (he, too, seems different from the rest).

However, in spite of the typical and deliberate suppression of information that makes explicit certain feelings she has, we can still get a sense of what moves Félicité and how she views the world.[9] This is generally true for the major characters in the *Trois contes*. As Raymonde Debray-Genette suggests in her detailed study of narrative techniques in the *Trois contes*: "Ce que l'on ne fait pas dire aux personnages, il faudra le leur faire manifester autrement; la parole non-dite est comme diffusée à travers toutes les autres formes du récit et les envahit."[10]

In the *Trois contes*, one of the most common ways Flaubert lets the reader participate in his characters' visions of things is by picturing their state of mind by association with descriptions of their surroundings. The role of description as a stylistic device for organizing the meaning of Flaubert's narratives in the *Trois contes* and elsewhere cannot be underestimated. Flaubert himself was very clear about its role in communicating the meaning of a text. He writes Louise Colet:

> Crois bien que je ne suis nullement insensible aux malheurs des classes pauvres, etc., mais il n'y a pas, en littérature, de bonnes intentions. *Le style est tout* et je me plains de ce que, dans *La Servante*, tu n'as pas exprimé tes idées par des *faits* ou des *tableaux*. Il faut avant tout, dans une narration, être dramatique, toujours peindre ou émouvoir, et *jamais déclamer*. (4: 10)

Albert Thibaudet and Erich Auerbach recognized, a long time ago, the importance of description in Flaubert when they suggested that for Flaubert the problem of representation consists *mainly* in establishing a complete identity between "la description matérielle et les sentiments des personnages" (Thibaudet), that Flaubert translates his characters' feelings into visual images that become a kind of dramatic presentation of a mental event (Auerbach).[11] Descriptions in the *Trois contes* are, generally speaking, strongly focalized through the characters; the reader has little problem identifying that what is described is seen through the character; for example, Virginie's communion and Victor's departure are seen through Félicité's eyes; Julien's hunts are described from Julien's point of view; Hérodias and Salomé are viewed, generally, through Herod. There are in the *Trois contes* other descriptions which are not as strongly focalized; I will be giving some examples shortly. Determining their function in the narrative becomes, as it is in the case of strongly focalized descriptions, subject to the larger issue of interpretation.[12]

On the whole, in the *Trois contes*, we can rely on descriptions to give us a sense of how characters like Félicité view the world. A problem presents itself, especially in the case of Félicité, when one tries to defend the claim, when one tries to supply "proof," so to speak, for a reading of Félicité as a conscious and desiring character. The drafts can be enlightening, but this is not always the case. In fact, they open up problems of their own.[13] The reason why it is difficult to argue for a reading of Félicité as a conscious and deliberate character is that critics (perhaps more than general readers) are inclined to speak of a fusion of point of view of character and narrator and tend to assign "exceptional" views to the narrator at the expense of Félicité. Jonathan Culler's remark that "it is patently clear that Félicité does not herself succeed in organizing and interpreting her experience" is shared by many.[14] Yet one would not be hard put to supply examples suggesting that Félicité is all too aware of the meaning of her existence, of her miseries as well as her joys, as when, at the summit at Ecquemauville, she stops in tears, reviews her life, and is overwhelmed by all her misfortunes. Obviously, however, if the interpretive assumption is that Félicité is too limited, too simple, too literal, to have what at times appears to be self-consciousness or what looks like an interesting perspective on things, then the point of view in question will be attributed to the narrator, since Félicité's thoughts and feelings are seldom recounted in her own words.[15]

In *Un Cœur simple*, as in the *Trois contes* as a whole, the distinction between what the character experiences and what the narrator expresses is, in most cases, artificial and tendentious. Moreover, by insisting on a separation, one tends to prejudice the reading in favor of seeing Félicité only in terms of an ordinary and simple-minded character; in other words, one tends to take the side of the dominant male bourgeois culture in *Un Cœur simple* whose views are represented by the fraudulent and pedantic Bourais. To think of Félicité as too banal or too shallow to have a point of view worth considering is to overlook the possibility that Flaubert might have provided the reader with an opening for interpreting Félicité's "simplicity" as a radical, though discreet, perspective on the world.

Flaubert does indeed give us a perspective on Félicité's way of thinking and of her desiring fantasies through, among other things, descriptions of her surroundings, as we see in the following passage where Félicité meets Théodore on her way home:

> [E]t du bras gauche il lui entoura la taille; elle marchait soutenue par son étreinte; ils se ralentirent. Le vent était *mou,* les étoiles brillaient, l'*énorme charretée* de foin *oscillait* devant eux; et les quatre chevaux, en *traînant* leurs pas, soulevaient de la poussière. Puis, sans commandement, ils

tournèrent à droite. Il l'embrassa encore une fois. Elle disparut dans l'ombre. (my italics)[16]

This beautiful scene is as much the description of the outside world as it is the description of the body of Félicité. The image of the enormous hay cart is a marvelous concretization of the body of desire oscillating from sensations, "le vent était mou," to the visible world, the twinkling of the stars. The image of the horses "traînant leurs pas" is full of the lazy sensuality Félicité is experiencing. Here, what is remarkable and poignant is that the horses find their way instinctively, "sans commandement." Throughout *Un Cœur simple,* scenes of pleasure are set in nature; moreover, they generally dispense with words.

More than a backdrop for the narrative of Félicité's life, nature is a maternal space and an image and metaphor of Félicité's body, of its sensation, as for instance the following scene at the seashore:

> Presque toujours on se reposait dans un pré, ayant Deauville *à gauche,* le Havre *à droite et en face* la pleine mer. Elle était brillante de soleil, lisse comme un miroir, tellement douce qu'on entendait à peine son murmure; des moineaux cachés pépiaient, et la *voûte immense* du ciel recouvrait tout cela. . . .
>
> D'autres fois . . . [l]es flots endormis, en tombant sur le sable, se déroulaient le long de la grève; elle s'étendait à perte de vue, *mais du côté de la terre* avait pour limite les dunes la séparant du Marais, large prairie en forme d'hippodrome. Quand ils [la famille] revenaient par là, Trouville, au fond sur la pente du coteau, à chaque pas grandissait, et avec toutes ses maisons inégales semblait s'épanouir dans un désordre gai. (21-22; my italics)

The huge hay cart and the gigantic parrot hovering above her head at the conclusion of the story are suggestive of the dilation of Félicité's sensations at moments of ecstasy. This scene at the seashore pictures for the reader the inner scape of pleasure. Félicité is in her element; there is hardly a movement or a sound, and everything is familiar and predictable. When, in the second paragraph, the eye is carried off to an imperceptible point, "la grève . . . s'étendait à perte de vue," it is quickly grounded by "mais du côté de la terre avait pour limite les dunes." Most everywhere in Flaubert's fictional work (though not in much of the *Correspondance,* for example, where he writes that nature inspires nothing but boredom), nature is linked with a sense of well being until, that is, it is touched by human hands. In *Par les champs et par les grèves*, in *Voyages aux Pyrénées et en Corse,* and elsewhere, repeatedly, the sea and the land viewed together in a single frame represent a privileged space, a space of unity and a shelter. The self can feel as one with nature in a kind of immense enclosure. But the experience of the infinite in Flaubert is troubling; this is why enclosures and limits are important. The infinite presents a threat of boredom and the threat of a loss of self. In Flaubert, one of the functions of description is precisely to limit or otherwise define and circumscribe the experience of the infinite, to strike a balance between the specific and the general, between the personal and the universal.[17]

In this scene that features nature as an immense maternal body, a womb (the sky covers the scene with its huge canopy), only the women are content; Paul experiences the vast though sheltered space as limitation and confinement. He, unable to respond in any way to this scene, is bored. On their return home, the decision is made to send him away to school. When he leaves, he is hardly missed by the women. The ideal, the scene of pleasure, is one that, as can be seen in this episode, alienates and excludes men. Nature and women are associated in *Un Cœur simple*, as are culture and men.

Another perhaps more pointed example of the way Flaubert communicates Félicité's vision is the scene on the way to the Liébard farm when the farmer, recounting events in the lives of the inhabitants of the region, mentions the name of Madame Lehoussais; she is the woman Théodore married in place of Félicité:[18]

> La route était si mauvaise que ses huit kilomètres exigèrent deux heures. Les chevaux enfonçaient jusqu'aux paturons dans la boue, et faisaient pour en sortir de brusques mouvements des hanches . . . La jument de Liébard, à de certains endroits, s'arrêtait tout à coup. Il attendait patiemment qu'elle se remît en marche; et il parlait des personnes dont les propriétés bordaient la route. . . . (18)

At this point, the farmer mentions Madame Lehoussais's name, and the scene that follows changes from the leisurely and lingering pace, suggested by the movements of the horses and the "et" of "il parlait des personnes," to a wild frenzy:

> "En voilà une Mme Lehoussais, qui au lieu de prendre un jeune homme..." Félicité n'entendit pas le reste; les chevaux trottaient, l' âne galopait; tous enfilèrent un sentier, une barrière tourna, deux garçons parurent, et l'on descendit le purin, sur le seuil même de la porte. (19)

The description is not so much grounded in what Félicité or anybody else sees but in the inner rhythm of her body; just as in the descriptions of the lazy and sensuous movements of Liébard's horses, and, earlier, in the description of the enormous cart swaying under the weight of its cargo.[19] These scenes and others like them are focalized, so to speak, from the inside. This inner focalization, or narrative omniscience, is a common strategy for illuminating for the reader a character's feelings and point of view.

Besides the descriptions (besides these "tableaux") which suggest her inner life, Félicité's attitude toward men in particular offers another perspective on her inner thoughts and feelings. How she manages her feelings in this respect is of special interest in gauging the radical and unsettling nature of her thoughts and actions. How are men depicted in *Un Cœur simple*? For the most part, they represent authority, both secular and spiritual. Their power is especially visible and dramatized in church, where they are portrayed as the leaders and defenders of the faith; there, too, the distinction between the two sexes, men's dominance over women, and men's penchant for violence are made most evident:

> Les garçons à droite, les filles à gauche, emplissaient les stalles du chœur; le curé se tenait debout près du lutrin; sur un vitrail de l'abside, le Saint-Esprit *dominait* la Vierge; un autre la montrait *à genoux* devant l'enfant Jésus, et, derrière le tabernacle, un groupe en bois représentait Saint-Michel *terrassant* le dragon. (25; my italics)

Flaubert, however, presents nearly all the male characters critically. Théodore is deceptive, callous, greedy, and cowardly. Bourais is revealed, in the end, to be a thief. Like Monsieur Aubain, he squanders and steals Madame Aubain's money. Paul is a failure professionally; he is an unthoughtful son who exploits his mother, and a meek husband to boot. Monsieur Aubain wastes his wife's fortune, then dies, leaving her and the children in considerable debt. In a passage in the drafts that Flaubert did not include in the final version, Monsieur Aubain is a thief and a gambler who is, moreover, unfaithful to his wife. The marquis de Gremanville is an alcoholic and a failure in life. As for Old Colmiche, he is known to have committed atrocities during the revolution. Does Félicité share Flaubert's critical view of the men of Pont-l'Evêque?

Throughout her life, Félicité regards men with suspicion and a few even with outright hostility. Théodore's betrayal and the unfeeling way he ends their relationship undoubtedly contributes to this resentment; yet the root of this feeling could go back even further, to her childhood. Félicité's father had been killed when she was very young. At one point during the composition, Flaubert considers the following account of her father's death: "Félicité Coindard était la huitième fille d'un pauvre maçon qui écrasé . . . sous un échafaudage." He then crosses this out and writes: "son père un maçon s'était tué en tombant d'un échafaudage." By using the possessive in "son père" and the reflexive ("s'était tué") Flaubert places the accent not on the "pauvre maçon" who is crushed (shall we say, passively and as if by some fault or negligence on his part) under the weight of a scaffolding but on the daughter he abandons when he "kills himself."[20] Shortly after her father's death, Félicité's mother also dies. As a result, Félicité and her sisters are forced to separate. Thus, the father's death begins the series of losses and misfortunes that will mark her entire life. It is, therefore, understandable that after Théodore abandons her, as did her father earlier, and she leaves for Pont-l'Evêque, Félicité would be drawn to Madame Aubain, "une bourgeoise en capeline de veuve" (11), a woman who shares a certain loss. In some of the drafts, Madame Aubain has just lost her husband when she meets Félicité; and one of the reasons given for Monsieur Aubain's death is that he, too, like Félicité's father, dies from a fall. Only, in his case, he dies following a fall from a horse. In the drafts, too, and quite apart from what this might imply, both Félicité's father and Monsieur Aubain share a reputation as "Franc-maçon."[21]

The struggle dramatized in *Un Cœur simple* is obviously a class struggle (and this struggle is clearly primary in the "straight" narrative). But the struggle is equally, though less obviously, a gender struggle in the "suspect," not-so-obvious text. The struggle that Félicité tries to overcome is both class and gender related. Similarities between most of the women and most of the men cut across class differences (there are exceptions which I go into later). So many details and events in the life of Madame Aubain, for instance, recall details and events in the life of Félicité. Lucette Czyba in her illuminating study of the treatment of women in Flaubert's novels has seen very clearly that there is in *Un Cœur simple* an attempt on the part of Flaubert to erase differences between the two women. Though I do not share Czyba's interest in demonstrating the duplicity and hypocrisy of Flaubert's view "of the common people" and the prejudices he shares with his own class against the servant, I agree with her conclusion:

Bien que le conte donne à voir l'aliénation et l'exploitation dont la servante est victime, on ne saurait le réduire à une allégorie de l'oppression subie par les classes populaires... Parmi les personnages féminins mis en scène par Flaubert, l'examen de celui de Félicité fournit un moyen privilégié de mesurer jusqu'à quel point la situation sociale du romancier conditionne sa vision du monde ... Car tout se passe comme si, constatant l'aliénation et l'exploitation dont Félicité est victime, Flaubert en réduisait l'importance en établissant entre elle et sa maîtresse un parallèle faussement égalisateur . . . Ce qui revient à affirmer la destinée irrémédiablement malheureuse des femmes, quelle que soit leur situation sociale.[22]

Flaubert was fully aware of this when he was writing, as the drafts show. He was aware that the two women were not sufficiently differentiated in concept, and yet the final text still shows strong similarities between them (age, cause of death, losses); the process of differentiation was not successful. Flaubert, also, tones down in the final text the harshness of Madame Aubain toward Félicité which we find in the drafts. It is as if in the course of writing, the idea of a bond between the women became an underlying concern for Flaubert. The *bourgeoises* are not, to any significant degree, the oppressors in *Un Cœur simple*. They are themselves presented as an oppressed class. This condition unites them. In the end, it is the *paroissiennes*, both the *bourgeoises* and their less prosperous counterparts, who choose to honor Félicité's death by setting up the principal altar in the courtyard of Madame Aubain, that is, under Félicité's window. (Madame Aubain had long been dead; only Félicité lived there. All concerned with the arrangements knew this well. The decision to place the altar in Madame Aubain's courtyard is a further indication that the two women, Madame Aubain and Félicité, are not differentiated in Flaubert's mind, and that they are not differentiated in the minds of the women of the community.) In the drafts of this episode, Flaubert relates the rivalry between two *bourgeoises*, each of whom wants the central altar placed in her own courtyard. In the final text, Flaubert eliminates the mention of any rivalry between the women. In so doing, he takes the accent away from dissention between the women and, instead, places the emphasis on Félicité herself and the honor bestowed upon her by the women of the community. Moreover, in the drafts, the women (the *commères*) who sit with Félicité during her last days are said to come to see her out of curiosity. This is not the case in the final text.

Since for Félicité men are a cause of unhappiness and unpredictability, the Aubain household, a household without a father, represents an ideal situation.

At the beginning, when she begins her service, she is disturbed by the "souvenir de 'Monsieur,' planant sur tout!"[23] It does not, however, take Félicité long to feel at home and happy with the family.

The episode of the bull in Part 2 suggests dramatically the way Félicité perceives men and how she is able to respond to their threat. On a peaceful night, as she, Madame Aubain, and the two children are returning home after an excursion to the farm, they are surrounded by a group of oxen. Madame Aubain and the children are petrified, but Félicité is able to calm them, and the oxen turn away. The walk home, however, holds a far more frightening surprise. As the family crosses a second pasture, it is pursued by a dreadful bull who had been hidden by the fog. Félicité fights him by throwing clods of earth at his eyes:

> Il baissait le mufle, secouait les cornes et tremblait de fureur en beuglant horriblement. . . .
>   Le taureau avait acculé Félicité contre une claire-voie; sa bave lui rejaillissait à la figure, une seconde de plus il l'éventrait. Elle eut le temps de se couler entre deux barreaux, et la grosse bête, toute surprise, s'arrêta. (16-17)

The oxen, or castrated bulls, in the first pasture are easily assuaged by Félicité. It is the bull, perennial symbol of male sexuality, who attacks the family. The beast's fury is in point of fact directed at the two women. The scene thus enacts the phantasm and fear of rape. This scene also re-enacts Théodore's attack on Félicité: "Au bout d'un champ d'avoine, il la renversa brutalement. Elle eut peur et se mit à crier. Il s'éloigna" (8). It should be noted that Félicité escapes and to a certain degree overcomes Théodore's assault, whereas Virginie's reaction to the bull's attack is nothing short of deadly: ". . . elle eut, à la suite de son effroi, une affection nerveuse" (17). Virginie's health deteriorates progressively, and she eventually dies.

In setting up a parallel between the two women's reactions, Flaubert might be said to comment on the mental and physical stamina of the peasant woman and contrast it with that of the privileged young bourgeoise. More appropriately, however, in so doing Flaubert invites the reader to view Virginie as Félicité's frail and vulnerable double; this identification is all too well highlighted in the episode of Virginie's communion when Félicité identifies both in soul and in body with the young woman. The incident of the bull is symbolic of the devastating effect of male aggression and sexuality on women; it stresses the importance of banishing men from the privileged space of the feminine.

Victor and Bourais represent two exceptions to Félicité's antagonism toward men. Victor is a complementary character to Virginie. Together, Victor and Virginie, and not the brother and sister Paul and Virginie, call to mind Bernardin de Saint-Pierre's couple.[24] It is Victor, for instance, and not Paul, who leaves for America where he, ironically, dies. More significantly, however, Victor and Virginie are linked in Félicité's heart: "un lien de son cœur les unissait, et leurs destinées devaient être la même" (36). This is perhaps the reason why immediately after Victor dies "Virginie s'affaiblissait. Des oppressions, de la toux, une fièvre continuelle et des marbrures aux pommettes *décelaient quelque affection profonde*" (40, my italics). After Victor's death, the drafts show Virginie interested in watching boats passing on the Seine (Victor is a sailor): "Ses yeux parcouraient les bateaux."[25] Perhaps this too explains why Virginie dies shortly after Victor; and why, after her daughter's death, Madame Aubain is obsessed by a recurrent dream of her husband, "costumé comme un matelot," holding Virginie's hand. The "sailor" stands more specifically for Victor; Monsieur Aubain was not a seaman.

Victor and Virginie make up a kind of spectral love story, certainly a very sketchy one. Félicité, as the author of such a story, can be said to set up a parallel between herself and Madame Aubain whereby she imagines herself as Victor's mother the way that Madame Aubain is Virginie's, hence reproducing the idealized relationship between Marguerite and Madame de la Tour of Bernardin's *Paul et Virginie*. This spectral story takes on an added meaning if we take into account Flaubert's problem in deciding on a name for the character of Victor. Théodore, Théodule, Emile, and Alexandre were all alternatives. The name Flaubert used most frequently before deciding finally on Victor was Théodule, a diminutive of Théodore, in other words, Félicité's first love. It is possible, therefore, that fantasizing herself as Victor's mother and identifying with Virginie, Félicité can be said to imagine herself as both mother and lover to Victor. Just as later Loulou, who reminds her of Victor, because he came from America, is also both a son and a lover.[26]

The second exception to Félicité's hostility toward men is Bourais. Her admiration for him can be considered the most damning flaw of her character. Like the rest of the bourgeois of Pont-l'Evêque, with whom she seems to share many values, Félicité looks up to Bourais; he represents to her the epitome of bourgeois rectitude and decorum. Thus, in spite of her kind and generous nature, she shows a marked prejudice against men who, in contrast to Bourais, are not proper and reserved, men who lead a life of dissipation. These are men like the marquis de Gremanville, who drinks, and like Fabu, who wants to teach Loulou obscenities. Félicité resents Fabu and unjustly accuses him of killing Loulou. Her accusation is based on nothing more than Fabu's tough manner and sexually suggestive demeanor. The narrator explains on Fabu's behalf that ". . . il ne fût pas cruel, malgré le tatouage de ses bras et ses gros favoris. Au contraire! il avait plutôt du penchant pour le perroquet" (53-54). On her deathbed Félicité, realizing that she has unjustly suspected Fabu, asks his forgiveness.

Félicité and Bourais represent dramatic opposites; we can understand them both better in the light of that difference. Bourais is, in a manner of speaking, the Homais of *Un Cœur simple*, but whereas *Madame Bovary* ends with Homais's triumph and Emma's disillusionment, the conclusion here finds Bourais ruined, humiliated, and ostracized, and Félicité triumphant. "Ancien avoué," Bourais is a man of the law. As a result, he enjoys the prestige associated with men who represent authority, legality, and institutional power. It is by virtue of this association that he is successful in concealing for a long time his illegal activities. Moreover, the bourgeois of Pont-l'Evêque also consider him an enlightened man. They are impressed by his knowledge of the law and of Latin; Madame Aubain seeks his advice on her children's education. The consideration they pay him is due primarily to his position in society, his manner, and the way he displays his knowledge. Always arrogant, he is less concerned with communicating information than with concealing it, with clarifying rather than with mystifying. Typical of his manner is the celebrated scene in which he responds to Félicité's question about the distance between Pont-l'Evêque and Havana:

> Il atteignit son atlas, puis commença des explications sur les longitudes;
> et il avait un beau sourire de cuistre devant l'ahurissement de Félicité.
> Enfin, avec son porte-crayon, il indiqua dans les découpures d'une tache
> ovale un point noir, imperceptible, en ajoutant: "Voici." (37)

The atlas, the pencil, like law and Latin, are symbols which the bourgeois, and Félicité, associate with knowledge and authority, that is, legal authority and the authority of the letter.[27]

The technical references Bourais uses, like the obscure language of the dogma that the priest pronounces, are meant to mystify their public. It is by mystifying that those in positions of power perpetuate the myth and the illusion that they alone have access to privileged sources of truth and knowledge. In this manner, the language of authority (relying on the perceived authority of language) becomes the tool of oppression and exploitation. This explains, in part, why language and representation in *Un Cœur simple* are linked with violence. For instance, Guyot, the first instructor of Paul and Virginie, is described as "un pauvre diable employé à la Mairie, fameux pour sa belle main, et qui repassait son canif sur sa botte" (14). Guyot is something of a celebrity in Pont-l'Evêque because of his "beautiful" handwriting regardless, it seems, of his mediocrity and vulgar manner. Moreover, the "illustrations" that Bourais offers the children for their education are filled with scenes of violence: "Elles représentaient différentes scènes du monde, des *anthropophages* coiffés de plumes, un singe *enlevant* une demoiselle, des Bédouins dans le désert, une baleine qu'on *harponnait*, etc." (14, my italics). The link between violence and representation is also manifest in church, where behind the tabernacle a wood carving represents Saint Michael slaying the dragon. The language of authority, therefore, is inherently linked with men, with institutional power, and with violence.[28]

Félicité is especially impressed by language and representation. The drafts are more explicit about that than is the final text. For instance, Flaubert writes regarding Félicité: "ça l'ébahissait que l'on pût dire *tout cela* avec de l'encre et du papier,"[29] or "Pour elle <c'était> comme un miracle," "il y avait dans l'écriture [quelque chose] de divin," "d'inaccessible"[30] and, yet again, that Félicité had a mystical respect for "l'écriture," (the scriptures, yes; but more specifically these "black marks"). When she sees the "For Sale" sign on the Aubain home, unable to read, she is wild with anger at the sight of these "papiers couverts d'écritures," "couverts de grandes lettres inégales noires."[31] Moreover, Félicité is just as impressed by illustrations and paintings as she is by writing; the portrait of Monsieur Aubain "l'émerveilla comme une chose magique," for she had never seen a portrait before that time.[32]

If Félicité does not respond to the Catholic dogma and falls asleep as soon as the priest begins, she is, on the other hand, moved and inspired by the Gospels. This is because the Gospels are not an impersonal and abstract text like dogma; their language is simple and, most importantly, familiar; the Gospels communicate through images of familiar things. Hence, they reach out to the heart and to the imagination:

Les semailles, les moissons, les pressoirs, toutes ces choses familières dont parle l'Evangile, se trouvaient dans sa vie; le passage de Dieu les avait sanctifiées; et elle aima plus tendrement les agneaux par amour de l'Agneau, les colombes à cause du Saint-Esprit. (26)

The Gospels teach her to love even more deeply than she would ordinarily. Yet does Félicité understand this text or is she subjectively transforming, even distorting its meaning? Perhaps Félicité does distort the meaning of the Gospels; but what is important for us here is that she has made the Gospels meaningful to herself; she has personalized them. It is by virtue of its accessibility to perception and imagination and hence to sentiment that the Gospels inspire Félicité to ponder, in her own materialistic terms, God and the world. Her probings are subtle and not without interest, even though she remains blind to symbolic and metaphoric relations:

Elle avait peine à imaginer sa personne; car il n'était pas seulement oiseau, mais encore un feu, et d'autres fois un souffle. C'est peut-être sa lumière qui voltige la nuit aux bords des marécages, son haleine qui pousse les nuées, sa voix qui rend les cloches harmonieuses; et elle demeurait dans une adoration, jouissant de la fraîcheur des murs et de la tranquillité de l'église. (26)

This passage is reminiscent of a passage in *Madame Bovary* in which Flaubert describes Emma's attitude and perceptions when learning the catechism: "Au lieu de suivre la messe, elle regardait dans son livre les vignettes pieuses bordées d'azur, et elle aimait la brebis malade, le sacré cœur percé de flèches aiguës, ou le pauvre Jésus qui tombe en marchant sur sa croix."[33] Clearly, Emma gets only sense satisfaction from looking at the pictures; the pictures allow her to feel more intensely not others, not the world around her, as is the case for Félicité, but herself. How much more interesting, sensitive, and venturesome is Félicité's response to religious representation when compared with Emma's.

Félicité is a kind of pantheist; she believes that God and the universe are identical, that God can take any form, hence, the dove or her parrot. Here, again, the drafts are more explicit. Flaubert points out that in her understanding of the Gospels, "le ciel ne se distinguait pas de la terre"; "Le symbole devenait [pour] elle la réalité stricte *ainsi* les objets [...] *n'était qu'un* reflet, une répétition, une continuité des choses *faites* divines"; and objects around her "acquièrent une importance poétique qu'elles n'avaient pas auparavant."[34] Félicité's mind is keen on establishing continuity. She asks questions and seeks answers to them; she is not a passive listener. The drafts show, too, a sort of progression in her speculations. Having realized that the Virgin, the Father, and the Angels were concepts she could understand, she begins to seek ways to make more concrete, and to her more real, the Holy Spirit: "Le St. Esprit lui semblait une personne plus étendue et plus subtile," "comment était sa véritable forme?"[35]

It is this imaginative and subtle Félicité that Flaubert contrasts with the likes of Bourais. Unlike Bourais, who speaks with an authority he borrows from the discourses of science, reason, and specialized knowledge, Félicité's understandings rely on imagination and intuition. Flaubert might be said to sympathize far more with Félicité's mental processes than with Bourais's. In his own life, Flaubert held a very critical view of people who assumed positions of authority in culture. He expressed his contempt for them in many of his letters and in his work in general. He writes the following letter to Caroline to console her about the negative reviews she received after the exposition of some of her art:

> Le public n'est pas si bête que ça. Il n'y a de bête, en fait d'Art, que 1) le gouvernement 2) les directeurs de théâtre 3) les éditeurs 4) les rédacteurs en chef des journaux 5) les critiques *autorisés,* enfin tout ce qui détient le Pouvoir est essentiellement stupide. Depuis que la terre tourne, le Bien et le Beau ont été en dehors de lui. (9: 24)

Flaubert is speaking here specifically of the relationship between art and power. It is safe to assume, however, that he would not have limited this particular characterization of power to art and art criticism. Bourais's fall in the end is the result of his inability to gauge properly the power of integrity and truth, "le Bien." Félicité may not impress us by her intelligence, for it is of a practical and intuitive nature. For example, she is very clever in the market place; she can use lies and tricks to get Loulou and attract Victor, and she is at times subtle enough to interpret or, more accurately, to misinterpret Théodore's fear of being inducted into the army as a sign of his affection for her.

However, what is most remarkable about her vision, and what, for some readers, passes as a sign of her simple-mindedness, is her tendency toward animism. She is, like Flaubert himself, inclined to endow objects and signs with life.[36] For instance, Loulou is as much alive to her in death as he is in life. Moreover, at Honfleur, she stands watching Victor's boat disappear into the horizon until she sees nothing but "une tache noire qui pâlissait toujours, s'enfonça, disparut" (34). Is it not possible that Félicité is remembering this particular scene when she asks Bourais to show her Victor's house in a similar black spot ("point noir") on the atlas? Also, Félicité keeps Virginie's hat after her death not because the hat stands for Virginie, but rather because the hat contains and preserves the traces of the girl's *movements*, her presence now rarefied: "Le soleil éclairait ces pauvres objets, en faisait voir les taches, et des plis formés par *les mouvements* du corps. L'air était chaud et bleu, un merle gazouillait, tout semblait *vivre* dans une douceur profonde" (48-49; my italics). Madame Aubain and Félicité open the closet and "des papillons s'envolèrent de l'armoire" (48). The clothes, the closet, and the room itself, like the spot on the atlas, vibrate with memory and with imaginative life.

Although Félicité's mind seems to be governed by effects of metonymy, of chance contiguity, there is more to it than that. As both Gérard Genette and Paul de Man have suggested in their studies of Proust, often what we call metaphor, that is, a perception of an essential similarity, depends on, is produced by, a metonymic effect of contiguity. Similarly, Jacques Derrida, in "Mythologie Blanche," points out that the function of metaphor, the trope of similitude, is to display properties and to relate to these properties on the basis of their resemblance, without ever directly or fully stating their essence; its function is to provide for a missing term, to represent the absent.[37] It is true that in Félicité's mind Virginie's hat stands for Virginie; yet the association is more than an accidental connection, for it is the image which helps evoke the girl's fullness of life, her presence now rarefied. Félicité succeeds in creating an illusion, a "metaphoric effect," of union and harmony with those she loves. The tendency of Félicité's mind is to create links, eliminate differences, as the examples above and as the example of Loulou show. This type of figuration, this way of relating to the world, gives her the sense of having recovered a lost and fragmented totality; she communicates this feeling to Madame Aubain, who responds to her, for the first time, with a physical embrace.

Czyba, in her study of women in Flaubert, shows that Flaubert's attitude toward women is mysogynous and at heart gynophobic. I agree with her when she writes that women of the bourgeoisie under the July Monarchy and the Second Empire are represented in Flaubert in a degrading fashion as alienated from male society by their education and their economic and political powerlessness, that these women are portrayed in traditional roles, and that "*Un Cœur simple* confirme et aggrave un certain nombre d'a priori sur la condition féminine bourgeoise déjà lisibles dans les romans antérieurs: maternité nécessairement synonyme de souffrance, guerre inévitable des sexes, hostilitée obligée de la bru à l'égard de sa belle-mère. . . ." I do not agree with her when it comes to assessing Flaubert's attitude toward the servant. I do not share her view that "[l]e texte tend à dégrader le dévouement de Félicité et à en montrer la vanité," that " [l]a piété de Félicité est moins dévotion à Dieu, qu'elle ne peut concevoir et dont elle n'essaie même pas de comprendre les dogmes, que le dévouement inconditionnel à ses maîtres," or that "[l]'attachement de Félicité pour Loulou est pathétique *et* grotesque."[38]

It would be wrong as well as reductive to view Félicité's inability to understand abstract notations and discursive signification as a sign of her naïveté and simple-mindedness. Some of the views elaborated by recent feminist writers offer a way to understand and appreciate Félicité's position and the subversive nature of her desires and her actions. I will focus principally on the thoughts of Hélène Cixous and Luce Irigaray (only in passing on Julia Kristeva and others), who can contribute to my thesis. In spite of their differences, they share many important views. I do not presume to argue the merits or the shortcomings of their views in or outside the feminist debate. I do not claim, moreover, that their model for a "woman talk" (a "parler femme") is the only option (or the best option) women have for self-expression. I use their model only because it illumines Félicité's case more faithfully than do others.

For Irigaray and Cixous, patriarchy has historically silenced the feminine and repressed in its historic accounts of Western culture this systematic exclusion of the feminine. They argue in their works that Western conceptual systems are dominated by masculine values. The masculine has been used as the model for all forms of exchange, especially discourse. In the process, the feminine, the mother especially, has been mutilated; its values and distinctive differences from the masculine have been suppressed and devalorized. This exclusion, suppression, and mutilation of the feminine, Cixous and Irigaray suggest, has been the chief strategy for perpetuating and consolidating over time the power of the masculine. They call on women to question Western assumptions in terms of that difference and to recover and valorize the feminine. Irigaray and Cixous have argued further that if women have a problematic relationship with language, it is primarily because discourse is governed by phallocentric concepts (presence, linear progression, unity, coherence, etc.); language has been created by men to fulfill their needs, to fill a lack which does not exist for women. This lack is tied, to a large degree, to men's incapacity to procreate, to create life, as women can. Hence, men's interest in discursive logic, language, and, more generally, political and social organizing can be explained by their desire to generate, to create, to represent themselves and the world, to reproduce themselves and mark their offspring with their name. In the process, they have established the masculine as a standard and as a locus of power.[39]

Men have used language, Cixous and Irigaray contend, as the chief instrument for carrying out this generative process. Women, on the other hand, are closer to the process of creation, which they enact through and by virtue of their bodies. Therefore, women do not perceive the impulse to create as a separate, exterior process, artifact, or system. Unlike men, who ignore bodily pleasure in their pursuit of theories and representations, what women lose in power, we are told, they gain in pleasure. Cixous calls for a feminine writing, a kind of writing that would break open the chain of syntax, escape the repression of linear logic and of narrative, and allow for the emergence of a language that would be close to the experiences of the body. Though both Cixous and Irigaray attempt to designate a "woman talk," both are troubled by the realization that to communicate outside the community of women, to communicate with the "other," women may have little choice but to use the language of the dominant masculine culture. While to be silent is not the solution, to speak is to fall prey, as always, to the foreign language of the dominant male structure; it is in a sense to continue the oppression and suppression of women.[40]

To answer this problem, Irigaray envisages for the future a feminine syntax which she calls not a language per se, but a field where subject and object are absent or random, where disorder and noise take the place of order and deceptive clarity. She writes, "Cette 'syntaxe' mettrait plutôt en jeu le proche, mais un si proche qu'il rendrait impossible toute discrimination d'identité, toute constitution d'appartenance, donc toutes formes d'appropriation."[41] This particular feminist ideology, with its emphasis on difference, not on similarity, between the genders and with its deconstruction of linguistic "competence" as a value and a mode of discourse, offers the best model from which to view and assess Félicité's radical subversion of the masculine. Félicité's animistic tendency to interpret, sense, or breathe life into inanimate objects and signs and her sympathetic imagination which makes her susceptible to identification with others seem to fulfill Irigaray's notion of a future feminine "syntax." More clearly, however, Irigaray's speculation makes us sensitive to the fact that Félicité's misunderstandings and/or disinterest in abstract thoughts and notations do not suggest a deficiency on Félicité's part but rather represent a uniquely feminine response to and provocative attitude toward representational conventions, conventions which she manages to undermine while seeming to heartily support.

Although we can speak of Félicité as exploited and oppressed by the patriarchal bourgeois system, she is not its passive victim. Moreover, she cannot be characterized as powerless and ineffective. Rather, she is deliberate and independent; she makes decisions and acts upon them. Many examples of this may be cited. After Théodore's betrayal, she takes the initiative and leaves town. It is Félicité who, drawn by Madame Aubain's widowed condition, approaches her in the hope of landing a position as her maid. (In an early draft, she is recommended to Madame Aubain by one of the farmers. As I pointed out earlier, Flaubert's original concept of Félicité's character undergoes a change, and we see her in the drafts progressively more independent and more deliberate in her actions than at first.) She requests and receives permission, at her late age, to receive her first Communion. She cunningly gets the neighbors to give the parrot to Madame Aubain, hence to herself. She succeeds in placing the stuffed Loulou in the altar in spite of the women's reluctance. She has no equal when it comes to negotiating with farmers. Generally speaking, it is Félicité, and not her mistress, who is in charge of the Aubain home. On the marquis's visits, for instance, Félicité is the one to decide when he has had enough and show him to the door. Similarly, she opens the door "avec plaisir devant M. Bourais." Clearly, the emphasis here is not on her duty as servant to act for her mistress. The Aubain home is like a web into which Félicité draws people and objects (the bric-à-brac in her room). She invites Victor to the house, feeds him, and mends his clothes, "heureuse d'une occasion qui le forçait à revenir" (31). Later, she locks Loulou inside the house and then in her room to protect him from Fabu's bad influence. Moreover, although she helps the Polish soldiers who come to her door, she is furious when one of them becomes too familiar and enters the kitchen in her absence. She is charitable and yet she remains profoundly territorial and independent.[42]

Félicité seems to have thoroughly assimilated the conventions and bankrupt values of the society around her; she finds it, for instance, incomprehensible that she should outlive her mistress and "natural" that like her, she should die of pneumonia. However, does Félicité really share the values of the bourgeois culture? She seems to. And yet if she succeeds in giving this impression, it is mainly because she so effectively parodies that culture, as the example of Loulou–Holy Spirit dramatizes so well. Her superior wisdom, be it akin to insight or intuition, moves her to act in such a way that we suspect that though her "heart" may in fact be in the role she is playing, it is also elsewhere. This suspicion becomes more certain after Loulou's death, when the bird takes on the attributes of a representational object, that is, when Félicité can express through him her "poetic" visions, her fantasies and desires. It is in fact through Loulou that Félicité expresses her most radical and unsettling nature, through him principally, that she is able, in the end, to outmaneuver and undermine the system which exploits her during her life.

Although Loulou can only repeat the clichés taught to him by Félicité, he seems to have a mind of his own, so to speak. He refuses, for instance, to play up to expectations: "Etrange obstination de Loulou, ne parlant plus du moment qu'on le regardait!" (52). Before anyone else in the community discovers Bourais's fraudulence, it is Loulou who humiliates and harasses him in front of the public:

> La figure de Bourais, sans doute, lui paraissait très drôle. Dès qu'il l'apercevait il commençait à rire, à rire de toutes ses forces. Les éclats de sa voix bondissaient dans la cour, l'écho les répétait, les voisins se mettaient à leurs fenêtres, riaient aussi; et, pour n'être pas vu du perroquet, M. Bourais se coulait le long du mur, en dissimulant son profil avec son chapeau, atteignait la rivière, puis entrait par la porte du jardin; et les regards qu'il envoyait à l'oiseau manquaient de tendresse. (53)

In this marvelous passage, the laughter of Loulou is magnified, repeated, by Loulou's echo and by the whole town. By mocking and ostracizing Bourais, in a way that Félicité herself never does, Loulou vindicates not only Félicité but the whole community. In a draft, Flaubert makes explicit that it is the women who observe from their windows the humiliation of Bourais and laugh.[43] We also learn later that besides his fraudulent financial dealings, Bourais is a morally depraved man; he has an illegitimate child and "des relations avec une personne de Dozulé" (64). This news makes Madame Aubain so ill that she dies nine days later—a sign perhaps that the hours they spent together were not entirely innocent ("il s'enfermait avec elle pendant des heures dans le cabinet de 'Monsieur,' et craignait toujours de se compromettre" (14). Like Monsieur Aubain (in the drafts), it seems that Bourais, too, was unfaithful to her.

As Félicité progressively loses her faculties, Loulou becomes more and more the mediator between herself and the outside world. It is through him that her need for love and self-expression is realized. While alive, he is, like Victor, both a son and a lover: "Ils avaient des dialogues, lui, débitant à satiété les trois phrases de son répertoire, et elle, y répondant par des mots sans plus de suite, mais où son cœur s'épanchait" (57). In the perfect reciprocity of this loving relationship, there is no place for an economy of exchange or of opposition. Félicité and Loulou are joined in pleasure. We see this so vividly in the conclusion of the passage just quoted where Loulou pecks her lips, as in kissing, and "les grandes ailes du bonnet et les ailes de l'oiseau frémissaient ensemble" (57). The words they send back and forth to each other with visible pleasure are not empty of meaning, although, of course, in a certain specific and correct sense they are; they are filled with sentiment, with affection. Yet, since these words are used without concern for their conventional sense, they trivialize to a great extent the conventional linguistic system by abusing and ignoring its procedures, by making it seem totally dispensable as a system of communication.

We can characterize these conversations as a form of "feminine syntax." Loulou, as has been pointed out by Shoshana Felman and others, is a figure for discourse.[44] More specifically, he is an androgynous figure of discourse, a figure for Julia Kristeva's "semiotic." The semiotic, according to Kristeva, is the "revival of archaic pre-oedipal modes of operation"; and, as I will argue shortly in my discussion of Loulou as fetish, Félicité fantasizes a relationship to the world that can only be characterized as pre-oedipal. Kristeva, unlike Cixous and Irigaray for instance, argues for a theoretical bisexuality of writing, for a dialectical struggle, in which the concept of the maternal coupled with the concept of the paternal makes possible the exploration of all aspects of signification. The semiotic is not exclusively attached to women, she points out. It predominates and is valued over the symbolic in certain texts, as, for instance, avant-garde texts like the texts of Mallarmé and Artaud. The feminine, she argues, enjoys a privileged relationship with the semiotic in a limited sense; it has a privileged relationship with the semiotic in the non-artistic, non-textual forms such as in pregnancy and childbirth, which Kristeva considers the equivalent of avant-garde art.[45] Loulou, it seems to me, can be profitably compared to Kristeva's semiotic, an androgynous figure for signification. For while Loulou trivializes masculine discourse and threatens, as I will show later, the position of the symbolic order, he is at the same time the emblem of that discourse and the chief vehicle by means of which Félicité expresses herself and undermines the standards of her oppressors.

When, after his death, he becomes the incarnation of the Holy Spirit, Loulou trivializes the authority of religious representation. That Félicité chooses a parrot to represent the Holy Spirit is surely startling and funny.

Nonetheless, seen the way she sees it, the parrot is really no different from the conventional dove; he is not less worthy or more ridiculous than the traditional symbol:

> A l'église, elle contemplait toujours le Saint-Esprit, et observa qu'il avait quelque chose du perroquet. Sa ressemblance lui parut encore plus manifeste sur une image d'Epinal représentant le baptême de Notre-Seigneur. *Avec ses ailes de pourpre et son corps d'émeraude*, c'était vraiment le portrait de Loulou. (62-63; my italics)

If there is irony here, it is directed not at Félicité nor at the concept of the Holy Spirit but at ridiculous stylistic representations of sacred objects in general. Félicité finds Loulou just as splendid and just as moving as these representations: "Quelquefois, le soleil entrant par la lucarne frappait son œil de verre, et en faisait jaillir un grand rayon lumineux qui la mettait en extase" (66).

Félicité does not mistake Loulou for the Holy Spirit. She is quite aware of deviating from convention, and what is more, she is convinced that the parrot, and not the dove, is the more appropriate representation for the Holy Spirit: "Le Père, pour s'énoncer, n'avait pu choisir une colombe, puisque ces bêtes-là n'ont pas de voix, mais plutôt un des ancêtres de Loulou" (63). We could mock her reasoning the way that Bourais would, and be amused by her excessively literal imagination, but we would be missing the point; we would miss the ideologically radical nature of her conceptions. Her conflation of the parrot and the picture of the Holy Spirit is in fact deliberate; Félicité has a method. Having bought a representation of the Holy Spirit of Epinal, "Félicité priait en regardant l'image, mais de temps à autre se tournait un peu vers l'oiseau" (63). She places the picture near Loulou "de sorte que, du même coup d'œil, elle les voyait ensemble. Ils s'associèrent dans sa pensée, le perroquet se trouvant sanctifié par ce rapport avec le Saint-Esprit, qui devenait plus vivant à ses yeux et intelligible" (63). A key word here is "intelligible." By modifying a convention that alienates her, Félicité can achieve the results both promised and denied to her by the convention. What she does in effect is to assume for herself the right and the privilege accorded only to men, to define, or redefine, to represent, in this case the Holy Spirit.[46]

In his by now all too familiar letter to Madame Roger des Genettes, Flaubert states without a trace of ambiguity that the ending of *Un Cœur simple* is not in the least ironic, but that it is "serious." We are not meant, and neither are we inclined, really, to ridicule Félicité's faith, although we tend to ridicule the form that it takes. What should be stressed instead is her resourcefulness and the way she triumphs in the end. That Félicité chooses a parrot as symbol of the Holy Spirit is not a sign of her blindness, literal or figurative, but rather of her superior insight, for what she, and Flaubert, expose through Loulou is the wholly contrived, arbitrary, mobile, and, here, comical and pathetic nature of representation, in particular, of religious representation. On a visit to Saint-Michel, Flaubert sees a painting of a bishop on his death-bed and writes:

> O sainte religion catholique, si tu as inspiré des chefs-d'œuvre, que de galettes, en revanche, n'as-tu pas causées! En contemplant cette épou-vantable toile, et en songeant que beaucoup l'ont pu regarder sans rire, qu'à d'autres sans doute elle a semblé belle, que d'autres enfin se sont agenouillés devant, y ont puisé peut-être des inspirations suprêmes, nous avons été pris malgré nous d'une mélancolie chagrine. Mais qu'y a-t-il donc dans le cœur de l'homme pour que toujours et sans cesse il se jette sur toutes choses et se cramponne avec une ardeur pareille au laid comme au beau, au mesquin comme au sublime? Hélas, hélas! rappelons-nous, pour excuser celui qui a fait cela et encore plus ceux qui l'admirent, nos prédilections maladives et nos extases imbéciles! Evoquons dans notre passé tout ce que nous avons eu jadis d'amour naïf pour quelque femme laide, de candide enthousiasme pour un niais ou d'amitié dévouée pour un lâche.[47]

It is inevitable that Félicité should be able to express her desires and exercise her autonomy by making a travesty of existing conventional forms rather than by creating some new form or some original concept entirely her own. The idea that women have to steal language from men (the way men think of themselves as having stolen fire from the gods) is a notion that several French feminists have expressed. The title of Claudine Herrmann's famous book, *Les Voleuses de langue*, points this out directly; and Cixous explains in an interview: "I found myself in the classic situation of women who, at one time or another, feel that it is not they who have produced culture . . . Culture was there, but it was a barrier forbidding me to enter, whereas of course, from the depths of my body, I had a desire for the objects of culture. I therefore found myself obliged to steal them . . . So that in a sense [culture] is always there [in the works], but it is always there in a displaced, diverted, reversed way. I have always used it in a totally ironic way."[48] Similarly, Irigaray suggests, because the system of representation is designed to alienate and silence the feminine and deprive it of its own autonomy, the only option available to women for self-expression in a patriarchal culture is through "mimetism," a reproduction deliberately assumed by the woman and that mimics masculine discourse not with the purpose of discovering the feminine difference but of uncovering how the/a woman is exploited:

> Il n'est, dans un premier temps, peut-être qu'un seul "chemin," celui qui est historiquement assigné au féminin: *le mimétisme.* Il s'agit d'assumer, délibérément, ce rôle. Ce qui est déjà retourner en affirmation une subordination, et de ce fait, commencer à la déjouer. . . . Jouer de la mimesis, c'est donc, pour une femme, tenter de retrouver le lieu de son exploitation par le discours, sans s'y laisser simplement réduire. . . . C'est aussi "dévoiler" le fait que, si les femmes miment si bien, c'est qu'elles ne résorbent pas simplement dans cette fonction. *Elles restent aussi ailleurs.* . . .[49]

The feminine gesture toward the unthinkable "elsewhere" that Irigaray suggests here is best understood by looking at Loulou in his role as a fetish in Félicité's economy of desire.[50]

Loulou dead and stuffed fits the anthropological definition of a fetish; namely, any inanimate object regarded as having magical powers and worshiped for that reason. It differs from an idol in that it is worshiped in its own character, not as an image, symbol, or occasional residence of a deity. Freud's theory of the fetish can deepen our insight of Félicité's attachment.[51] The problem with using Freud's theory is that he was careful to leave to the side the question of feminine perversion, and he ascribes fetishism, which is the very nucleus of perversion, to an accident of the masculine phallic phase. Certainly it is the case that women have their share of perversions, fetishism not excluded even if theoretically it remains unrecognized as such by psycho-analysis. In any case, for our purpose, a case for feminine fetishism can be built by following Freud's model of masculine fetishism.

For Freud, generally speaking, the fetish is a token triumph over the threat of violence, namely, the threat of castration. Freud stresses that the fetish is not just a substitute penis; it is a substitute for a particular and quite special penis that was very important in childhood but was later lost. The fetish is designed to preserve it from extinction. This particular penis is the one the little boy once believed his mother had. Because the boy does not want to relinquish that belief, he continues to believe his mother has a penis, but that it is no longer the same as it was before. Something else, the fetish, has taken its place, has been substituted for it. To the extent that the boy identifies with his mother and fears her fate (the father has castrated her), the fetish represents a triumph over that fear. Hence, the fetish represents both the realization and the denial of a certain reality, the mother's castration; the ego has split itself as a means of defense. The fetishist enjoys yet another advantage; since the meaning of the fetish is not known to others, the fetish is not forbidden to him and he can readily obtain the sexual satisfaction attached to it. To understand how the fetish works in the girl's case, we must understand first how she deals with the threat of castration which is central to Freud's argument.

According to Freud, the castration complex is as strong in girls as it is in boys, though its content cannot be the same for both. But the girl's realization that her mother has no penis makes her feel wronged by the mother, whom she blames for her condition. As a result, the lack of a penis in the mother is a sign of the mother's, hence, of all women's, weakness with regards to men. Thus, Freud's scheme suggests that the boy does not need to hate his mother to proceed to the next phase of sexual adjustment, as the girl does. At the onset of the oedipal crisis, the girl begins to transfer her early attachment and love for her mother to her father. Having lost, so to speak, her penis, she nevertheless continues to want it ("penis envy") and seeks to obtain it from her father, then later from her husband, in the form of a baby. In Freud's scenario, as has been often pointed out, the girl never adequately resolves the oedipal crisis. Freud contends that only the birth of a male child really gives the woman the penis she is longing for, and adds that a woman will likely be content in her marriage only when she can mother her husband and turn him into her own penis.

What is the nature of the feminine fetish? And does it have the same operative value for a girl as it does for a boy? Is it a victory for her over the threat of castration? It should be if, as indeed Freud claims, girls fear castration in the same way boys do. It would be an error to conclude too hastily that in her case, the fetish is a substitute for the father's penis. The weight of Freud's discussion hinges, appropriately, one might add, on the proposition that the fetish is a substitute for a very particular and special penis, namely the mother's. The argument that the penis in question is the mother's relies on two quite convincing tales that (1) all children, boys and girls, are attached first and foremost to their mother before they transfer their attachment to their father and (2) that both boys and girls initially believe that the parents of both sexes have a penis. Therefore, just as Freud claims that it is in the case of the boy, the fetish in the case of the girl serves to preserve the notion of her mother as intact, whole. At the same time, it preserves her (as it does the boy) from the fear and the threat of castration or violence at the hands of the powerful father. The boy's fetish is a substitute for the mother's penis, or a denial of its lack in the same way that it is for the girl. In the girl's case, this operation has an important consequence; the fetish preserves the daughter's love and esteem for her mother (since the father has taken, or threatens to take, nothing away from her); it has eliminated the impetus to debase the mother which would have constituted penis envy, and a complex of inferiority vis à vis men. The fetish is having a penis of one's own, to reword an already reworded phrase. Where there is no lack, there is no desire; the father has nothing to offer the girl, and his violence is kept at bay; hence, we find him in *Un Cœur simple* absent from scenes of desire and emerging in phantasms of fear and violence.[52]

This scenario, by the same token, describes a procedure whereby the feminine subject forfeits her chance at acquiring language; she misses out, so to speak, on the symbolic.[53] But the rewards are clear. The fetish serves the positive role of allowing the feminine to envisage itself in a masculine-dominated world as intact, independent, ideal. Indeed this is the unthinkable gesture Félicité points to, the unthinkable that imagines a world where the mother is unviolated, valued, perfect; this is the pre-oedipal state. There is more than a denial of sexual difference in Félicité's fetishism; in the process, she *restores* the essential bond with the mother by the suppression of the masculine.

It should be obvious that Loulou alive carries a different value from Loulou dead. Alive he is a "son" and a "lover," a testament to Félicité's conventionality, her yearning for a male child and a lover. Loulou becomes a fetish, a positive and subversive sign, only after his death when she has him stuffed and endows him with the properties of an artifact (the etymology of the word *fetish* is from the Latin *facticius*, "made by art"). It is only as a representational object, then, that Loulou becomes the expression of Félicité's radical desire, her gesture of self-assertion and defiance. Loulou alive is still phallically determined; Loulou-fetish is Félicité's design, an imaginative strategy, a willed and creative arrangement, whereby she assures herself of happiness in this world and salvation in the hereafter by outmaneuvering masculine reference and law. Thus, Félicité learns or borrows from the masculine culture a valuable concept and tool, namely, how representation serves desire. Representational conventions offer her a way of shaping and hence controlling reality. This is an understanding that Emma Bovary, for instance, lacks and that Félicité is perceptive enough to sense and profit from. Emma is happy only when she recognizes in her own life the fictional representations she has encountered in literature. Félicité knows how to reproduce (not merely recognize) these fictions in her life (recall, for example, the way that she fictionalizes the relationship between Victor and Virginie, herself and Madame Aubain). By using Loulou as her personal sign, she shows a determination not to accept the world on its own terms, but on hers. Emma's fantasies, moreover, are strongly marked by a lack. She envies the masculine condition and perceives the feminine as a mode of passivity and impotence. In other words, she privileges the masculine.[54] Félicité's fantasies are not fantasies of equality and of sameness but of difference. She desires and achieves the exclusion of the masculine from her world and from her fantasies.

One gets a different perspective of the significance and specificity of Félicité's fetish when one looks at it through the sociologically determined accounts of penis envy and castration complex best exemplified in the following response to Freud by Elizabeth Janeway. Janeway asserts that no woman envies a penis or, by extension, fears castration of a penis she never had to begin with, except insofar as penis stands in her mind for:

> something else that men enjoy: namely autonomy, freedom, and the power to control her destiny. By insisting, falsely, on female deprivation of the male organ, Freud is pointing to an actual deprivation and one of which he was clearly aware. . . Women were evident social castrates, and the mutilation of their potentiality as achieving human creatures was quite analogous to the physical wound.[55]

If, as Janeway says, the penis represents power and autonomy, then the fetish has meaning in the economy of desire only if it is designed and perceived as not a less powerful but a less threatening and more personal and secret substitute, or figure, for the all powerful penis. Hence, by definition, the fetish would have the same effect as the penis, or what it stands for, namely, power, but without assuming the same form. The fetish, therefore, allows the fetishist to borrow, or plug into, the power it lacks from the dominant signifier, which is unaware of the fetishist's design. By appropriating the power invested in the penis, the fetishist can be said to deflect power away from its conventional source, to decentralize it and thus undermine its authority and its effects. In addition, since the fetish is a secret signifier, whose meaning is not likely to be discovered by other people, especially the power source that is tapped, the fetishist experiences the subterfuge as pleasurable, liberating, and, above all, safe from dangerous reprisal. In Félicité's case, the fetish works to undo a debilitating and alienating convention by reconstructing it in a context more familiar and less inhibiting (the parrot for the dove). This reconstruction might be perceived as limited, since it borrows heavily from the convention (the parrot and the dove are both birds, after all). But this type of borrowing is a radical enterprise. It consists in undermining the *exclusiveness* and supremacy of the dominant signifier and, possibly, sets the stage for others, also not institutionally supported, to play the game.

Who are these "others" in *Un Cœur simple*? Before Félicité dies, we find la mère Simon waiting in the wings to assume Félicité's role. In an early manuscript version, la mère Simon is an alcoholic not to be relied on for the care of Félicité. Flaubert's intention was undoubtedly to stress Félicité's bad fortune and intensify the reader's pity for her. By changing la mère Simon's portrait, however, from one of a wretched loser to that of an unfortunate yet kindly, devoted, and understanding woman, like Félicité herself, Flaubert allows for an unambiguously positive and hopeful sense of community between the two women (recall, too, that the three women who sit by her side at the end were, in the drafts, with her out of curiosity). La mère Simon conveniently loses her grocery business at about the time Félicité can no longer do things for herself. As with Félicité and her alter ego Loulou (and later with Saint Julien), the process of physical and economic disintegration is a sign of, and a necessary step toward, transcendence and salvation. La mère Simon cares for Félicité the way that Félicité once took care of le père Colmiche: for instance, she comes every morning, splits wood and pumps water; at Félicité's deathbed, la mère Simon calls for the doctor and remains until Félicité dies, thinking to herself that one day she too will have to pass this way; she understands and respects Félicité's attachment to Loulou and, touchingly, brings the bird to the bed for a last farewell.

To describe Félicité's and la mère Simon's last moments together, Flaubert places them in a setting at once restful and vibrant, reminiscent of the scene at the seashore, and the scene between Félicité and Madame Aubain in Virginie's room, both quoted earlier. Although they are indoors, in Félicité's room, nature seems to envelop them with its warmth and its life: "Les herbages envoyaient l'odeur de l'été; des mouches bourdonnaient; le soleil faisait luire la rivière, chauffait les ardoises. La mère Simon, revenue dans la chambre, s'endormait doucement" (69). Three "kindly women" sit around Félicité while she is given extreme unction; like la mère Simon, they understand and respect Félicité and defend her intentions next to Fabu.

The women of Pont-l'Evêque form a sisterhood of sorts; this includes the *bourgeoises* as well, as I have indicated earlier. When a controversy arises as to where to place the central shrine of the procession, the women of the parish designate Madame Aubain's courtyard. They might as well have asked to place it under Félicité's window, for that is exactly what they meant; Madame Aubain had been dead for several years and no one lived in the house except Félicité. Moreover, Flaubert clearly suggests that the ceremony that unfolds under Félicité's window is staged for her, to honor her passing. The narrative of the procession which culminates beneath her window is carefully orchestrated to reflect or to announce the different phases of Félicité as she nears death.

Orchestration is Flaubert's poetry, his metaphors; and this passage, along with the agricultural fair in *Madame Bovary*, is one of the most successful. Félicité follows the procession mentally. Her delirium subsides when she hears it approaching. The beginning of the description of the procession shows all the townspeople, women and children as well as men, as they make their way to Félicité's courtyard. When they arrive around the bend, her agony begins; a cold sweat moistens Félicité's temples, and at the highest moment of her agony a fusillade shakes the window-panes as if to announce that Félicité is near the end. All the people, now gathered beneath her window, are as silent as the beating of her heart; all kneel, and as the incense wafts upward and through her window she takes her last breath, inhales it sensuously, mystically, as her heartbeat gently comes to a stop. The final vision of Loulou in the sky ends the dialectic between the two spaces, the courtyard and the room.

Looking at the details that constitute the description of the altar beneath her window, we begin to suspect that Félicité may not, indeed, be alone in endowing ordinary things with sacred overtones:

Des guirlandes vertes pendaient sur l'autel, orné d'un falbala en point d'Angleterre. Il y avait au milieu un petit cadre enfermant des reliques, deux orangers dans les angles, et, tout le long, des flambeaux d'argent et des vases en porcelaine, d'où s'élançaient des tournesols, des lis, des pivoines, des digitales, des touffes d'hortensias. Ce monceau de couleurs éclatantes descendait obliquement, du premier étage jusqu'au tapis se prolongeant sur les pavés; et des choses rares tiraient les yeux. Un sucrier de vermeil avait une couronne de violettes, des pendeloques en pierre d'Alençon brillaient sur de la mousse, deux écrans chinois montraient leurs paysages. Loulou, caché sous des roses, ne laissait voir que son front bleu, pareil à une plaque de lapis. (71-72)

Are some of these objects fetishistic like the parrot? Perhaps. Moreover, as with the objects in Félicité's room, the items undoubtedly have a personal and sentimental value to the individual who has placed them there;[56] even if they did not already have a special meaning, their inclusion alone in the altar would, ipso facto, confer a sentimental or a sacred value upon them.[57]

The objects in the altar are there by virtue of an institutional convention which allows them to be displayed. But by permitting this, the system loosens the structure and allows for the expression of radical desires, the kind of subversive practice Félicité engages in, practices which dismiss, if they do not in fact challenge and secretly usurp, the authority and prescriptions of the system. These fundamentally radical desires are not less radical for being common. The priest who gives in to Félicité's request to have the dilapidated body of Loulou in the altar is showing kindness to her; but he cannot begin to suspect what Félicité has in mind, that is, how she perceives Loulou. It is ironic and comic, that to show her appreciation to the priest, Félicité bequeaths Loulou to him at her death. This is not a pathetic gesture and must be seen as a possible gesture of forgiveness (she does the same for Fabu). This gesture is a recognition of the "other" as a possible interlocutor in a real dialogue. The priest, after all, was receptive enough to her request to place Loulou in the altar.

The altar is the artistic expression of the women of the parish. The women are responsible for the arrangements of the ceremony, under the direction of the officiating priests. By masculine standards, the composition is surely barbaric; it is excessive and lacks harmony; its center, or "heart," "un petit cadre enfermant des reliques," and the two orange trees at the corners, meager attempts at symmetry and design, are overwhelmed by, among other things, the many types of flowers coming from all directions with their different colors and different containers. Can the altar be read as saying something about "feminine style"?

Cixous and Irigaray, among others, are concerned about the question of a specifically feminine style. However, they have tried to refrain from defining it. Cixous, for example, points out that it is impossible to "define" a feminine practice of writing "for this practice will never be theorized, enclosed, encoded—which does not mean that it doesn't exist."[58] Cixous wants to save feminine style from being incorporated in masculine (i.e., theoretical) discourse. So does Irigaray when she suggests that a "parler-femme" cannot be explained: "il se parle, il ne se méta-parle pas."[59] This is because a feminine style, for Irigaray and Cixous, cannot be inscribed as such in any theory, except indirectly, when it is standardized against male parameters; the masculine will always serve as a model for speaking about the feminine.

To a certain degree, the altar, and Félicité's room, fit Irigaray's and Cixous's qualified notion of a feminine style by their lack of concern for organization, balance, and their predilection for movement, excess, and over-statement. In the altar, the disproportionately small central frame and the large orange trees at the corners, tokens of masculine principles of organization, cannot possibly counterbalance the overwhelming surge and impulse toward movement and chaos. This joyful and uncontrolled composition flies in the face of the standard for a well-wrought artistic product, but it works. It works, like the dialogues between Félicité and Loulou, in the sense that it communicates a feeling of exuberance and pleasure, and, most importantly, it succeeds in conferring a special meaning to common, everyday personal objects in the altar by granting them legitimacy as sacred objects, or objects touched by the sacred. These are legitimized, as I said earlier, by virtue of this area of tolerance in the system which women, out of necessity, are keen to sense and exploit.

Ironically, it seems that Loulou is the most "artistic" image, the most understated item in the altar. Although in reality the stuffed bird was falling apart, "les vers le dévoraient; une de ses ailes était cassée, l'étoupe lui sortait du ventre" (69), to the point that even the parish women thought it improper for Félicité to include him, all we see of him at the end is his blue forehead, "like a plaque of lapis lazuli," surrounded by roses. Like a symbolic image, this blue spot will expand to reflect and occupy the sky, where Félicité sees an immense Loulou hovering above her head. Félicité does not die a solitary death, nor does her goodness go unrecognized, at least by the women of Pont-l'Evêque, who celebrate her death with the grandeur and the sentiment reserved for martyrs and saints.

3

Murdering the Father: Re-writing the Legend of Saint Julien l'Hospitalier

For Flaubert, as Michal Peled Ginsburg remarks, "narrating is never simple; it requires a ruse."[1] *Saint Julien*, like *Un Cœur simple*, is a text which offers two equally valid and incompatible interpretations, a straight and a suspect reading. On the one hand, Julien's itinerary can be read as following faithfully the model of hagiographic narratives. The narrative can be read as the story of a man who sins but who, after immense suffering and repentance, achieves salvation. On the other hand, Julien's sin can be read as the expression of an unrelenting hostility toward his parents, especially his father and the law which he represents. This hostility is not directed at himself, as is the case in the straight narrative, but against civilization. Like "simplicity" in Félicité's case, Julien's sin is the means by which he succeeds in undermining and transgressing the law of the father. The paradigm of "sainthood," like the paradigm of "simplicity" in *Un Cœur simple*, helps him cover up, so to speak, his intentions and win in the end.

G. F. G. Lecointre-Dupont's preface to the Alençon manuscript of the legend of Saint Julien relates that it was customary for medieval scribes to embellish and amplify the legend they were transmitting in order to interest their worldly audience in the stories of men who devoted themselves to the service of God. He calls this added part of invention, embellishments, and amplifications the scribes' "pieuse fraude," suggesting that what changes they had undertaken were made in the spirit of the model at hand, that the "fraud," in other words, did not subvert the model's meaning, its moral message, but that it merely rendered the narrative more interesting to its new audience.[2] In addition, Lecointre-Dupont points out to his nineteenth-century readers that the story of Saint Julien could be considered the French version of the life of the legendary Oedipus. By calling the reader's attention to the fact that the story of Saint Julien is the story both of a parricide and of a saint, Lecointre-Dupont possibly hoped to interest his audience in the story he, in his turn, was adapting for their benefit.

Having consulted Lecointre-Dupont's text, could Flaubert have missed noticing the potential for irony in Lecointre-Dupont's characterization of the hagiographic text as a "pious fraud"? In any case, Flaubert's predilection for ironic situations is well recognized. We have an especially telling example in *Pyrénées et Corse,* Flaubert's account of his travels with Maxime du Camp:

> Nous revenions de Saint-Mandrier, que nous avons visité, guidés par un de ses médecins, M. Raymond fils; on m'y a fait admirer une église toute neuve, bâtie par les forçats, j'ai admiré le coup de génie qui a fait construire un temple à Dieu par la main des assassins et des voleurs.[3]

It is in this spirit that Flaubert conceived *Saint Julien,* as the letters in the *Correspondance* on the *Trois contes* suggest. For instance, Flaubert was adamant that his publisher Georges Charpentier include in the text an illustration of the stained-glass window picturing Saint Julien from the cathedral of Rouen. Effectively, Flaubert wanted to baffle and outrage his readers, as we gather from the following passage in a letter to Charpentier:

> Je désirais mettre à la suite de *Saint Julien* le vitrail de la cathédrale de Rouen. Il s'agissait de colorier la planche qui se trouve dans le livre de Langlois, rien de plus. Et cette illustration me plaisait *précisément* parce que ce n'était pas une illustration, mais un *document* historique. En comparant l'image au texte on se serait dit: "Je n'y comprends rien. Comment a-t-il tiré ceci de cela?" (8: 207)

The Goncourts also relate a significant conversation between Flaubert and Charpentier in which the latter asks the former if he has not changed his mind about including the illustration from Langlois's book, an illustration which, Charpentier adds: "c'est vous qui le dites—n'a aucun rapport avec votre livre?" Flaubert's answer does not come as a surprise: "Oui, parfaitement, et c'est bien à cause de cela."[4] It bears pointing out that the distinction Flaubert makes between his version of the legend and the representation in the stained-glass window does not allude at all to compositional or aesthetic differences. It does not suggest, for example, the superiority of the verbal medium over the visual: "this illustration pleased me *precisely* because it was not an illustration, but a historical *document*" (my translation). Note Flaubert's emphasis.

In placing the two versions side by side, Flaubert hoped somehow to place the reader in a situation where one of the readings would involve rethinking the meaning of the traditional hagiographic representation, the "document," whereby a parricide becomes a saint by appealing to God for forgiveness through self-sacrifice and repentance. The inclusion of the representation with the text invites the reader to wonder whether Flaubert's text develops or distorts the familiar conventional story. Either way, the effect of Flaubert's subtext is to undermine the hagiographic text (the document) if only by highlighting the saint's sin, his violence, his eccentricities.

Curiously, and even more perversely, Flaubert wanted Charpentier to place the illustration *after* the text, undoubtedly to serve as a visual index to the last words of *Saint Julien*: "Et voilà l'histoire de Saint Julien l'Hospitalier telle à peu près qu'on la trouve sur un vitrail d'église, dans mon pays," with the "more or less" sounding a sustained ironic note.[5] Flaubert, the consummate ironist, must have conceived *Saint Julien*, at least in part, as a deviant, unorthodox version of the traditional narrative; a story that would unsettle more than confirm.

It is not surprising that *Saint Julien*, and the *Trois contes* as a whole, whose composition interrupted the writing of *Bouvard et Pécuchet*, should be written in the same spirit found in that major project of demystification, the *Dictionnaire*:[6]

Ce livre [the *Dictionnaire*], complètement fait, et précédé d'une bonne préface où l'on indiquerait comme quoi l'ouvrage a été fait dans le but de rattacher le public à la tradition, à l'ordre, à la convention générale, et arrangé de telle manière que le lecteur ne sache pas si on se fout de lui, oui ou non, ce serait peut-être une œuvre étrange et capable de réussir. (2: 237-38)

A few years later, Flaubert wrote Louise Colet:

La préface surtout m'excite fort, et la manière dont je la conçois (ce serait tout un livre), aucune loi ne pourrait me mordre quoique j'y attaquerais tout. Ce serait la glorification historique de tout ce qu'on approuve. . . . Cette apologie de la canaillerie humaine sur toutes ses faces, ironique et hurlante d'un bout à l'autre, pleine de citations, (qui prouveraient le contraire) et de textes effrayants (ce serait facile), est dans le but, dirais-je, d'en finir une fois pour toutes avec les excentricités, quelles qu'elles soient. (3: 66-67)

More than 20 years later, Flaubert's concept of a work celebrating traditional values, order, and morality, aimed at making the readers wonder if perhaps they were being made fools of, is implemented, but with more subtlety perhaps. For in *Saint Julien*, Flaubert is able to subvert the moral function of the legend while making the narrative conform to the paradigm of Christian hagiography. As with *Un Cœur simple*, he succeeds in this task by writing a text that allows itself to be read equally well as both a straight and a subversive account. On close examination, the neat dichotomy sinner/saint upon which rests the straight reading reveals itself to be perhaps nothing more than a false opposition, as is often the case with Flaubert, an empty vehicle for masking the obsessive and narcissistic impulses of a neurotic rebel whose cause, so to speak, is the destruction of culture and, ultimately, of life.

The activity of interpretation, in particular, the problem of whether or not to interpret, to fill the gaps and supply a meaning to a discourse charged with irony, is both a thorny problem and a central one to consider in approaching Flaubert.[7] The activity of interpretation is invariably featured in his work not only as it addresses the reader's concerns and procedures but often dramatically in the plot itself where, outside the *Trois contes*, it is generally shown to be a weakness, a sign of delusion, and a tragic flaw in the character. With the exception of a few, like Félicité for example, nearly all of Flaubert's major characters suffer from an inability to adapt to the world in which they live. The art or inclination to imagine, and hence to interpret, or to misinterpret, the world, to redefine conventions and conventional limits, provides them with the only way they have of making the world a more intelligible place. Although it is often argued that Emma's unrealistic notions of love and social realities result in her tragic outcome, it remains nonetheless true that her misconceptions represent the only way she can ever imagine living her life; when her illusions are destroyed, so is her life. Although the activity of interpretation in Flaubert's work may be suspect as an epistemological tool, it nonetheless constitutes the only way the characters in his novels can exercise their subjectivity in a world they perceive as overrun by mediocre ideals and inane and morally bankrupt authority figures. The activity of interpretation is posited, therefore, both as a quality (and, in the *Trois contes*, as a strategy) and as a weakness; it is a sign of a rich, imaginative life as well as of a character's delusions and errors of perception or of knowledge. It may result in disappointment and failure, as in Emma's case, or it may be the means to find fulfillment in life, as in the case of Félicité. Hence, Flaubert's texts at once valorize and undercut the interpretive impulse of his characters and of his readers, acknowledging in this way that their compulsion to interpret, to find or construct meanings, is a means of salvation, as it is also a source of both pleasure and frustration.

Saint Julien is exemplary in this respect; quite apart from its display of the doubtful nature of interpretation, it shows, as does *Un Cœur simple*, that the self's realization, the process by which the subject creates a meaning for itself, constitutes a re-reading and a re-writing of the self upon an already written and alienating world-text (masculine-text in *Un Cœur simple*, father-text in *Saint Julien*).

The question of interpretation is posed at the outset of the narrative of Julien's life. Two messengers make prophecies at his birth concerning his future. The first appears to his mother as she is lying in bed after giving birth and announces that her son will be a saint; the second appears to the father and tells him that his son will be an emperor. Both parents are not sure they really heard and saw the messengers. Yet there is a difference between the mother's reaction and the reaction of the father. The mother, a devout woman, does not doubt the content of the message itself; she is simply not sure whether to attribute it to a dream or to reality. On the other hand, the father is inebriated and exhausted from celebrating when he meets the messenger at the gate; it is a foggy night and the messenger is stuttering. Therefore the father attributes his vision to lack of sleep. Both parents keep the news of their encounters to themselves, the mother fearing that she will be accused of the sin of pride, while the father's more mundane concern is to avoid possible ridicule. Not surprisingly, the narrator does not credit one vision over the other, and he is careful not to discredit them while inviting the reader to entertain an explanation based on the gap that is opened between the two opposed and doubly doubtful hallucinated visions. It is difficult to overlook the fact that each parent sees and hears exactly what he or she wishes, that each prophecy is in accord with the temperament and desire of the respective parent. The religious mother sees a hermit who tells her that her son will be a saint, while the father, a worldly man and an adventurer, sees a gypsy with flaming red eyes and silver bracelets around his arms who tells him that his son will be an emperor.

Psychology or prophecy? Desire or fate? Can these two interpretive possibilities be Flaubert's way of saying, as Enid Starkie has pointed out, that in Flaubert character is indeed fate?[8] Or are we justified in thinking that by leaving the question open, Flaubert undercuts both, as well as any attempt to look behind the facts, the straight text, for the origin and the motives of Julien's behavior? As Leo Bersani has put it, "psychology is as interpretive as hagiography . . . neither is more 'original' than the other, and both illustrate the same tendency to multiply fictions about human experience."[9] In this sense, *Saint Julien* offers the reader at least two valid ways of interpreting Julien's behavior. We have, on the one hand, the mother's interpretation, or the hagiographic text, and, on the other, the father's text, the worldly text in which Julien is featured as a heroic warrior and a prosperous man. By the end of his life, Julien will have fulfilled both of his parents' wishes, prophecies, texts. However, he will not accept himself as the object of his parents' desires, and he will have succeeded in re-writing their texts, realizing himself as a being apart, with desires of his own.

When we note that Julien is a peculiar sort of character, that he seems to lack "presence," and that he has no ego;[10] when we find him displaying both passive and aggressive types of behavior, or when he strikes us as selfless yet inordinately concerned with his own guilt; in other words, when Julien's behavior strikes us as contradictory and bizarre, we are witnessing the confrontation between Julien's desire and that of his parents, their image of him. The text of the parents tells the story of a Julien estranged from his own desires, a subject who takes the other's desire, namely, the parents', for its own. Julien's text, however, is neither the story of a saint nor that of an emperor; it is the narrative of a subject striving to differentiate and disengage itself from the oppressive and fiercely tenacious influence, curse, design, of his parents and of the world they represent. However, his text, like all texts, is not an entirely original one. Rather, it relies on models borrowed from the father and from Jesus Christ; Julien, as Félicité does with masculine culture, uses the power he is rebelling against, causing it to overturn and undermine itself. Julien's mother can be said to provide a model for the son only insofar as she is identified with Christ and Christian values and not the other way around. Once Julien discovers his passion for hunting, the mother's place is taken by male religious figures; for example, before he kills his mother, Julien leaves her for a priest. Similarly, he later leaves his wife to join with the leper, that is, Jesus Christ. *Saint Julien* is the story of a son's struggle against his father and his law.

More than in any previous version of the legend, including the Romantic versions of Langlois and Lecointre-Dupont which he drew on, Flaubert emphasizes and expands appreciably the accounts of Julien's childhood, his obsession with hunting and violence, and his extreme sense of guilt.[11] In so doing, Flaubert opens the text to a psychological reading, a fruitful approach as evidenced by the number of exegetes who follow its procedures.[12] Thematic concerns such as the desire/fear of committing the parricide, the important part played by dreams, the dreamlike quality of certain actions, the obsession with hunting, as well as a general sense of suffering and uncertainty experienced by Julien, point to psychoanalysis as an appropriate grid for talking about the character's desires.[13]

To get a sense of where Julien's desires lie, one must stay close to the scenes which reveal desire at work. *Saint Julien* is a tightly structured text; one can even say that it is an exercise, a "pensum" as Flaubert called it, in the management of detail. Structuring elements such as parallelism, opposition, continuity, and return of scenes, figures, images, while serving an aesthetic function, act as efficient ways of foiling the lack of actual change in the character. From the moment Julien kills the mouse in the chapel until the time he ascends to Heaven in the arms of Jesus Christ, his desires, his obsessions, even his predicament, remain fundamentally unchanged; they merely manifest themselves differently.

Saint Julien is divided into three parts, with the first two parts structured along lines of opposition. Interestingly, and conveniently, each part features a different habitation, each suggesting, in turn, the kind of relationship Julien has with the world and the way that he experiences life. The movement from the first to the third suggests his trajectory toward self-definition. Similarly, as will be shown in my conclusion, the *Trois contes* is made up of three stories (or three parts), each of which describes a different historical period, but which repeats the character's rejection of the masculine and of civilization; *Un Cœur simple* and *Saint Julien* are parallel and reverse stories; the poor and unloved orphan girl and the privileged and adored son both strive for the same goal: undermining the father's authority and law. *Hérodias*, or the last part, synthesizes and represents more clearly the movements and the themes of the first two stories and brings them to a close.

The first part of *Saint Julien* opens with the description of the parental castle, situated in the midst of the woods, on the slope of a hill. The castle, with its four pointed towers resting on a solid rock foundation, conveys a sense of permanence and solidity, while its position on the slope of a hill also suggests the eventual decline of the world it represents and encloses. Inside as well as outside there is a visible sense of order. Natural elements such as water, vegetation, and wild life are channeled and controlled: "De longues gouttières, figurant des dragons la gueule en bas crachaient l'eau des pluies vers la citerne" (77); there is a garden with figures wrought in flowers and a vine-covered arbor. The castle is separated from the outside by its central location in the middle of the woods, by a moat, and by a second enclosure beyond the moat. This enclosure contains two distinct functional parts: the orchards and flowers are contained in one area, which accomodates games and leisure activities, while beyond it, on the other side, we have an area which contains the more vital and necessary functions, like the production of food and the habitation of the animals. This last enclosure is in turn surrounded by grazing land which is itself enclosed by a solid thorned hedgerow.

The narrator, starting from a point way above the ground, zooms down to a center in the woods, the castle, and out from the castle to five different circles of enclosures. The description of a peaceful, ordered, and controlled universe is accompanied by images of defense and caution: the castle is surrounded by a moat, one enclosure is surrounded by stakes, the other by thorns. This is a sheltered and prosperous world. The tapestries, like the flowers in the painted earthenware pot and the figures wrought in flowers, imply that all is stylized and civilized.

Solidly anchored in the world, well protected, sheltered and prosperous, this is indeed a privileged place. Yet Julien, after leading an ordered and seemingly happy childhood, will feel compelled to flee, and he will, ultimately, disrupt and destroy this world. After he abandons home, his parents leave to search for him; when they find him, they are old and very poor. One ought not, however, readily assume that life in the parental castle is necessarily happy. Protection and prosperity may be a sign of comfort, but they are also a sign of a world which has lost its vitality, a stagnant world. Walls protect, but they also imprison.

Until the episode in the chapel, Julien has been an exemplary child; he is patient and obedient to his parents and his tutor, the monk. He exhibits no signs of violence or defiance. Julien, however, will experience his first compulsion to kill when seated between his parents in a chapel during mass. Looking up, he sees a little mouse moving about the altar; he is troubled by it and devises a strategy to get rid of it. The irruption of the desire to kill is a sign, here, of the emergence of a differentiated self, the formation of an identity in an activity apart from that of the parents or the monk, a secret activity.[14] From this point on, Julien begins to exhibit signs of defiance. He rejects the highly ordered and structured environment of his home. Moreover, he has contempt for the timid rituals with which he is associated. The easy, unchallenging nature of the communal hunt leaves him indifferent:

> Souvent on menait dans la campagne des chiens d'oysel, qui tombaient bien vite en arrêt. Alors des piqueurs, s'avançant pas à pas, étendaient avec précaution sur leurs corps impassibles un immense filet. Un commandement les faisait aboyer; des cailles s'envolaient; et *les dames des alentours conviées avec leurs maris, les enfants, les camérières, tout le monde se jetait dessus, et les prenait facilement.* . . . Mais Julien méprisa ces commodes artifices; il préférait chasser *loin du monde,* avec son cheval et son faucon. (90, my italics)

When Julien discovers hunting, he sets himself apart from the rest of society. What then is the relationship of hunting to society, to civilization? In Julien's mind, the way individuals hunt reflects the way they experience life. Thus, the men and women who make up the society of which he is a member, like the parental castle of which they are part, represent a petrified, stagnant, social order. It is a society at peace; life had been peaceful for so long, sheltered from outside dangers and estranged from the vital energies of nature. Julien's parents and their entourage engage in a stylized form of hunting; hunting, to them, is a controlled activity. On the other hand, hunting as Julien practices it is a radically antisocial activity; it is what distinguishes him from the rest. It is also, as will be obvious later, the expression of a repressed hostility toward humanity itself. Hunting is not only the act which results in the parricide, it is also, and perhaps primarily, a manifestation of Julien's desire to destroy civilization and to return to a primitive, even primal, form of existence.

Part 1 closes with the stag's prediction that because he has wantonly killed so many animals, Julien will, as a result, kill his father and mother. Obsessed with the stag's prediction, and fearing or wishing ("si je le voulais, pourtant?") that the stag's words will come true, he decides to run away from home.

Part 2 opens with the quick account of Julien's heroic adventures as a warrior of great renown. Like a medieval hero, he fights at once for Christianity and for his country. As a reward for having saved an important kingdom, he is offered the emperor's daughter in marriage. After the wedding, he moves into a beautiful castle overlooking the sea.

Julien's second home is the reverse architectural image of the parental castle. The first is northern, the second in the Moorish style. Angular shapes are replaced by domelike forms; there is a general softening of contours. In contrast to the sunny brilliance of the first, objects here are enveloped in soft shades. An aesthetic of the "natural" gives the impression that nature is less controlled than in the northern castle. Natural elements, however, are contained by an architecture which *imitates* nature and uses it to a much greater extent to stylize the shapes of its environment. The flowers, for instance, do not merely stream down to the gulf but, instead, are contained by terraces; the thin columns supporting the domes are compared to reeds; the decorative bas-relief imitates stalactites, and the sunlight enters through incrustations in the walls and illuminates the soft darkness of the rooms.

Like the castle where he was born, the Moorish castle is an enclosed and isolated space. Built on a promontory facing the sea, it is nonetheless closed-off at the horizon by mountains ("des montagnes, qui fermaient au loin l'horizon") and protected from the rear by a forest shaped like a fan. Both castles have enclosures. However, the enclosures of the northern castle are man-made and defensive, while the enclosures of the Moorish castle are natural. The sense of serenity, luxury, and above all sensuality conveyed by the wife's castle derives from an atmosphere of lulling repetitiousness, as, for example, in the images of the continually blue sky and the swaying trees. When we follow these images with the image of the perfume of orange blossoms, flowers, and the sea, we have circulating in this space a listlessness, a torpor capable of overwhelming and engulfing the senses, and in turn the will. This would have been a privileged scene for Félicité, a space of the feminine; but it is not so for Julien. Not surprisingly, Julien is melancholy; he weeps; the "echo of a sigh" that one hears is an allusion to his sighs echoing through the marble hallways. Julien feels as stifled and confined here as he did in his parents' castle. Here, however, he has repressed his desires; in a sense, his desires must remain invisible like the enclosures of his second home. Importantly, however, the wife's castle reveals the beginning of a breakdown, a process of dissolution, whereby matter and enclosures become progressively less solid, less reified.

The two dominant themes of Part 2 are melancholy and impotence. Julien abstains from hunting for fear of fulfilling the stag's prophecy. Since his marriage, he is no longer a warrior. He spends his days in his wife's company, or he daydreams about running free in deserts and through forests hunting down animals. One night, his wife convinces him to go hunting once again.[15] However, on this first night out he cannot kill or wound a single animal. He returns home full of rage and, taking his parents for his wife and a lover, kills them. They had arrived at the castle in his absence and, ironically, the object of his wife's "hospitality," had been placed in her bed for the night. Once Julien has committed the parricide, he leaves his wife and his home and heads up into the mountains and there finds his third habitation.

It is a simple hut built on a muddy and slippery terrain. Built of clay and tree trunks, it is the least solid of the three homes. Located on the shores of a big river which is both violent and stagnant, it stands in contrast to the inviting seascape of the marital home. This is a space of decomposition; two elements are basic to this environment: water and soil. The sun never appears here. In contrast to the solidity and hardness of the parental home, we have, instead, a slimy, slippery place. The elements are not stylized or even controlled as in the castles; in fact they are formless and vague: he sees in front of him pale pools of water, muddied water, greenish masses, and, in the spring, swirls of dust. In contrast to the white marble Moorish castle with its delicate architectural details, and its flowers and fragrant atmosphere, this world reeks of decay. The winds neither elevate nor circulate the air; instead, they trap the odors in whirlwinds of dust.

In a sense, this home is no less confining or enclosed than the other two homes. Julien feels the same sense of being imprisoned, since he must escape elsewhere: through his memory, he tries to recall the happy days of his youth surrounded by his father and mother, but as soon as he conjures up this scene, the scene of the murder also, irrepressibly, comes to his mind.

Just as devastating as Julien's imagination, which cannot help but reduce a happy family scene to a morbid one, are the descriptions which clearly point to an inexorable process of decomposition and decay. Whereas we started with a solid, anchored, sense of the world, or at least a sense of a permanent world, we now have a vision of a world reduced to its primordial matter, that is, mud. But the hut and the leper are not the concluding images of the story. The ending is a cosmic spectacle; Julien, still in the arms of the leper, expands to the point of dissolving, literally, into the firmament. Thus, as in *Un Cœur simple*, transcendence translates into a supreme exaltation of the senses, a dilation of being, with matter, or the world, no longer serving as a point of reference. It is clear that, from the parental castle to the hermit's hut, form in space decomposes *because* it is in the world, as if life contained the germ of its own negation. This movement from form to the disintegration of form is a projection of Julien's desire to annihilate the world. Julien's fantasies, however, will become more manifest and his actions will reveal themselves to be the expression of a willful consciousness when we examine crucial scenes which seem complete in themselves but which, when unraveled, yield valuable insights into the character.

Part 1 and Part 2 of *Saint Julien* are nearly inversions of one another (as are *Un Cœur simple* and *Saint Julien*). The three major hunting scenes in Part 1 parallel three descriptive passages in Part 2. The first passage (quoted below), which will be referred to as the goat episode, is at the *beginning* of the great hunting episode in Part 1. It parallels the passage at the *close* of Part 2 which marks the end of Julien's hunting adventures.

> Trois heures après, il se trouva sur la pointe d'une montagne tellement haute que le ciel semblait presque noir. Devant lui, un rocher pareil à un long mur s'abaissait, en surplombant un précipice; et, à l'extrémité, deux boucs sauvages regardaient l'abîme. Comme il n'avait pas ses flèches (car son cheval était resté en arrière), il imagina de descendre jusqu'à eux; à demi courbé, pieds nus, il arriva enfin au premier des boucs, et lui enfonça un poignard sous les côtes. Le second, pris de terreur, sauta dans le vide. Julien s'élança pour le frapper, et, glissant du pied droit, tomba sur le cadavre de l'autre, *la face au-dessus de l'abîme et les deux bras écartés.* (93-94; my italics)

This passage from Part 1, at the height of Julien's success as a hunter, already strikes an ominous note. The vision of Julien, slipping and lying face down with both arms spread out in a sign of the cross, fallen over the corpse, prefigures that in Part 2 of Julien after he has murdered his parents: "Il resta, pendant la messe, à plat ventre . . . les bras en croix, et le front dans la poussière" (122).[16] After his parents' burial, he takes the road leading to the mountain. In the goat scene, he descends from the mountain to get closer to his prey. The mountain summit is a privileged place for Julien (indeed, for he is a Romantic hero); the valley, on the other hand, is where the rest of humanity dwells; the parents' castle, it will be recalled, is on a slope, in a downward position. Symbolically, the valley is the place where the parricide is enacted. It is, moreover, the place where other orgies of violence and death, symbolic parricides, occur.

The second major parallel hunting scenes are, in Part 1, the description of Julien's tremendous speed and confidence as a hunter, and in Part 2, the scene where he decides to go out hunting again after a long period of abstinence and realizes that he is unable to kill any animals. The passage from Part 1 reflects the ease with which Julien kills his prey; it occurs in the daytime and happens as in a dream. Appropriately, the woods he enters are shaped like an arch of triumph. Julien shows no pity for the animals he kills. The passage from Part 2 occurs in the night; it is a nightmare. Julien hesitates. His reflexes are slow, his vision is blurred. He is overwhelmed, paralyzed. When he leaves the forest, he is "like a blind man." The animals escape him. His arrows do not affect them. They mock his attempts, humiliate, encircle, and frighten him. "Une ironie perçait dans leurs allures sournoises. Tout en l'observant du coin de leurs prunelles, ils semblaient méditer un plan de vengeance" (117). What a striking reversal of the scene in Part 1 just before he kills the great stag and his family, where it is he who encircles the animals. In Part 2, from his first steps in the forest enjoying the soft grass and balmy air, Julien is seen, as he experiences himself, from the inside, bound to phantasms of fear, guilt, irony. He is the hunted hunter or a haunted hunter, haunted by his guilt for having massacred so many animals, a crime whose consequences, he suspects, will affect his parents' fate.

The third parallel episodes are Julien's encounter with the great stag and his family in Part 1 and the parricide in Part 2. When he comes upon the stag, the doe, and her fawn, Julien has just slaughtered a herd of stags huddled together in a "valley" ("Le rebord du vallon était trop haut pour le franchir" [96]). The stag's family corresponds to Julien's family. The stag is the image of the father; when he looks at Julien, his eyes are "like a patriarch and like a justicer" (98). The doe, "blond like dead leaves" (97), recalls his blond mother as it alludes to her fate, "dead"; she will cry looking up at the sky as if to God. Her voice is qualified as human. Why does her cry exasperate Julien? And why does Julien, who would correspond with the fawn, shoot the fawn *first*? If the stag's and the doe's descriptions are clues relating them to Julien's parents, can the word *tacheté* which is used to decribe the fawn be given a special significance that would tell us something about Julien?

On comparing the goat scene and the stag episode, we notice that the figure of the child is absent from the goat scene. Hence, the episode of the stag signals the recognition of the self in a picture of the world: the Lacanian mirror stage. The goat scene is, also, a prefiguration of the phantasm, or desire, of parricide even *before* the encounter with and the prediction of the stag. The qualifier *tacheté* works on both the literal and metaphorical registers. The fawn that Julien promptly shoots is spotted as opposed to the solid and contrasting coloring of the parents; that means that the fawn, like Julien himself, is marked by the dual and opposing characteristics of both parents (white/black and religious/secular). Metaphorically, the fawn is spotted or, as the French *tacheté* suggests, stained, as in guilty of sin. When he kills the fawn, Julien kills the child in himself and thus asserts his independence from his parents. But, by the same token, by killing the fawn, he also kills this version of himself that is guilty of desiring his parents' death and his own independence from them; in other words, killing the fawn is both an assertive gesture of independence and a self-reproach, a self-inflicted punishment for wishing his independence and their death.

Looking again at the stag episode, we notice that Julien is in an important manner unable to kill the great stag. In spite of the affirmation that upon being shot the stag "gently closed his eyelids, and died" (98), the stag, his phantasm, returns. For when Julien kills his parents, he is terrified to hear the bellowing of the great black stag. Moreover, when he looks closely at his father's cadaver, "il aperçut, entre ses paupières mal fermées, une prunelle éteinte qui le brûla comme du feu" (121). The father, also, is not quite dead; his phantasm returns, like that of the stag, when, looking into a fountain, Julien confuses his image with that of his father. In fact, if we go back again to the goat scene we notice that Julien stabs one goat only and that the second goat escapes him and falls to its death. The figure always escaping Julien is the father. On the other hand, the mother, represented by one of the wild goats, is constantly left behind, killed.

Once back home after his encounter with the stag, Julien is overwhelmed with exhaustion and becomes ill. The mother is replaced by the monk. Similarly, in Part 2, after the parricide, Julien leaves his wife behind and replaces her, in a sense, by the leper.

The parricide occurs after his unsuccessful hunting scene when, unable to kill any animals, Julien decides to return home to his wife. On his way he comes upon some red partridges fluttering around. He throws his cloak over them like a net, but when he uncovers them he finds only one; rotten, it seems to have been long since dead.[17] The dead and rotten partridge, like the spotted fawn, is principally the introjection in Julien's consciousness of the abject nature of his own character. It is a prefiguration of the parricide and Julien's sense of guilt. When he finally actually kills his parents, they seem already dead. Yet lying in their death bed, they appear to keep "some eternal secret." What secret can they be keeping? This "secret," like the father's half-closed eyelids, is an imagined reproach, a self-reproach, and a threat. The scene of murder is expanded, its impact reinforced by the brilliant images of blood and sun. These are images of the consummation of desire. The sun reflected through the scarlet stained-glass window multiplies visibly the effect of the crime. The reflection of blood fills the room, surrounds the family. Julien is in a womblike space.[18] Contemplating his act, he is appeased as if this act were the culmination of an overwhelming repression. He examines the father's body to see if there is some mistake. He then goes to the mother's side and raises her head, "la tenant au bout de son bras roidi, pendant que de l'autre main il s'éclairait avec le flambeau. Des gouttes, suintant du matelas, tombaient une à une sur le plancher" (121). Tension has liquified into pleasure.[19] The mother who was once so stern, now melts, so to speak; and Julien, in a pose of dominance and control, watches her. This is a scene of pleasure at the final physical dissolution of the mother. It will take more than the act of murder itself to kill the father. Lucette Czyba, who has written a lucid and documented account of Flaubert's mysogenia, has written: " Flaubert sublime par l'art son propre fétichisme et tire souvent des effets plastiques les plus fascinants pour le lecteur de ce qui a été le plus profondément refoulé par son inconscient . . . L'esthétique . . . déréalise la scène et, gommant la matérialité dangereuse du corps féminin, évacue le malaise qui lui est associé."[20]

Although the actual parricide occurs at the end of Part 2, it is prefigured in the stag and in the goat episodes as well as in the scene in Part 1 when, seated between his parents in the chapel, Julien sees a mouse and resolves to kill it. The latter scene is the primal scene of parricide; killing the mouse is a deferred action meant to be directed against the parents. From this moment on in the narrative, animals are substituted for the parents: for instance, in Part 1, Julien leaves home when, confusing his mother's headpiece with a stork, he almost kills her.[21] Later, on the night he actually commits the parricide, he is compelled to go out hunting when he hears the "yelping" of a fox. The fox should remind us of the father, "always wrapped in a foxskin cape"; in the same scene, the "light footsteps" and what appeared to him to be animallike shadows were, clearly, his parents arriving. When reaching the castle after the unsuccessful hunt, animals lacking, "il aurait voulu massacrer des hommes" (118).

No reading of *Saint Julien* can fail to note the paradigmatic relation between animals and the parents.[22] This relation, however, can be extended to include the substitution of animals for human beings in general. Before Julien kills the black stag and his family, he kills a herd, that is to say, a society, of deer: "Des cerfs emplissaient un vallon ayant la forme d'un cirque; et tassés, les uns près des autres, ils se réchauffaient avec leurs haleines que l'on voyait fumer dans le brouillard" (95). Julien is excited and starts to shoot: "Il se fit des enfonçures dans leur masse; des voix plaintives s'élevaient, et un grand mouvement agita le troupeau" (96). There is more to Julien's desiring fantasies than the death of his parents. From the beginning, his deepest desire is to live outside of society. As a child, he discovers hunting and becomes aware of his superiority; hunting distinguishes him from the rest. His heroic career in the world as a warrior is a barely disguised sublimation for his desire for violence against society. As a warrior he finds the medium for legitimizing his passion, and discovers that society's aim is to devitalize even, or, perhaps, especially, heroes. Like his father, who after many adventures married a woman "de haut lignage," Julien also marries and finds himself in a role resembling that of his father. Peace characterizes Julien's kingdom as it did his father's. Unable to go out hunting, he fantasizes radical plots against humanity. Placing himself in the position of the first man, Adam, surrounded by animals, he imagines killing them by merely spreading his arms. Or, imagining himself as Noah, the man responsible for perpetuating or founding anew the human race, and the rest of the animals, for that matter, he fantasizes shooting deadly arrows at the animals as they enter, two by two (the parental couple as origin) into the ark.[23] Julien's fantasy is to put an end to the world as it is coming into being, a nihilistic fantasy. The desire is powerfully radical in that it attempts a reverse genesis and a return to a primal, pre-oedipal, presymbolic state. The parricide, therefore, is a sign of a more general rejection.

Sartre, in his examination of *Saint Julien,* asks in frustration: "Where does the sainthood of this slaughterer of man and beast, parricide to boot, come from?"[24] If he is truly worthy of sainthood, if we are to believe that he has changed from sinner to saint, we should be able to find in Part 3 some indication that a change of heart has taken place. Instead, we find Julien continuing to display hostility toward mankind—but on the sly.

Part 3 relates for the most part Julien's remorse, his alienation, and his suffering. A relatively small place is devoted to featuring his services and his charity; moreover, he never turns to God for forgiveness. By placing so little emphasis on his redeeming qualities and so much on his sin and his fantasies of violence, Flaubert plants the seeds for a reading that would seriously undercut the authenticity of Julien's conversion from sin to saintliness. Julien's abrupt and total reversal of attitudes toward people and animals, his change from sadism to masochism, from violence to love, and from arrogance to humility, imposes an order which is essentially ironic; Julien in Part 3 is not very different.[25] He has not sublimated but only repressed the desire for violence and omnipotence. This is an important distinction; it suggests that the desire remains; only the language and outward manifestations of the desire change. This explains why the acts of love and charity toward people and animals produce the same effect as violence and contempt: "Il contemplait avec des élancements d'amour les poulains dans les herbages, les oiseaux dans leurs nids, les insectes sur les fleurs; tous, à son approche, couraient plus loin, se cachaient effarés, s'envolaient bien vite" (124-25). Violence and love are equivalent at heart. In Part 2, Julien the warrior endangers his life to save the weak, yet is spared from death. Similarly, in Part 3, Julien the hermit tries to help the weak and he is saved from death. The difference is that in the latter case Julien's motivation for undertaking these services is the desire to somehow be killed in the process; ironically, it is undertaken less in the spirit of selflessness and charity than the attempts related in Part 2.

From the episode of the mouse in the chapel, Julien is depicted as a solitary character who suffers in the presence of others. In Part 1 he leaves his parents; in Part 2, his wife. In excluding the wife from participating in Julien's travails when in all previous versions of the legend she accompanies him and is saved by Christ along with him, Flaubert radically shifts the legend's meaning, since he stresses not only Julien's solitariness but also a most unchristian attitude, his egocentricity. In Part 3, we find that Julien has very successfully maneuvered himself into a position of more complete isolation; he discovers that by telling people his story, they will avoid him. To commit the crime, assume the responsibility, and ask for punishment seem to be the mechanisms for a more complete isolation.

> Quelquefois, au tournant d'une côte, il voyait *sous ses yeux* une confusion de toits pressés, avec des *flèches* de pierre, des ponts, des tours, des rues noires s'entrecroisant, et d'où *montait* jusqu'à lui un bourdonnement continuel.
>
> Le besoin de se mêler à l'existence des autres le faisait *descendre* dans la ville. Mais l'air *bestial* des figures, le tapage des métiers, *l'indifférence* des propos glaçaient son cœur. (123-24; my italics)

Julien's living on the mountain and his elevated perspective on various manifestations of ordinary life (a sight from which he recoils), as well as the recurrence of terms such as *flèches* and the "beastlike" faces of the people, suggest the precarious nature of the repression of violence, and of Julien's disdain for the commonplace. Men and animals are still associated with one another in his mind. Julien's grief is real, but his humility and sincerity are a pose. Even after he has established himself on the banks of the river and devoted himself to the task of ferrying people across, violent images are often on his mind: the severe cold weather conditions "inspiraient un besoin fou de manger de la viande" (128). He daydreams about the happy scenes of his childhood: "et la cour d'un château apparaissait, avec des lévriers sur un perron, des valets dans la salle d'armes, et, sous un berceau de pampres, un adolescent à cheveux blonds entre un vieillard couvert de fourrures et une dame à grand hennin; tout à coup, les deux cadavres étaient là" (129).

One of the most important scenes in Part 3, and certainly the most complex, is Julien's encounter with his father's image in a fountain. This is a pivotal scene. It comes at a point when Julien's suffering and his feeling of alienation are so acute that he decides to commit suicide, and it is followed, significantly, by his discovery of a vocation. He finds an old boat by a river, a river so dangerous that no one for ages has attempted to cross it, "et l'idée lui vint d'employer son existence au service des autres" (127). Between the decision to commit suicide and the decision to devote his life to serving humanity something crucial must have occurred. What happens when Julien looks into the fountain and confuses his image with that of his father? And why upon seeing his father's image does he refrain from committing suicide when, as George Moskos has rightly said, the sight of his father should, instead, drive him to suicide?

Ostensibly, we might see the encounter with the father as Julien's introjection of the father's grief: "il lui fut impossible de retenir ses pleurs" (126). In so doing we would be saying that he is able to transcend this grief and, on a very deep level, forgive himself. But Julien does not forgive himself; this is clear. He continues to feel great remorse *after* the encounter in the fountain. The parricide continues to haunt him mercilessly. The explanation is elsewhere.

When at first Julien looks into the fountain, he has no ego to speak of; he is ravaged by remorse. When he mistakes his own reflection in the pool for that of his father, something begins to congeal in his mind. Lacan tells us that the ego is formed by the subject's acquisition of an image of himself based on the model provided by the other. The other, here, being (not the specular image of the subject but) Julien's father, the figure of legitimacy and authority.[26] Recall that Julien's father is a respected and loved member of the community. He dispenses justice to his vassals and settles his neighbor's quarrels. By taking himself for his father, "C'était son père; et il ne pensa plus à se tuer" (126), Julien provides himself with what up to this point he lacked, namely, a sense of himself as whole, as unified, as legitimate. The image of the father represents the "ideal other," the image of the integral and unalienated self.

The mirror stage is a fundamentally narcissistic experience; narcissism is contemporaneous with the formation of the ego and implies an affirmation of life. Narcissism always entails the exploitation of someone else's life, Lacan suggests; it is always done at someone else's expense. Freud makes a useful clarification in this regard. He relates the concept of narcissism to the notion of libidinal cathexes and postulates that the more ego-libido (i.e., the libido which cathects the ego) is used, the more object-libido is depleted: "The ego is to be regarded as a great reservoir of libido from which libido is sent out *to* objects and which is always ready to absorb libido flowing back *from* objects."[27] Every exchange, every "unit," of libido, so to speak, is accounted for in the subject; libido, like matter, cannot be destroyed; it survives in different forms. Hence, for the subject, the as yet unconstituted subject, to succeed in perceiving itself as whole and perfect (like the ideal other), he must believe that he has robbed the other of a precious ego-sustaining substance. However, the experience of totality and the ensuing feeling of triumph resulting from the encounter with the mirror is accompanied by the realization that this "ideal" ego reflected in the mirror is, and always will be, the other, that the subject is symbolically castrated. Consequently, the relationship established in the mirror is fundamentally one of hostility and rivalry. The encounter with the father gives Julien a *provisional* identity, a sense of power, but it does not offer the means to triumph over him once and for all. This will be accomplished when Julien meets the leper. Like Félicité, who "steals," or "mimes," from the masculine culture the means to subvert it but only succeeds when she has transformed what she has appropriated into a form that is meaningful to her, Julien, too, will only succeed when he has transfigured the identity he has robbed from his father to suit his goals. The ego is derived through a process of transformation.[28]

We can appreciate the full import of Julien's identification with his father, and with Christ, only if we understand the process of identification in terms of differentiation. Julien's encounter leads to his discovery of a vocation modeled on the father: the father is a hospitaler; he welcomes travelers and weary pilgrims to his castle, feeding and rewarding them generously. But Julien's vocation as ferrier and hospitaler imitates poorly, or incompletely, his father's role. Julien, we have seen, alters the model, empties it in fact of its content and meaning: the father acts out of genuine charity, love, and respect for his fellow man; we really have no reason to suspect his intentions. Julien, on the other hand, humbles and sacrifices himself in the service of others as a means of asserting his difference, and assuring his continued separation from the rest. Julien just simply does not love his fellow man; and this is the essential and important difference between himself and his father.

To triumph once and for all over the father, over his influence and law, Julien will have to apply the other model with which he is marked, namely the Christian model. It is this model that will play the determining role in the realization of Julien's desire to surpass and otherwise kill the father. Here, the leper/Christ is an important figure.

Several critics have viewed the leper as a figure for the father. William Berg, for instance, sees the leper as the ghost of Julien's father and suggests that were it not for the narrator who "cuts off Julien's ascension in midflight and brings him soundly back to earth" where "the Oedipus 'complex' can be transcended," Julien would have fallen back to dependency and passivity, and no reconciliation with the father would have been possible. Berg reads the ascension scene negatively, as a psychic regression, and views the narrator as yet another figure for the father by virtue of his "position as creator and purveyor of order."[29] To George Moskos, the ending of the story suggests a reconciliation between the father and the son: through the union with the leper, Julien becomes himself the " 'Father' giving birth to his 'Son' Christ, out of his own body and mind."[30] Whether one views the leper as a representation of Julien's father, a figure of Julien himself, as does Shoshana Felman,[31] or of "all the previous characters,"[32] his function in the economy of Julien's desire remains the same. The leper's most significant attribute is that he *changes into* Jesus Christ and that through him Julien himself is transformed, becomes one with Christ. Hence, the leper is, primarily, the figure of transformation, and difference.

As a personification of the degradation and disintegration of flesh, the leper is a figure of "abjection" as Julia Kristeva describes the term. The "abject" is a primitive structuration of difference anterior to castration. It is related to the mother; the abject of abjects is the mother, she remarks. It eludes the paternal and appears as soon as the symbolic and social dimension of man is constituted.[33] Kristeva's conception of the abject is consistent with the view I have taken that the leper/Christ represents the culmination of Julien's desire, his renunciation of civilization. He reflects Julien's desire to undo the process of culture and return to a pre-oedipal, imaginary stage. Moreover, the scene of

Julien's union, his fusion with Christ at the end of the narrative, is Julien's fantasy of a return to the body of the mother, to the place of his conception. Thus, the leper emerges as the figure for the ego in opposition to the father. Like Loulou/fetish in *Un Cœur simple*, the leper in *Saint Julien* is an androgynous figure, a figure of transformation, a sign of the mobility of desire. Both the leper and the bird represent victory, real or fantasized, over the father and over the threat of castration. In terms of the linguistic analogy, this return to the mother in *Saint Julien* is a renunciation of language; it implies a view of signification, in Kristeva's term, as semiotic production (where the concepts of the paternal and the maternal are integrated). The body of the mother/leper becomes a metaphor for "poetic language," the "semiotization of the symbolic" (Kristeva). This process becomes more explicit in *Hérodias,* where the voice of Iaokanann wells forth from the cave (feminine space) to condemn and harass Hérodias and Herod, representatives of civilization.

Julien does not want to assume his father's role. Had he wanted to, the story would have ended at the point where he encounters the reflection of his father in the fountain, or shortly after. This is not the case. Julien's desire is to kill his father and to assume a more ideal identity. Consequently, he identifies with and, later, literally fuses into Christ. For Christ offers him an example of how he can subvert the father; this is why it was important for Flaubert to distinguish the father from the mother, to identify the mother with Christ and the religious, while the father is identified with and remains that which is essentially nonreligious, the secular.

How might Julien perceive the figure of Christ? To put it differently, what is it about Christ that he identifies with? It is, namely, the image of Christ as the rebellious son who renounces his earthly father and mother, rejects the family triangle, and substitutes for it an idealized construct, the Trinity, whereby the three are conceived as One; in other terms, he is drawn to the image of Christ the man who redefined and, in a sense too, defied the concept of God the Father as One. Moreover, Julien finds his inspiration in the historical figure of Christ: the man who envisioned new values, and a world beyond, for humanity; who admonished humans to call no man father on earth, and to acknowledge only one Father, the one in Heaven. Yet, although Julien models his life, in a certain respect, on that of his father, and on that of Christ, one ought to keep in mind that he has also transformed and emptied both models of their value. This is why Michel Grimaud can write, "The whole story, in fact, seems to be in a kind of moral and religious vacuum, in no way a justification of the ways of God to man."[34] This is also why Sartre is right to say about Julien, "This member of medieval Christianity believes only in nothingness."[35]

Freud's understanding of the impulse behind the conception of Christianity helps in a way to see more clearly just exactly what draws Julien to this model. For Freud, Judaism is to Christianity what the father is to his son. Therefore, by questioning Judaism and challenging it, Christ can be said to have challenged the supremacy of Judaism as a religion, and, in the process, killed the father (Freud recognizes that it was in all likelihood Paul and not Christ who was responsible for the major conceptual changes that distinguish Christian and Jewish theologies). As a result, Freud believes that Christianity represents the return of the repressed, that is to say, in part, the return of the scene of hostility against the father and a return to the scene of his murder. Freud claims that in Christianity, the Father "took second place; Christ, the son, stood in his stead, just as in those dark times [primeval times when the brother horde killed the father] every son had longed to do."[36] Self-sacrifice and the assumption of guilt that Christ takes unto himself for the rest of humanity could only mean, for Freud, that the son had to expiate some terrible sin; that terrible sin had to be the murder of the father. The importance and centrality of the notion of original sin in Christianity can only be justified, according to Freud, if indeed the son was responding to a powerful feeling of guilt brought about by the murder of the father.

Freud's interpretation of Judaism and Christianity, like my own interpretation of Julien's "saintliness," is based on the assumption that in our civilization, at least, an account of the individual's struggle for selfhood is nearly always, at heart, a response to the father, and a challenge to his supremacy.

As with Félicité, Julien, whose name also implies happiness, can be said to have triumphed over the father. There is no irony in their names. Looking at the details of their lives, at the many episodes of suffering which mark them, we may not be convinced that Félicité and Julien have led happy lives. We cannot fail to be convinced, however, that they have fulfilled their desires. In this lies their happiness. Both have led very discreet and very successful revolts and both find themselves, in the end, just where they had always wanted to be. In the end, Julien is close to his desire and lifelong fantasy; matter has dissolved into pure vision, and he triumphs over his worldly father through a perfect union and identity with Christ the son.

In *Saint Julien*, Flaubert made use of the hagiographic model, emptied it

of its moral function, reversed its main thrust, and forged a work committed
to revealing the self-serving nature of its, of all, fictions.

* * *

Saint Julien interrupted the pressures and disappointments of trying to
write an "impossible book," *Bouvard et Pécuchet*. Flaubert was despondent,
he felt "empty," and he was having serious doubts about his capacity to write
the simplest sentence. *Saint Julien* became a way of testing himself, of trying
out his hand at an "easier" project. The work was conceived as a "pensum,"
an exercise in writing. Thus, like *Hérodias* and, to a certain extent, like *Un
Cœur simple*, it lends itself to an autobiographical reading, to a view of the
story as the narrative of Flaubert's conception of language and of the writing
process. In a general sense, Julien's itinerary can be read figuratively as a
reflection of Flaubert's own itinerary as a writer.[37] For instance, at the outset
I suggested that the descriptions of Julien's three habitations illustrate a thematic process whereby form gradually becomes less rigid and then is reduced
to matter, how finally, matter (the landscape and the leper) in turn is transformed to vision. This process of dissolution is a figuration of Flaubert's
phenomenological obsession with the fear, and the desire, of drowning in a
kind of undifferentiated liquid matter.[38] I have described this inclination as a
projection of Julien's desire to annihilate the world, as a desire to return to
a primeval, pre-oedipal existence. Writing is, for Flaubert, a way of undoing,
of destroying the world, of imagining it away. This relationship to the world
is not unique to Flaubert. But in Flaubert's work it is invariably expressed
metaphorically, as a dissolution of the material world or as the breakdown of
an organized conception of the world.

More specifically, hunting must have seemed to Flaubert a particularly
exciting metaphor for writing. Julien's arrow cannot be dissociated from its
twin image of the writer's pen. By describing Julien's success and failure at
the hunt, Flaubert was himself acting out the feelings of both exhiliration and
frustration he experienced during the act of writing. Flaubert wrote:

> J'en conçois pourtant un, moi, un style: un style qui serait beau, que
> quelqu'un fera à quelque jour, dans dix ans ou dans dix siècles, et qui
> serait rythmé comme le vers, précis comme le langage des sciences, et

avec des ondulations, des ronflements de violoncelle, des aigrettes de feu; un style qui vous entrerait dans l'idée comme un coup de stylet, et où votre pensée enfin voguerait sur des surfaces lisses, comme lorsqu'on file dans un canot avec bon vent arrière. La prose est née d'hier; voilà ce qu'il faut se dire. Le vers est la forme par excellence des littératures anciennes. Toutes les combinaisons prosodiques ont été faites; mais celles de la prose, tant s'en faut. (2: 399)

Flaubert's ideal style is one that would penetrate the reader, convey the idea, with the precision of a surgical instrument. It is a common assumption, supported by Flaubert's own assessment of his writing, that his work is marked by two distinct styles, the style he used for the "lyrical," "romantic," or "oriental" novels and the style he used for the "realistic" novels where, by his own accounts, he "searches for and digs out truth," and "likes to point out the little facts as vigorously as the big ones" (2: 343-44); the latter style characterizes what Flaubert termed his contemporary novels, novels like *Madame Bovary* and *L'Education sentimentale* that are concerned with common reality. Flaubert had written: "J'ai la vie ordinaire en exécration"(4: 125) and "Je suis né lyrique" (3: 375). There is in Flaubert the fantasy that somehow lyricism is more "natural" to him; and the fantasy, too, that it is somehow a style that he finds easier to execute. He worked hard at whatever style he chose to use in his novels, which takes nothing away from the fact that he felt more comfortable, more in his own skin, that he found greater enjoyment in writing the lyrical novels than in writing those concerned with contemporary subjects. Moreover, one can make a case that Flaubert complained less about writing *La Tentation* and *Salammbô* than he did about writing *Madame Bovary*, *L'Education sentimentale*, and *Bouvard et Pécuchet*. It is a fact, for example, that when he was working on the corrections and revisions of *La Tentation,* he focused on removing and tempering what he had written "spontaneously," or with ease. Flaubert's "affres du style" were the result of a critical regard and his suspicion of spontaneity and "eagle flights" of the imagination. It is curious that contemporary settings made Flaubert more self-conscious about his language, more demanding of its effects.

Julien's guiltless pleasure at the hunt in Part 1 reflects Flaubert's sense of power and ease when he wrote in the "lyrical" style. Yet, although Flaubert very often distinguished between "lyrical" and "vulgar" styles, his writing efforts were nearly always directed at trying to balance and temper the two tendencies. Prose can be as complex as poetry, Flaubert pointed out. He wrote

Louise Colet regarding *Madame Bovary*: "Toute la valeur de mon livre, s'il en a une, sera d'avoir su marcher droit sur un cheveu, suspendu entre le double abîme du lyrisme et du vulgaire (que je veux fondre dans une analyse narrative)" (2: 372). It is telling that though he admired, certainly with reservations, both Balzac and Chateaubriand, he feared at times that his style was a hybrid of the two. Clearly, Flaubert sought a more complicated effect than the "blending" of romantic and realistic styles.

Lyricism can be likened to Julien's success at the hunt in Part 1. Julien's arrows never fail to reach their targets, to kill the animals. Hunting, like writing in the lyrical vein, is carried out "with the ease one experiences in dreams." It gives the hunter/writer a sense of omnipotence, the confidence that he can easily capture animals/reality. The facility with which reality is annihilated makes this activity and this style so pleasurable. On several occasions, Flaubert expresses to Louise Colet the immense pleasure he experiences when writing in the lyrical mode. For example, he writes to her about the second version of *La Tentation*: "Prenant un sujet où j'étais entièrement libre comme lyrisme, mouvements, désordonnement, je me trouvais alors bien dans ma nature et je n'avais qu'à aller" (2: 344-45). Why then must Flaubert renounce or even temper his lyricism? Why must Julien give up hunting?

If Flaubert must check his lyricism, if he always feels the need to return to the discipline he requires of himself in order to write on contemporary subjects, it is only partly because he wished to make his task a difficult one in order to valorize his craft, as Sartre suggests, and only partly because his friends, Bouilhet and Du Camp, encouraged him to do so. It is also because, like omnipotence in hunting, once the hunter/writer has developed a conscience, lyricism cannot survive, except when repressed and sublimated. The conscience which the writer develops tells him that lyricism, like hunting, is a window on the writer's own desires and not a window on the world. Lyricism is a form of self-indulgence, a return to nature, to his nature, to "désordonnement." In the letter cited above to Colet about *La Tentation*, Flaubert goes on to explain to her that although he wrote some beautiful passages using this style, his work lacked an important ingredient; namely, a unifying element: "Comme je taillais avec cœur les perles de mon collier! Je n'y ai oublié qu'une chose, c'est le fil." Lyricisme is disorder; it does not build structures but encourages the fragmentary, the discontinuous, and the excessive. This is the reason why Flaubert cannot, in all conscience, allow it to continue. The writer's desire should not be, in Flaubert's mind, the object of his work, and writing must be approached like an exact and exacting science;

the work of art must have unity and coherence—the value of unity and coherence in a work of art is repeated so often in Flaubert's correspondence that we cannot take it lightly. Thus, the censure of lyricism/hunting is a self-censure which renders, as a consequence, the hunter/writer impotent—at least temporarily.

When in Part 2 Julien returns to the hunt, he is unable to kill a single animal: "Il rencontra dans un ravin un taureau furieux. . . . Julien lui pointa sa lance sous les fanons. Elle éclata, comme si l'animal eût été de bronze; il ferma les yeux, attendant sa mort. Quand il les rouvrit, le taureau avait disparu" (115). Is this bull real or is it a phantom? Julien sees many more animals: "Julien darda contre eux ses flèches; les flèches, avec leurs plumes, se posaient sur les feuilles comme des papillons blancs. Il leur jeta des pierres; les pierres, sans rien toucher, retombaient" (115-16). Julien's arrows do not penetrate. His arrows are like butterflies. The "flèches avec leurs plumes" suggests the writer's pen, the "feuilles," writing paper, and the "papillons blancs" on a black night, words. There is another example in Flaubert where the written word is expressed in terms of butterflies on a contrasting background; it is in the coach scene of *Madame Bovary*. "Une fois, au milieu du jour, en pleine campagne . . . une main passa sous les petits rideaux de toile jaune et jeta des déchirures de papier, qui se dispersèrent au vent et s'abbatirent plus loin, comme des papillons blancs, sur un champ de trèfles rouges tout en fleur."[39] In a letter to Louise Colet, Flaubert compares sentences to the rustle of leaves in the forest: "Il faut que les phrases s'agitent comme les feuilles dans une forêt, toutes dissemblables en leur ressemblance" (4: 52).

Lyricism, as Flaubert conceives it, that is in opposition to realism, takes too much for granted about language's relationship to the world, to the self, to its referent. If arrows/language do not capture the animals, as they once did, it is because the notion of word to world fit has become problematic. Why this has happened is not entirely clear. Does the problem reflect concern about the inadequacy of language for capturing the world (the referent) or is this difficulty a sign of a more radical questioning, the calling into question of the very notion of an objective and stable reality? The answer is likely to be both.

Flaubert is a deliberate writer. Determining and shaping the meaning (or meanings) of his narratives is an essential part of writing. Numerous entries in the *Correspondance* attest to the importance of controlling language. "Les affres du style" and the search for "le mot juste" consist in trying to find the appropriate words to suggest the idea. Every sentence, every word, and indeed every phoneme, as Flaubert saw it, contribute to the text's meaning: "Au point où j'en suis, la phrase la plus simple a pour le reste une portée infinie. De là tout le temps que j'y mets" (3: 20).

Though, as I pointed out in the introduction, Flaubert tended to idealize and simplify classicism, he held it as a standard for himself and for others.[40] For Flaubert, one of the fundamental concepts of classicism in literature was the notion that words can be and are transparent vehicles for the expression of ideas, so that problems encountered in writing could only mean that the ideas themselves were not clear in the writer's mind. Repeatedly and throughout his career, Flaubert voiced his concern for the proper fit between thought and expression. He labored to follow this precept. If he succeeded in his attempt, it was not without doing major violence to that notion. For "ideas" in Flaubert's work do not have the same "clarity" as they do, say, in La Bruyère's or Montesquieu's works. They are not communicated directly but are insinuated. Flaubert is not a classical writer; his experience with language did not leave him with the sense that it was the transparent medium he imagined it would and ought to be. His aesthetic pronouncements are on some major points in conflict with his practice, as Claire-Lise Tondeur has argued.[41]

Can we, then, interpret Julien's sense of guilt about his fear/desire to kill his parents as Flaubert's guilt about his deviation from the classical writers he so admired? For Flaubert, classical style and classical ideology represent unity, coherence, universality, and transparence (adequation of form to content). In many ways, this classical ideal is a projection of Flaubert's desire for order, totality, and permanence. Classicism, to this extent, would be for Flaubert a metaphor for the law, or for the father within patriarchy, the signifier of unity and self-sufficient authority. Lyricism, that is to say, excess, unrealistic scenes and events, implausible plots, the depiction of violence, these are condemned by classical aesthetics, and they would be represented by the mother/leper, the pre-symbolic figure for the abject. Mitchell Greenberg, in an interesting study which compares the classical and the baroque, suggests that in classicism, excess is excluded from the represented universe; it is repressed. He adds that this repression of the excessive, "very similar to those repressions that form the parameters of an 'individual,' allow for the notion of the text as a finished, whole, integral representation, but also identify it as a separate, alienated, and therefore 'discontinuous' production."[42] Greenberg relates the classical text to the image/model of the father and suggests that repression in classical form is so great, "the tension so high, the tribute to the Father so burdensome, that fantasies of the most horrific destruction surface in its rhetoric." "It is not for nothing," he argues, "that the 'end' of Classicism, its final bloody chapter, is the Revolution and that the most salient, most spectacularly symbolic act . . . was precisely the . . . parricidal beheading . . . of the 'Père du peuple.' "[43]

To be sure, nothing could be further from Buffon's and La Fontaine's styles than lyricism. Moreover, Flaubert never thought of classical style as a form of self-indulgence, as he did of lyricism; quite the opposite, in fact. But when Flaubert was questioning lyricism, could he have been thinking all along not about lyricism, per se, but about the classical conception of language as the unproblematic medium of signification, as the "crystal" through which meaning shines like a bright light, as he put it? In other words, could it have been not too clear in Flaubert's mind what it was he was rebelling against? Could Julien's guilt feelings about his desire to break his relationship with, to destroy, his past be the way Flaubert expressed his uneasy alliance with the aesthetics of the past, not of Romanticism but of classicism? Flaubert's admiration for classical writers is without doubt a very earnest feeling. Those aspects he admired and did carry out in his own work are, for example, the classical writer's sensitivity to the sounds and rhythms of language, the virtue of economy in expression, as well as the classical author's "pudeur," his reserve and distance from his creation. But the differences are many. For example, Flaubert did not have the same notion of the "vraisemblable" as did classical writers; he did not write for a public he expected would respond to his work; his notion of "universality" did not have the same implications. In classical aesthetics, "Le critérium de l'universel est basé sur l'opinion la plus largement admise," explains Tondeur. "Mais pour Flaubert il est la quintessence de la réalité quotidienne, dépouillée de toute contingence et qui permet de révéler ce que cachent les apparences et la réalité."[44] Moreover, he was convinced that truth is a matter of perspective. Flaubert may have shared the aesthetic theories of classicism, but he could not in practice apply them without doing violence to himself, to his "nature."

Flaubert's "affres du style," it seems to me, are the result of trying to incorporate, to reconcile, the classical concept of language as an unproblematic medium for reflecting ideas and feelings with the as yet not fully conscious awareness that language is more likely to distance and distort these ideas than to reflect them. In other words, language serves both to express intentions and to distort those intentions by creating a surplus meaning, a supplement, an excess.

Flaubert speaks of classical style with nostalgia, barely aware, if at all, how different in execution his own style is. Flaubert is a writer at the crossroads of classicism and modernism. It is in the nature of such a position to reveal an ambivalent, even a confused sense of one's relationship to the literature of the past.

In Part 3, Julien discovers a vocation which reflects in a dramatic and suggestive manner Flaubert's "affres du style." Julien's thankless job of transporting people and animals back and forth across a "muddy river" using a "heavy boat," is his only way of making life bearable. It is his only means of transcending the world he hates so intensely. Similarly, Flaubert could never envisage himself engaged in the world, outside literature. Only writing gave a sense of purpose to his life. The boat and the river are images for the act of writing just as Julien's vocation is a metaphor for Flaubert's literary vocation:

> A chaque coup d'aviron, le ressac des flots la [la chaloupe] soulevait par l'avant. L'eau, plus noire que de *l'encre,* courait avec furie des deux côtés du bordage. Elle creusait des abîmes, elle faisait des montagnes, et la chaloupe sautait dessus, puis redescendait dans des profondeurs où elle tournoyait, ballottée par le vent.
>
> Julien penchait son corps, dépliait les bras, et, s'arc-boutant des pieds, se renversait avec une torsion de la taille, pour avoir plus de force. La grêle cinglait ses mains, la pluie coulait dans son dos, la violence de l'air l'étouffait. . . . (130-31; my italics)

For Flaubert, language is an abstract medium, but it is equally a material reality. This is apparent in his concern for the sound of sentences, for the importance of reading out loud. Words mean, but they exist in the physical world, too. As I pointed out earlier, language is a tool which the writer manipulates in order to express his intention, but it is equally autonomous and unpredictable. The passage quoted above brings to mind several examples in the *Correspondance* where Flaubert describes writing as a laborious activity. He tells of how he would sweat, his heart would palpitate, and how, upon completing a particular scene, he would be exhausted and out of breath. For Flaubert, writing is a physically strenuous exercise: "J'ai des abcès de style et la phrase me démange sans aboutir. Quel lourd aviron qu'une plume et combien l'idée, quand il faut la creuser avec, est un dur courant!" (2: 326). Flaubert often describes writing in terms of a body maneuvering in difficult waters. He wrote for example: "La continuité constitue le style comme la constance fait la vertu. Pour remonter les courants, pour être bon nageur, il faut que de l'occiput jusqu'au talon le corps soit couché sur la même ligne. On se ramasse comme un crapaud, et l'on se déploie sur toute la surface, en mesure, tête basse et serrant les dents. L'idée doit faire de même à travers les mots" (3: 401); and "Quand je considère mes plans d'un côté et l'Art de l'autre, je m'écrie comme les marins bretons: 'Mon Dieu, que la mer est grande et que ma barque est petite'!" (1: 349). The activity of writing is a physical experience, a difficult effort at navigation, and language has a will of its own, so to speak. Jean-Pierre Richard puts it very succinctly in the concluding remark of his work on Flaubert: "Ecrire, c'est nager en soi, mais c'est nager *à contre courant*."[45]

The leper in *Saint Julien* is emblematic of language in all its materiality. It is Kristeva's semiotic; the figure for a language that is close to the body, a language which disrupts the order and clarity of the symbolic by its "non-expressive articulation." The leper, like the semiotic, is the figure of a radical reorganization of the values of the symbolic. It is, in the economy of Flaubert's aesthetics, not unlike his notion of a poetic prose, a prose whose style valorizes the aesthetics of poetry with its emphasis on rhythm, sounds, allusion.

Flaubert writes: "La perle est une maladie de l'huître et le style, peut-être, l'écoulement d'une douleur plus profonde" (2: 391). The words *lèpre* and *perle* are near anagrams of one another. The pearl may be beautiful and the leper a horrible and diseased figure; both, however, remain a testament of the very difficult and painful process of representation in general and of poetic prose in particular.

4
Reading the Landscape of Desire and Writing

Hérodias might strike readers, at first glance, as an odd addition to the triptych. Instead of focusing on one character, Flaubert focuses on three, Hérodias, Herod, and Iaokanann; and he seems more interested in events and situations than in the characters' responses to these events and situations. Moreover, the outside world, the physical environment (landscapes, interiors, costumes, etc.), dominates his attention more so than in the previous stories. At first glance, too, the story is likely to give readers the sense that the subject matter is more enigmatic, that the characters' motives are more puzzling than in *Un Cœur simple* and *Saint Julien*. But this is mostly an impression. It is true that the political issues and the subjects of race and religion are, at least the way Flaubert sketches them here, difficult to understand and appreciate. However, we do not need to understand these issues to see that in writing *Hérodias* Flaubert was addressing some of the same concerns we find in *Un Cœur simple* and *Saint Julien*. *Hérodias* echoes and completes the two stories in a way that makes this story a perfect conclusion to the work.

The sense of mystery that seems to envelop the narrative is in real terms superficial. It is ironic that *Hérodias*, this seemingly enigmatic work, does not contain a subversive subtext as do the previous two stories. In fact, what Félicité and Julien do on the sly, Iaokanann expresses directly. The father as a character is absent; he presents no threat as he does in *Un Cœur simple* and *Saint Julien*. Moreover, the civilization which he represents is, in the context of *Hérodias*, in its death throes. Iaokanann sings ("bellows") the end of the old order. *Hérodias* is, as I will argue in the conclusion, more explicit in expressing the principle ideas and themes which have been of central concern in the two previous chapters; the characters' hostility toward civilization, and Flaubert's fantasy of a language that would be close to the body, are both dramatized more directly and more explicitly in *Hérodias* through Iaokanann's condemnation of Herod's and Hérodias's culture, and through Iaokanann's voice, specifically.

Flaubert was disappointed by the cool reception the critics gave *Hérodias*. Generally speaking, they thought the work difficult to read, its meaning obscure.[1] It did not compare well with either *Saint Julien* or *Un Cœur simple*, the latter being viewed as a masterpiece. But Flaubert's disappointment aside, he was not himself without doubts concerning it. "Il y manque je ne sais quoi. Il est vrai que je n'y vois plus goutte! Mais pourquoi n'en suis-je pas *sûr,* comme je l'étais de mes deux autres?" (7: 383). The sense that something in the story is lacking finds expression in the work itself on both thematic and symbolic levels. *Hérodias* is fundamentally the story of an absence, namely, the absence of Christ, the figure always referred to but never materializing in the text. It is also the story of a failure, Herod's failure to understand the meaning and the importance of the prophet's message.

It is a story about mysticism and mystery written in the style and using some of the dramatic procedures appropriate to a mystery story. Oddly enough, however, the mystery is anything but mysterious, to its Western readers, at least. The suspense is only rhetorical, since the reader knows who Iaokanann is, knows that he is announcing the coming of the Messiah in Jesus Christ, and knows that the prophet's head will be the prize for Salomé's dance, to mention just the major events. The entire tale is built around predictable events and falsely enigmatic pronouncements. Mystery is a foil. To be sure, the real drama is not on the level of plot. It is to be understood as part of a preoccupation with desire, with language and writing. *Hérodias*, this most abstract of Flaubert's works, is reflexively about art (this is equally true of *Un Cœur simple* and *Saint Julien*). It is as if Flaubert, in writing the story of Herod's conflict, perceived and elaborated an allegory of the writing process—concerned as he was at the time about his inability to write.

Due in part to its theatrical nature and in part to the large number of characters presented, there is a great deal of talking in *Hérodias*. Most of what accompanies this verbal activity reflects a mixed variety of beliefs which, on the whole, have no common reference. Herod's banquet is a good example. Conversations, there, represent a plurality of points of view which when stated are either ignored or questioned by others. For example, Marcellus describes to Jacob Mithraic baptism, while Jacob urges him to become a follower of Jesus. Or, when Aulus's captain informs him about events which presumably ought to concern him, "extraordinary events," Aulus's attention is elsewhere, divided "between the Proconsul and what was being discussed at the adjoining tables" (185). Religious beliefs are especially undermined. For example, temples and pilgrimages are referred to in the casual way people speak of famous exotic sites they visited while on vacation: "Un marchand d'Aphaka ébahissait des nomades, en détaillant les merveilles du temple d'Hiérapolis; et ils demandaient combien coûterait le pèlerinage" (190). Religious discourse is juxtaposed with details of the food served: "On servit des rognons de taureau, des loirs, des rossignols, des hachis dans des feuilles de pampre; et les prêtres discutaient sur la résurrection" (190). For the most part, there is a great deal of talking, but little communication. Flaubert condenses the meaninglessness of the conversations at the banquet into an image which associates metaphorically these conversations with a "fog," with vapor: "Plusieurs causaient debout, au milieu de la salle; et la vapeur des haleines avec les fumées des candélabres faisait un brouillard dans l'air" (191). Are Iaokanann's words, which irritate as much as they inspire, exempt from this characterization?

In addition to serving as background to Herod's drama, the religious theme serves a structural function. With the exception of Herod, it organizes the characters along the lines of insiders and outsiders of the faith, those who believe that the Messiah has arrived and those who are either hostile or indifferent to such a belief. Language generally serves the two groups in different ways. This difference identifies the characters, accordingly, as either closer to or further from the truth the prophet proclaims.

Iconography and certain other visual forms of representation, such as dance, clothes, make-up, are important means of expression for outsiders. Icons are especially valued, and they are believed to have magical powers. But, though icons may be magical, they can be tools of political and psychological dependency and manipulation, too. They are an essential part of the discourse of power, of civilization, against which Iaokanann cries out in his wrath. In Herod's eyes, the coin inscribed with the emperor's image which is meant to protect Herod's life, saves him from death. However, it also assures Hérodias's victory over him. During the feast, Herod is threatened by a group of men, and so in fright he quickly pulls out the magical coin given to him by Hérodias "et, l'observant avec tremblement, il la présentait du côté de l'image" (194). As a result of this gesture, Hérodias herself immediately appears in all her glory, indicating by her arrogant posture and position that she dominates Herod: "[E]t du haut de la balustrade qui dominait Antipas, avec une patère à la main, elle cria" (195). This appearance sets up Salomé's dance and Iaokanann's subsequent decapitation. Herod might think that he saves his life when he pulls out the coin, indeed he may be right, but what he does in effect is to precipitate the very end he has been forestalling.

In this same scene, Hérodias, standing between two sculptures representing monsters, is compared to Cybèle, mother of the gods and personification of the forces of nature, standing between her lions. This is surely meant to strike us by its contradiction, for there is nothing "natural" about Hérodias. With her highly stylized demeanor, she represents above all the disfiguration of nature, the travesty of the feminine. It is not she but Iaokanann who represents the feminine. Similarly, the "stone monsters" at her sides are disfigured and petrified representations of Cybèle's lions. Outsiders, like Hérodias, do not have an immediate relationship with the natural world. They place value on artifacts in which, on the contrary, natural elements are controlled or disguised. Thus, when Aulus expresses dissatisfaction with the food at the banquet ("les mets étant vulgaires, point déguisés suffisamment!" [193]), the statement is meant to reflect poorly on Herod and to imply that this provincial ruler is not sufficiently civilized.

Icons are symbols of worldly power; they are symbols of man's role in shaping and dominating nature. However, they are, in the context of *Hérodias*, limited when compared to speech. They do not, for instance, operate like the "natural" objects which inspired them, as we see in the following description of Herod's room:

> Le jour tombait par un grillage, se développant tout du long de la corniche. Les murailles étaient peintes d'une couleur grenat, presque noir. Dans le fond s'étalait un lit d'ébène, avec des sangles en peau de bœuf. Un bouclier d'or, au-dessus, luisait comme un soleil. (155)

The golden buckler suspended atop Herod's bed which is compared to the sun does not shine like the sun. Rather, the gold underscores the light of the sun but fails to illuminate the false ("painted") world. If Herod's icon fails to function like the natural object which presumably inspired it, it is primarily because unlike the natural light of day which spills out generously over the outside world, the icon's light illuminates nothing but itself ("luisait"). Moreover, in the scene where Iaokanann appears for the first time, the sun is said to be "glinting on the tips of the tiaras," suggesting, in a manner of speaking, that the natural sign scorns and duels with its earthly symbolic representation. Iconographic representations only remotely allude to nature and are, therefore, in the context of the religious thematics of *Hérodias*, a profane form, a sign of the culture's aberration from nature and from God.

Insiders, on the other hand, are closer to nature. They value the land, lead simple lives, dress simply, and renounce all forms of artifice. Phanuel, one of Iaokanann's sympathizers, is described as "stoical in appearance"; he dresses in white and walks barefooted. Jacob, another sympathizer, is "pale" and "humble." Phanuel reads the future in the stars, thus implying that he can read natural signs, that he can recover God's meaning. As it turns out, his interpretation is accurate when he predicts the prophet's death. Although insiders do not have a monopoly on speech, it is effective only for them. When Jacob cries out Iaokanann's name, "Antipas se renversa comme frappé en pleine poitrine" (188); and when the cave in which Iaokanann is imprisoned is opened for the first time, and even before he can raise his voice loud enough to be heard at a distance, Hérodias, at the other end of the palace, hears it: "Vaincue par une fascination, elle traversa la foule" (171). The prophet's voice has the power to draw her, and others, like a magnet.

Iaokanann's voice is compared to natural sounds: the roar of a lion, the sounds of thunder and lightning. It can strike with an overwhelming impact: "La voix grossissait, se développait, roulait avec des déchirements de tonnerre, et, l'écho dans la montagne la répétant, elle foudroyait Machærous d'éclats multipliés" (176). His voice is also eloquent and inspired. His speeches exhort men to return to the land, to a simple life, and to renounce the vain pursuit of pleasure:

> Ses discours, criés à des foules, s'étaient répandus, circulaient; elle [Hérodias] les entendait partout, ils emplissaient l'air. Contre des légions elle aurait eu de la bravoure. Mais cette force plus pernicieuse que les glaives, et qu'on ne pouvait saisir, était stupéfiante; et elle parcourait la terrasse, blême par sa colère, manquant de mots pour exprimer ce qui l'étouffait. (151)

Iaokanann is vicious in his attacks on Hérodias. Yet, in spite of the strength of her personality, she is incapable of expressing, at least through words, the anger she feels. She will, however, succeed in expressing both her hatred and her fear of him indirectly, by using Salomé as intermediary, as medium. Again, it is as if words have an impact when used by insiders but not when used by outsiders. Typically, however, Flaubert throws in an ironic commentary. When Mannaëi, who execrates Iaokanann, curses the temple of the Jews, he is mocked by the narrator for believing that "les mots avaient un pouvoir effectif" (145). But words do have an effect when used by insiders like Iaokanann, for example.

For the most part, speech enjoys a privileged place in *Hérodias*. Iaokanann's voice, and his words, are meant to express the absolute proximity of an ideal and divine presence. No irony undercuts Iaokanann's words. Flaubert gives his pronouncements authority and recognition. As if, in accordance with the Aristotelian and medieval Christian thinking, among all forms of expression, the voice came closest to nature, to mind, to soul, to truth.[2] As if, the least material and visible, it were deemed closest to the signified—all other signifiers remaining derivative, secondary, fallen. Yet, though privileged by their proximity to voice, it is precisely because Iaokanann's words are still only words, still only signifiers, that we can understand the cryptic and often repeated remark: "Pour qu'il croisse, il faut que je diminue." It is only when Iaokanann's words stop referring to what is missing that Christ (the one missing) will emerge as presence. In the allegory of language, Iaokanann is to Christ what the signifier is to the signified. Both become one (are one), in the sign, when Salomé, whose function in the allegory will be clear shortly, negotiates for Iaokanann's head.

How ought we interpret Christ's absence from the narrative? Does it imply that the signified cannot be represented as such? Or does it, less radically, suggest the difficulty (not impossibility) of figuring the signified?

Flaubert wrote in a letter to Madame Roger des Genettes that *Hérodias* had nothing to do with religion, that he was interested above all in the "mine officielle d'Hérode (qui était un vrai préfet) et la figure farouche d'Hérodias, une sorte de Cléopâtre et de Maintenon" (7: 309). At least initially, character was what interested Flaubert in the subject of *Hérodias*. The dynamic confrontation between the three main characters interested him, and so he applied equal lighting on all three. What is striking, however, is that he placed only slightly less emphasis on minor characters like Aulus and Phanuel. The result is a highly colored and intense atmosphere. With the exception of Herod, the characters are one-dimensional and static, their motivations easy enough to understand. Though for the reader, character may be what is least interesting in *Hérodias*, in Flaubert's work, character is always the best place to focus for getting at the text's meaning. It is, therefore, useful to turn to the characters, especially to Herod. Herod's indecisiveness and seeming lack of motivation give his character some interest and depth. In effect, without him, there would be no drama. Hérodias and Iaokanann may strike Herod as fascinating and mysterious, but for the reader it is Herod who stands apart as the most enigmatic character. It is difficult to understand why the title refers to Hérodias when Hérodiade (a title Flaubert considered) or Herod would have been more appropriate.

Hérodias opens with the description of the citadel of Machærous hanging over the abyss. Herod, on the terrace, is contemplating the surrounding terrain. He is thinking about his past and anticipating the problems of the future when he is twice interrupted from his reverie. The first interruption is Iaokanann's voice—although Herod is not so sure he has heard it ("J'avais cru l'entendre!" [143]). The prophet's voice is like the voice of Herod's conscience. It is, at first, hidden, uncertain, and mysteriously vague. After this interruption, and after having been reassured by Mannaëi that the prophet was still in his underground cell, Herod sighs in relief and continues his reverie: "Tous ces monts autour de lui, comme des étages de grands flots pétrifiés, les gouffres noirs sur le flanc des falaises, l'immensité du ciel bleu, l'éclat violent du jour, la profondeur des abîmes le troublaient" (145). This time he is interrupted by Hérodias who, "d'une voix forte, secouant le Tétrarque" (146), announces news of their victory concerning a political matter. The two voices, Iaokanann's and Hérodias's, represent the two poles of Herod's desire, the two paths he is reluctant to choose between.

Throughout *Hérodias,* Herod is portrayed as a passive man. He is too tired to rule, too tired even to think. But mostly, he is a scared man. He is afraid of his wife and feels threatened by Iaokanann, Mannaëi, Vitellius, the Arabs, and others as well. Essentially, Herod is afraid to die. All around him, characters with little or no power assert their beliefs and allegiances. Only Herod is hesitant and confused. He is caught at the crossroads of two powerful and mysterious forces and is incapable of defining his own position. Ideally, Herod would prefer not to take a position. But the force of the events, determined mainly by Hérodias's resolve to kill Iaokanann, compels him out of his passivity and into action. The prophet's death is ironically and tragically effectuated by a promise made, lightly, by Herod's irresponsible use of language. If Herod's promise to grant Salomé's wish is tragically effective, it is because Herod is not wholly an outsider. He remains, in fact, closer to Iaokanann than to Hérodias up until the time he sees Salomé and is seduced by her. Salomé brings Herod out of his passivity. It is desire, finally, that breaks the stalemate and dispels the tension of the conflict mounting within Herod. But what exactly does Herod desire? And how do Iaokanann and Hérodias figure in this desire?

Although Herod's dilemma can be viewed as a conflict between political power and worldly pleasure, on the one hand, and his longing to escape from the world, on the other, this explanation misses the point. The real conflict resides in the fact that both Hérodias and Iaokanann have qualities which captivate Herod. From Herod's point of view, Hérodias offers more than political influence and power. Clearly, Herod no longer has any political ambitions. What continues to draw him to her is her magical qualities. When, for example, Phanuel predicts the death of an important man, Herod, thinking that the prediction could only be referring to himself, runs to Hérodias for help: "Il eut l'idée de recourir à Hérodias. Il la haïssait pourtant. Mais elle lui donnerait du courage; et tous les liens n'étaient pas rompus de l'ensorcellement qu'il avait autrefois subi" (179-80).

Herod is above all an aesthete and a dreamer. Hérodias is visually suggestive and erotic. She surrounds herself with visually stimulating objects which captivate Herod and make him dream: "Quand il entra dans sa [Hérodias's] chambre, du cinnamome fumait sur une vasque de porphyre; et des poudres, des onguents, des étoffes pareilles à des nuages, des broderies plus légères que des plumes, étaient dispersées" (180). Hérodias is ruthless and cunning, too. Realizing that as she ages, her grip on Herod is likely to diminish, she trains her daughter Salomé in the art of seduction. Salomé and Hérodias are functional doubles. Both the daughter and the mother represent an aesthetic of artifice. If Hérodias's room were to represent a metaphoric and unnatural womb, Salomé would be its most accomplished product. Highly adorned, the mother and the daughter are emblems of an opposition to nature. This visual quality with its accompanying sense of mystery and eroticism is the reason for Herod's fatal attraction to both women.

Turning to Iaokanann, Flaubert presents him as a powerful and threatening figure. In that sense he resembles Hérodias. He is, however, depicted more as a wild animal than as a man, as a "natural" not a "civilized" creature. He is the figure for the feminine. She, on the other hand, as I pointed out, is presented as a perversion of nature, a monster and a monstrosity (recall that her relationship with Herod is characterized as adulterous and incestuous).

Iaokanann's first appearance comes after much suspense. What fascinates Herod and attracts him to Iaokanann is his awe-inspiring voice and the visionary stir produced by it. Iaokanann represents an aesthetic of eloquence. His lyrical speeches set Herod dreaming about possibilities which both frighten and seduce him. Iaokanann evokes apocalyptic visions of the violent overthrow of the world as well as utopic, redemptive visions of a beautiful and struggle-free existence for mankind. His voice, like an instrument, can be "sweet, gentle, melodious" or it can be deep, wild, and terrifying; it is always moving and unsettling to those who hear it.

Herod is a collector of exotic and beautiful objects which he keeps hidden in underground caves: the marvelous collection of arms, the magnificent white horses, the "treasure" Vitellius is after and which may be, in a symbolic sense, none other than Iaokanann himself. These prized possessions, like the prophet's eloquence and visions, and like Salomé's sublime dance, are the only source of fascination and pleasure in Herod's life. Iaokanann's passion keeps him in touch with a source of vitality and energy which Herod, in his profound passivity and impotence, lacks. But, more importantly, it is both Iaokanann's visions of the coming of a new world and the eloquence of these visions which seduce Herod. Herod's penchant and weakness, his desire for beauty and his profound need to escape the world, place him in the problematic position of having to choose between two equally moving and inspiring modes of aesthetic flight, namely, the visual and the verbal. In the contest between images and words, the visual triumphs. Salomé's dance determines Herod's choice and assures Iaokanann's silence. What is it about the visual that gives it the edge in Herod's fantasy?

According to Flaubert, Salomé's dance was the most difficult passage he had to write in *Hérodias*: "Je suis malade de la peur que m'inspire la danse de Salomé! Je crains de la bâcler" (7: 14). Salomé's dance is choreographed to be at once visually striking and erotic in its effect on Herod. Watching her, Herod is "lost in a dream." She comes onstage veiled and mysterious. When she drops her veil, she appears in her role as Hérodias: "C'était Hérodias, comme autrefois dans sa jeunesse" (196). Salomé is highly adorned. She wears a provocative costume and stark facial make-up. Like the icons, referred to earlier, Salomé is fraudulent. She is not Hérodias, but an imitation of the mother in her youth. To underscore this fraudulence, Flaubert uses similes 11 times in a relatively short space to describe the variety of roles which Salomé takes on during the performance. Vitellius compares her to Mnester the pantomime—she produces signs without using the privileged medium, the voice.

In her dance, Salomé represents a series of figures and displays a variety of moods, different emotions. Her movements express youthful exuberance and gaiety as well as languor and sexual frenzy. One must note, however, that she expresses through her performance roles and moods quite different from anything she can experience herself. When she opens her mouth to speak, she does not speak in the voice of the graceful and sexually stimulating dancer she has just been portraying, but in the voice of the awkward, childish, and silly girl she actually is. The performer and the performance are not bound to each other. The performer is, therefore, free from any responsibility regarding the effect (erotic or tragic) that she produces. Even before watching her dance, Herod had, on separate occasions, noticed Salomé from a distance and was fascinated by her figure as she posed or moved gracefully against different backgrounds. In the allegory of language and writing, Salomé stands suggestively for the concept of form in art.

The white horses, Herod's most prized possessions, have much in common with Salomé. Like Salomé herself, they have been kept separate, in hiding. Like her, too, they are youthful, agile, striking in form. They are highly adorned, painted, made-up:

> Ils avaient tous la crinière peinte en bleu, les sabots dans des mitaines de sparterie, et les poils d'entre les oreilles bouffant sur le frontal, comme une perruque. Avec leur queue très longue, ils se battaient mollement les jarrets. Le Proconsul en resta muet d'admiration.
>
> C'étaient de merveilleuses bêtes, souples comme des serpents, légères comme des oiseaux. Elles partaient avec la flèche du cavalier, renversaient les hommes en les mordant au ventre, se tiraient de l'embarras des rochers, sautaient par-dessus des abîmes, et pendant tout un jour continuaient dans les plaines leur galop frénétique; un mot les arrrêtait. Dès que Iaçim entra, elles vinrent à lui, comme des moutons quand paraît le berger; et, avançant leur encolure, elles le regardaient inquiètes avec leurs yeux d'enfant. Par habitude, il lança du fond de sa gorge un cri rauque qui les mit en gaieté; et elles se cabraient, affamées d'espace, demandant à courir. (167-68)

These horses are more than living weapons in Antipas's armory. The description falls on the beauty of their form, on their overwhelming desire for movement, for space, for freedom, on their childlike and irresponsible joy. They are frivolous and mindless creatures, much as Salomé is. They are attached only to their keeper, Iaçim, who alone controls them, as Hérodias does Salomé. Like Salomé, the horses represent the concept of form in art. Form in *Hérodias* embodies tremendous energy and beauty and is associated at the same time with mindlessness, meaninglessness, irresponsibility.[3]

Iaokanann, in contrast to the horses, calls out for a return to order, to duty, to responsibility, allegiance to a unique truth. He promises the cessation of all desires. If Salomé and the horses are striking for their physical perfection, for the beauty of their form, Iaokanann, in contrast, is physically vague and repulsive. When he speaks, his words strike those who hear them as filled with a secret meaning, set them thinking, and stir feelings within them. The prophet stands in relation to Christ as the signifier stands to the signified, as was pointed out earlier. He is, also, emblematic of content, of meaning.

Herod and Phanuel, too, are intrigued by the prophet's words. But whereas Phanuel discovers the meaning of these words and understands the parable, Herod does not. In a sense, Herod has opted for freedom over responsibility, for form over meaning. Fascinated by form, Herod sees but does not perceive beyond his immediate desires and fears. He mistakes Phanuel's prediction that a great man will be killed on the night of the banquet as referring to himself, and when Mannaëi repeats to him the mysterious words of the prophet, "Pour qu'il croisse, il faut que je diminue," Herod is intrigued, but does not try to interpret what they mean: "le Tétrarque était las de réfléchir" (145). An aesthete but not an interpreter of signs, Herod does not make the effort to understand, to go beyond or behind his fascination, beyond the mystery. Thus, he fails to grasp the significance of Iaokanann's message. If Herod had understood the parable, he might have gained a useful insight, namely, that the willingness to sacrifice the self is a necessary step for achieving salvation, that is, for eternal life, the only resolution possible for Herod's fear of death. By missing the clue, Herod fails to exercise power over his destiny. Herod's failure is a failure of interpretation which itself stems from a failure of character. Herod, a figure for the writer, is also, as I said in the introduction, a figure for the type of reader who, fascinated by style or by questions of form, ignores clues about the work's meaning. Félicité and Julien are able to subvert the system precisely because they know how to interpret the models provided by the dominant order; they interpret these models on their own terms. Herod cannot escape the system because he is blind to its procedures; he is too tired to deal with problems.

In *Hérodias*, Flaubert dramatizes a symbolic confrontation between conflicting impulses within himself as an artist. By representing the confrontation between Hérodias and Iaokanann in terms of a pressure to value content in art over aesthetic concerns, Flaubert acts out the terms for understanding the conflicting pressures at work during the act of writing. Form and content are two faces of the same coin; it is impossible to speak of one without, at the same time, implicating the other. These are the terms in which Flaubert conceived form and content, as many passages in the *Correspondance* reveal.[4] The notion of Flaubert striving to write a book about nothing (a goal expressed, among others, by Jean Racine in his preface to *Bérénice*), with his arduous work on form, on style, is taken by some critics as the final word on Flaubert's goals and values in art. However, Flaubert's letters aside, an allegorical reading of *Hérodias* as a sort of archeology of the written text suggests that Flaubert's notion of form is within the classical norm. Form is that which shapes ideas and makes communication possible. It is the visible and material manifestation of desire; and writing, I want to show now, is a kind of bringing to the surface of that desire.

In *Saint Julien* and *Un Cœur simple,* the narratives end on a grandiose celestial scene: Julien is lifted up to Heaven in the arms of Jesus Christ and Félicité hallucinates joining with a gigantic Loulou hovering above her head. *Hérodias,* however, begins, more or less, where the other two leave off. It begins on an elevation beyond the mountain tops and above the clouds: "Les montagnes, immédiatement sous lui [Herod], commençaient à découvrir leurs crêtes, pendant que leur masse, jusqu'au fond des abîmes, était encore dans l'ombre. Un brouillard flottait, il se déchira, et les contours de la mer Morte apparurent" (140). As the narrative unfolds, the description progresses to the lower and deeper regions (caves) before the final scene in which the prophet emerges from the cave and is carried horizontally on land, toward a new place at the dawn of a new age for humanity, "A l'instant où se levait le soleil" (203). It is as if, looking for specificity about the fullness of being, about the nature of desire, in metaphors of elevation and transcendence, and not finding it, Flaubert decides to take a different approach, to use a different metaphor.

Spaces are symbolically meaningful in Flaubert. There are in the landscape of *Hérodias* topographic layers which suggest the following divisions into figurative spaces: (l) the exterior or surface space, the topography of Herod's kingdom, as well as his palace, (2) the intermediate space, the cave where Iaokanann is interred, and (3) the deepest level, the white horses' cave. This topographic structure will serve as a visual model of Flaubert's conception of language and writing.[5]

Often, when reflecting on writing, Flaubert makes a neat distinction between the outside, "dessus" or "surface," and the inside, "dessous" and "profondeur." He writes, for example: "Le lecteur ne s'apercevra pas, je l'espère, de tout le travail psychologique caché sous la forme, mais il ressentira l'effet" (5: 3); "Il faut faire . . . des tableaux complets, peindre le dessous et le dessus" (3: 158); "Il y a des constructions souterraines à tout. Ce n'est qu'une question de surface et de profondeur. Sondez et vous trouverez" (8: 373); "J'ai fait nettement, pour mon usage, deux parts dans le monde et dans moi; d'un côté l'élément externe . . . ; de l'autre l'élément interne que je concentre afin de le rendre plus dense et dans lequel je laisse pénétrer, à pleines effluves, les plus purs rayons de l'Esprit, par la fenêtre ouverte de l'intelligence. Tu ne trouveras pas cette phrase très claire; il faudrait un volume pour la développer" (1: 278); "La couleur dans la nature a un esprit, une sorte de vapeur subtile qui se dégage d'elle et c'est cela qui doit animer par en-dessous le style" (3: 263); and, "Sois sage, travaille, fais-moi quelque grande belle chose sobre, sévère, quelque chose qui soit chaud en-dessous et splendide à la surface" (1: 311). One can find many more references such as these.

The best discussion of the terms inside and outside (or depth and surface) is given by Jean-Pierre Richard in his brilliant essay on Flaubert. Richard suggests that the act of writing brings to the surface the elements that constitute the subject's inner being, namely, nature, instincts, habit. He suggests further that the "surface" of the written text represents the sentence, the written, the visible aspect of the sign, whereas the depth is the primary, nonlinguistic impulse which motivates Flaubert to write in the first place.[6] Flaubert's text, Richard points out, is made up of layers, of spaces which proceed downward from the most stylized and structured to the least, that is to say, to nature, to instincts, to being.

Hérodias illustrates the process by which language, in Richard's words, solidifies and condenses the writer's impulses. In a figurative sense, the outside space in *Hérodias* corresponds to the surface layer of the text. The outside is occupied by a highly civilized culture whose characteristic mark is the value it places on controlling and shaping nature. To this extent, the outside space reflects the most stylized aspect of the work of art, namely, the layer of text that is most visible, most material and formed, in other words, the written. Furthermore, the topography of the outside, with its calcified and massive landscape and architecture (temples, monuments, cities, dispersed in the landscape) and the general sterility symbolized by the desert landscape, recalls Flaubert's notion of the work of art as an inert and monumental artifact existing in the midst of a desolate environment, in the midst of society: "Les livres ne se font pas comme les enfants, mais comme les pyramides, avec un dessin prémédité, et en apportant des grands blocs l'un par-dessus l'autre, à force de reins, de temps et de sueur, et ça ne sert à rien! Et ça reste dans le désert! mais en le dominant prodigieusement" (4: 239-40).

Some critics have interpreted this passage as implying the death of the subject: the pyramid suggests that what is within the structure (the book) is stillness and death—the pyramid is a monument to death which encloses within it a dead body. The passage has also been interpreted to mean that there is no meaning within but only structures that mean. Read in context, however, it refers particularly to the laborious and deliberate process of composing books. Although at times Flaubert compares books to buildings, walls, and monuments, he more often imagines a "within" of the aesthetic object which lives and breathes like its counterpart in the real world. For instance, admiring a bas-relief in the Parthenon, Flaubert exclaims in admiration: "On dirait qu' il [un des seins d'une figure] va se gonfler et que les poumons qu'il y a dessous vont s'enfler et respirer" (2: 298). There is a "within" to representation, something that moves in both the literal and affective sense of the word. I like to think of this within as the narrative's subtext, that which is suggested through style, mostly, but in other ways as well. For if style itself did not tease the mind and the sensibility, procedures for unearthing meaning(s) as subtle as those we find in Flaubert would not be noted by many readers. The successful passage, Flaubert pointed out repeatedly, is one that makes it possible for the reader to sense that inner movement ("tout le travail psychologique") on the surface of the text. Both the bas-relief and the pyramid passages stress the distinction between the inside and the outside of a work of art and imply that the outside is the space of the written, of style, of the visible and material aspect of the sign.

Is there something moving within the volcanic mountain upon which Machærous stands? Or, is what is inside dead? Death in *Hérodias,* it should be underscored, is not within but without. This is suggested in the dramatic opening of the story describing the citadel of Machærous facing the Dead Sea, and in the images of doom and destruction in the terrain, images which obsess Herod. There is, however, movement inside, and it is deep within the mountain in two distinct places: Iaokanann's cave and the horses' cave. It is in the innermost interior, in a cave *deeper* than the cell where the prophet is situated, that we find Herod's white horses:

Un souffle d'air chaud s'exhala des ténèbres. Une allée descendait en tournant; ils la prirent et arrivèrent au seuil d'une grotte, plus étendue que les autres souterrains.

Une arcade s'ouvrait au fond sur le précipice, qui de ce côté-là défendait la citadelle. Un chèvrefeuille, se cramponnant à la voûte, laissait retomber ses fleurs en pleine lumière. A ras du sol, un filet d'eau murmurait. (167)

This passage is strikingly different from anything we find before it in *Hérodias*. It is the first time, for instance, that nature appears as a vibrant and living space. There are plains just beyond the cave in what is described here as the "précipice." It is also the first time that we have a description of actual vegetation, flowers. These flowers "en pleine lumière" contrast with the rigidity of the "fleurons" of the "crown of stone" that are suspended over the abyss, in the opening description of *Hérodias* and with the stylized "festons d'anémones" of Hérodias's costume. In the horses' cave, words are not uttered. We are told that "le Proconsul en resta muet d'admiration." The sounds are "natural." Iaçim communicates with the animals by projecting "du fond de sa gorge un cri rauque," and nearby, on the ground "un filet d'eau murmurait" (167-68). Moreover, this space opens up perspectives of freedom. The young horses "pendant tout un jour continuaient dans les plaines leur galop frénétique . . . elles se cabraient, affamées d'espace, demandant à courir" (168).

The cave is only superficially the place where Herod hides his most secret possessions for fear that Vitellius would claim them for himself. Its vaguely drawn outline, the frenetic mobility of the horses, and the fact that it is located even further down from Iaokanann's cave are indications that the horses' cave is, like Iaokanann's cave, a space of symbolic proportions. Partly, it is a spatial figure for the horses themselves, a place of self-generating energy. The very young horses are emblematic of unbridled desire, of bodily sensations, of libido. They intimate the body's desire to move freely, irresponsibly, in limitless space ("précipice," "abîme"). These and other points raised earlier regarding the horses' proximity to nature and the fact that no words are uttered in this cave are indications of the pre-linguistic, pre-oedipal status of this symbolic space. The horses and the horses' cave, respectively, are figurative representations of desire and the body of desire. So are Iaokanann and Iaokanann's cave. To this extent, these are all figures for the feminine; they are uterine symbols. As Luce Irigaray points out, the feminine is related to the concept of space, the woman/feminine is a place; it is the place from which all men originate.[7] In the allegory of language and writing, the horses and

Iaokanann can be viewed as metaphors for Julia Kristeva's semiotic, which she describes in these terms: "The semiotic is a distinctive, non-expressive articulation; neither amorphous substance nor meaningful numbering. We imagine it in the cries, the vocalizing, the gestures of infants; it functions, in fact, in adult discourse as rhythm, prosody, plays on words, the non-sense of sense, laughter."[8]

Interestingly, though not surprisingly, the horses are not devoid of artifice; they are, like Salomé, "painted." Thus, even as Flaubert located in his imaginary the locus of desire and conceived it as the original impulse of a pre-linguistic space, he was already also perceiving it as yet another sign in the chain of signifiers. Indeed, this suggests that Flaubert had a *suspicion* (perhaps more vague than not) that the notion of origin might be problematical, that representation might have primacy over experience and that the feminine is already always contaminated by the symbolic; as Kristeva points out, the concepts of the maternal, the body, and the paternal are always coupled in signification.

How does the original impulse (the horses) find its way, so to speak, to the surface of the text? In other words, how is desire transformed, how is it "figured," in the language of the text? This appears to be the function of the intermediate space, Iaokanann's cave, or more exactly, Iaokanann's voice. Iaokanann is less a man, less a character, than a voice trying to communicate with the outside. In terms of the linguistic analogy, Iaokanann's voice can be related to that mechanism in the process of writing whose function is to make words reflect as truly as possible the desiring and signifying impulses. For Flaubert, this mechanism is the *gueuloir*.[9] As was pointed out earlier, Flaubert was dissatisfied with *Hérodias*. However, he did praise its quality as a great *gueulade*, a term by which he meant that the story read well out loud, a quality that he always attributed to the superior work of art. He wrote to Turgenev about *Hérodias*: "Que sera-ce? Je l'ignore. En tous cas, ça se présente sous les apparences d'un fort gueuloir, car en somme, il n'y a que *ça:* la Gueulade, l'Emphase, l'Hyperbole. Soyons échevelés!" (7: 369). Similarly, he wrote his niece: "La nuit, dans le 'silence du cabinet,' Monsieur se monte tellement le bourrichon qu'il arrive à la 'fine frénésie et fureur.' Après tout, il n'y a que ça de bon. Mais il ne faut pas que la mécanique en claque" (7: 375). He wrote to Madame Régnier about *Hérodias*: "C'est un gueuloir, et que j'aurai plaisir à vous dégoiser" (7: 376). He wrote to Maupassant: "C'est peu 'naturaliste,' mais 'ça se gueule,' qualité supérieure" (7: 377).

Reading *Hérodias* as a dramatization of the forces and spaces in Flaubert's text suggests a parallel between Iaokanann's voice and Flaubert's *gueuloir*. Iaokanann attacks Herod's civilization on the ground that it is morally corrupted. He calls for a return to the source, to God and to nature. In the same way, the *gueuloir*, the writer's voice, assures that the language of the text does not lose touch with its source in life. This source, if we accept the symbolic reading of the horses' cave, is synonymous with desire and with the senses. Thus, the *gueuloir* instills live-liness into the text through the writer's body, his voice, his breath. The *gueuloir* animates language. Yet clearly the *gueuloir* does more than that; it is more than a reading of the text. It is part of the writing process, the mechanism by which Flaubert tested, corrected, and balanced his words and sentences so as to make certain they did not become cold and lifeless. This is, in a sense, what Flaubert means when he says, for example, that "les phrases mal faites ne résistent pas à cette épreuve [au gueuloir]; elles oppressent la poitrine, gênent les battements du cœur, et se trouvent ainsi en dehors des conditions mêmes de la vie."[10] It is by means of the *gueuloir* (that is, of Iaokanann) that desire (the horses) is shaped into language, that it emerges from the depths to the surface. Because the voice is a phenomenon of the writer's body, it attaches language to the experience of the body. The *gueuloir* is voice and language, or body and language, linked together; it is language animated by the voice. It serves to measure and structure Flaubert's sentences in a way that makes them not just reflect but also shape the unstructured impulses from within, impulses which no structure however rigid can completely suppress.

Iaokanann serves as a link between the outside/written and the inside/ desire only up to Salomé's dance. In other words, the link is severed by the dance. The performance is a figurative description of the act of writing, and Salomé herself is a figure for the trace of desire (the horses) on the surface of the text. Salomé is, as was pointed out earlier, a reflection of the white horses. Yet, there is a difference between them. For while Salomé represents the corrupt double, the double in the world, the horses represent the fantasy of purity and innocence sheltered from the world. Hence, Salomé represents the trace of an origin (the horses) in the text. But, at the same time, she also represents the idea of transformation, of difference from the origin—Salomé takes the form of a sex goddess. As for the instincts and impulses, the free energy associated with the original impulse, it is shaped, choreographed in Salomé's performance for the purpose of creating an effect, of seducing the audience. For while the horses most surely experience desire, we are aware that Salomé only mimes it. In other words, she *represents* desire. Salomé's performance symbolizes the act of writing just as Iaokanann's severed head (now that it has surfaced as a result of the dance) represents the sign. In other words, it is through the act of writing that the signifier (Iaokanann) and the signified (Christ) are joined and become one in the sign (Iaokanann's head).

The final movement of Salomé's dance is an abrupt and violent pose, a frightful image of fragmentation, a decapitation of sorts, like Iaokanann's decapitation. With her leggings falling over her shoulders, her face appears disembodied, dissociated from the rest of her figure:

> Sa nuque et ses vertèbres faisaient un angle droit. Les fourreaux de couleur qui enveloppaient ses jambes, lui passant par-dessus l'épaule, comme des arcs-en-ciel, accompagnaient sa figure, à une coudée du sol. Ses lèvres étaient peintes, ses sourcils très noirs, ses yeux presque terribles, et des gouttelettes à son front semblaient une vapeur sur du marbre blanc.
>
> Elle ne parlait pas. Ils [Salomé et Hérode] se regardaient. (198-99)

Salomé's eyes communicate a kind of nonverbal meaning. They point to something. But to what exactly? Similarly, during the banquet, Iaokanann's head is passed around for all the curious to see and Mannaëi places it in front of Aulus, who is awakened by it: "Par l'ouverture de leurs cils, les prunelles mortes et les prunelles éteintes semblaient se dire quelque chose" (202). We are reminded of the scene of parricide in *Saint Julien* when the father's "prunelle éteinte" seems to be communicating something to Julien. All these looks are pregnant with meaning, or at least we feel that Flaubert implies that they are. Yet, typically, he does so without making the precise meaning explicit. What we might want to do in the face of this silence is to interpret, or we might choose not to.

In this reading of *Hérodias* I have been suggesting that the signified (Christ) is not represented metaphorically as an absence of meaning but as a mystery that can and ought to be (judging by Herod's example) unraveled. Admittedly, the examples of the eyes communicating to one another and of the horses' ambiguous status as emblems of a pre-linguistic space are both suspicious and unsettling. For while the eyes can be rightly viewed as rhetorical devices for underscoring the general sense of mystery and incomprehension that sets the tone for the story, one cannot help but suspect that they may be, in a vague way, pointing us, pointing Flaubert, to the enigmatic and problematic nature of the signified.

Like Herod, Flaubert is a man at the crossroads of two currents which both appeal to some aesthetic concern within him. As we saw in *Saint Julien,* Flaubert held two antagonistic notions of language and wrote with both these imperatives in mind: the classical notion of language as the medium through which ideas or feelings are reflected and the modern tendency to question the meaning of existence, the primacy of being over representation, and the capacity of language to communicate. Without undermining the importance of representation, the thrust of the allegory in *Hérodias* confirms the primacy of being, of desire, and reassures Flaubert that the difficulty of representing the plenitude of human experience and of desire is due to the inadequacies of words, of art, and of style, specifically. After all, the heavy head of the prophet, a figure for the sign, is symbolically heavy with disseminating potential.

Hérodias, Un Cœur simple, and *Saint Julien,* like Flaubert's work in general, express Flaubert's radical distrust of language. But the *Trois contes* differs from the rest of Flaubert's production in that it also expresses the pleasure and the sense of power that the writing self experiences when using (and abusing) language. Rimbaud called for a new language to express the new sensibility. Flaubert's more conservative call was for the expansion of the expressive space of language. Language did not need to be reinvented; prose would learn from poetry how to bring language closer to the body, to sounds and rhythms; style would suggest the complexities and dualities of human nature, of thought, and of desire.

Conclusion:
Straight and Suspect Texts:
A Poetics of Transgression

Et qui est-ce qui s'apercevra jamais des profondes combinaisons
que m'aura demandées un livre si simple?
                                    —Flaubert, *Correspondance*

Ce livre, tout en calcul et en ruses de style... Ce sera peut-être un
tour de force qu'admireront certaines gens (et encore en petit
nombre).
                                    —Flaubert, *Correspondance*

Le style, l'art en soi, paraît toujours insurrectionnel aux gouvernements et immoral aux bourgeois.
                        —Flaubert, "Hommage à Louis Bouilhet"

One cannot write a conclusion, least of all on Flaubert, without feeling
somewhat slighted by his famous remark that "l'ineptie consiste à vouloir
conclure." Having said this, however, I would like to add that Flaubert's
remark on the subject of conclusions is itself a conclusion. Unlike Gide, for
whom life and art offered contradictory yet equally viable and equally
interesting possibilities for experimentation and for thought, Flaubert held
relatively fixed views on existence, art, love, politics. The *Correspondance* is
full of assertions and of "parti pris." Flaubert seemed perfectly at ease making judgments, writing maxims, in other words, concluding. Even when he
described himself as a man made up of "compartiments" and when he referred
to himself as a man of dualities, he did not speak of this with delight but with
concern, as if of a flaw in his nature. Although his work at times dramatizes

multiplicity and indeterminacy, it is far from celebrating them. As with Saint Antoine, they are presented as symptomatic of an obsessed and troubled self. The mobility and multiplication of desire are the causes of anxiety, the anxiety of a loss of self, a loss of center. Nothing is further from the Flaubertian universe than Gidean "disponibilité." Nothing is more desirable for the Flaubertian ego than stasis, unity, coherence.

To be fair to Flaubert's intention in discrediting conclusions, however, it must be said that when he remarks that conclusions are a sign of "stupidity," he is thinking of conclusions as the tendency in some people to simplify and expedite the meaning of complex issues and subtle distinctions. For Flaubert, to close in on meaning in order to make a point seems a sure way of rendering the complex and the diverse superficial. "La conclusion, *la plupart du temps*, me semble acte de bêtise. C'est là ce qu'ont de beau les sciences naturelles: elles ne veulent rien prouver" (3: 154; my italics). There are no points to make; there are only depths to expose. In a curious remark where he compares writing to reading, Flaubert expresses what he admired in the art of La Fontaine and La Bruyère: "Comme ils lisaient lentement! Aussi toute leur idée y est, la forme est pleine, bourrée et garnie de choses jusqu'à la faire craquer" (3: 150). There is in Flaubert a predilection for images and states of fullness, totality, and completion. As if these were the signs of a superior sensibility, of moral and intellectual integrity and perfection. For Flaubert, the role of good readers, like the role of good writers, is to work slowly to unearth the rich deposits which are alluded to in the depths, and at the surface, of a given text or of a given experience. If conclusions are undesirable, for Flaubert, it is because they seem to simplify the complex reality of things.

Flaubert's view on conclusions is not informed by an ontological questioning of the possibility of concluding, of knowing. After all, conclusions are a sign of "stupidity" only "most of the time." His remarks on the subject betray an elitist bias. They imply that only an enlightened few are justified in this practice; all others he suspects of superficiality and dogmatism. Flaubert's attitude stems from a fear that conclusions, regardless of who makes them and regardless of how they are arrived at, are likely to be accepted at face value as truth by most men. Underlying this fear is an uneasiness about what he suspected was a dangerous democratizing of knowledge and of intellectual authority. Much of what informs Flaubert's responses to social and aesthetic issues can be linked to a disillusionment with what he felt to be the leveling of moral, aesthetic, and political values brought about by democratic principles and ideals. Though, as Sartre has remarked, Flaubert shared many of the values of the bourgeoisie, a class to which he belonged, he could only envisage this class as mindless, deficient, and morally bankrupt. Moreover, he could only imagine it as a victorious, socially and politically dominant class. In the works prior to the *Trois contes,* the victory of the bourgeoisie, or of the dominant class, over the individual is a common theme. In the *Trois contes,* however, Flaubert emphasizes the victory of the individual over the class in power.

What are the motives and what are the implications of this victory for Flaubert's art? In this chapter, I will address these questions. I will also try to develop the arguments I made throughout this book in light of bringing the three stories to bear on one another, finding their common ground and their unifying elements. The three stories were written consecutively and they were intended to compose one volume. I believe that there is much to be gained from reading them together as a unit. Finally, I will show how what I have called the straight and the suspect narratives fulfill Flaubert's aesthetic ambitions by helping to reconcile his allegiance to the classical ideal of art as a pure reflector of thought with notions of language and representation which are at odds with this ideal.

This conclusion began by taking up the subject of conclusions; it will be partly concerned with highlighting the importance of the *Trois contes*'s three endings. Flaubert may have undermined discursive conclusions, but he took special care and pleasure in writing the endings of his novels. Conclusions in Flaubert's work are highly thought out and carefully executed passages. Generally speaking, Flaubert conceived and wrote his concluding passages before he had developed other important features of the work. Once written, they were rarely altered. When he did change them, the changes were for the most part minor. They nearly always involved stylistic refinements, attempts to make the flow of images and sounds more harmonious or, in the case of *Hérodias*, more rhythmical. Flaubert's conclusions are not primarily aimed at befuddling the reader, as is often argued. Rather, they are meant to put the reader in awe of Flaubert's mastery of orchestration, style, effect; equally important, they are meant to make the reader think about the meaning of the work. If Flaubert's conclusions strike us as open ended, undetermined by explicit authorial intention, it is because this is the best way to make us think about what we have been reading. The endings of *Le Père Goriot* and *Le Rouge et le noir*, for example, are not less enigmatic. How is the reader meant to interpret Rastignac's challenge or Julien Sorel's shooting? Balzac and Stendhal are not more helpful to us in determining the meaning of their conclusions than is Flaubert.

The relative lack of changes which conclusions underwent in Flaubert is all the more striking since he worked and reworked his material obsessively. *Un Cœur simple* is a case in point. The ending changed little, while the conception of the characters, especially that of Félicité herself, experienced significant alterations. As I have pointed out in the chapter on *Un Cœur simple*, in the earlier drafts, for example, Félicité's stupidity is more awkward, more dense. She is an opinionated person. She can be openly angry and hateful toward others. She expresses herself far more forcefully and more directly than in the final text. On the whole, her character is more bold than in the final text, where the description is far more nuanced and the character, enigmatic. Flaubert's conception of Félicité goes through changes not only throughout the drafts but, also, in the final text itself. For example, it has to strike the reader as quite odd that this sensitive and emotional woman who is capable of so much love and suffering throughout the story is described at the beginning as "une femme en bois, fonctionnant d'une manière automatique" (6). If we find this characterization so misleading, it is not because the character of Félicité unfolds slowly. It is not, moreover, because Flaubert wants, somehow, to motivate us to regard her differently at the end from the way we regarded her at the beginning. There is a conceptual flaw and an obvious incongruence in this description of Félicité which others have noted as well.[1] However, I think that it is justified given the exigencies of Flaubert's imaginary. If Flaubert missed this particular incongruence in his characterization of Félicité and neglected to correct it during numerous subsequent revisions, it is because this detail plays a fundamental role in the economy of Flaubertian desire. Félicité, like Saint Julien and Iaokanann, must follow the itinerary of the Flaubertian model for transcendence and fulfillment. This seemingly "wooden" woman will have to give up her, so to speak, hardness in order to be transformed into pure desire in the union with the parrot / Holy Spirit. The disintegration or dissolution of form as a sign of the progress of Flaubertian desire toward transcendence is a central model and metaphor in his work. It is a movement that can be traced in all three of the stories as well as elsewhere in Flaubert's work. I have attempted to illustrate its dynamics in the chapter on *Saint Julien*. It can be traced cogently in *Un Cœur simple,* where Félicité's faculties are slowly eroded, and in *Hérodias,* where Iaokanann's decapitation becomes an emblem and a figure of this process.

René Girard may not be right in suggesting that *all* conclusions are the "axle" around which novels turn.[2] But it is certainly true that for Flaubert, endings and the effects he wanted these endings to produce were often the clearest and, to his mind, the most meaning-ful parts of his projects. From *Madame Bovary* on, they serve to give the reader a clue for interpreting the meaning of the characters' lives, the meaning of the work.

It has been suggested that the conclusion of *Un Cœur simple* is not a true conclusion, that is to say, it does not recall the beginning and it fails to put the elements of the story together in a meaningful way for the reader; it opens rather than closes the text of Félicité's life to interpretation. It has been further suggested that the famous incipit of the story, "Pendant un demi-siècle, les bourgeoises de Pont-l'Evêque envièrent à Mme Aubain sa servante Félicité" (3), is a phrase one expects to find at the end of the story and not, where it is, in the beginning; placing it at the beginning suggests that the narrative of Félicité's life will not be developed further, that her life is presented as a closed case.[3] This may be so. But the reason we might feel this way is that, for Flaubert, though conclusions are the end of the character's itinerary they, just as surely, are meant to offer the reader an opening for interpreting the life of that character, to give it and the work itself meaning. The conclusion of *Un Cœur simple* is a conclusion in the sense that it is the culmination of the character's itinerary, the end of the narrative of her life. The incipit, on the other hand, like the characterization of Félicité as an inanimate or "wooden" creature, must necessarily limit and fix the indentity of the character. It must do so because, as I have suggested above, it is in the nature of Flaubert's imaginary to depict the intinerary of a character and the progress of a narrative as the slow unfolding and transfiguration of form into something more amorphous, more rarefied and idealized. The movement of writing is always for Flaubert a kind of opening, an "épanouissement." Thus incipits close and limit in order that the rest of the work can more dramatically open and expand.

This expansive movement serves to reinforce the narrative unity of the *Trois contes.* Each of the three stories ends on a victorious note which is accompanied by an image of expansion and dilation. In *Un Cœur simple,* Flaubert ends the narrative of the character's life with an evocative image of enormous proportions; the skies open and reveal Loulou as a "perroquet gigantesque." In *Saint Julien,* though the story itself concludes with an evocation of the narrator/scribe with both feet planted on the ground of his native town contemplating the stained-glass window depicting the saint, the character's itinerary culminates with the leper and Julien embracing and expanding together, "et celui dont les bras le serraient toujours grandissait, grandissait, touchant de sa tête et de ses pieds les deux murs de la cabane. Le toit s'envola, le firmament se déployait" (134-35). Both endings represent a union of the character with the desired or idealized other (Félicité and Loulou, and Julien and the leper). That other is itself represented as a union of two figures (Loulou–Holy Spirit and leper–Christ). The identification of these two figures with one another is the end result of the characters' effort, their strategy, for making reality (Loulou and the leper) coincide with illusion, with its idealized and desired double (the Holy Spirit and Christ). In the process, the particular and the personal are legitimized and the universal and abstract are made more personal and more effective, thus allowing the characters to fulfill their desires and fantasies.

What about the conclusion of *Hérodias*? On the surface, it would seem to be different from the other two stories. But, like *Un Cœur simple* and *Saint Julien*, *Hérodias*, too, ends with an image of expansion and dilation. Only, here, the expansion is not, as in the two previous tales, ascending and vertical; it is descending and horizontal. *Hérodias*, as I have pointed out in the last chapter, starts on an elevation (as opposed to the other two tales, which end on an elevation). It starts where the itineraries of the two others end (in the skies) and it carries through these last two movements to their conclusion; the conclusion of *Hérodias* descends or lands, so to speak, the narrative of the *Trois contes*. This movement had been already sketched in the conclusion of *Saint Julien* where Flaubert, the writer/scribe, brings the narrative down to where he and his readers stand.

The ending of *Hérodias* is not only the conclusion of *Hérodias* itself, as it most surely is. But it is also the conclusion of the *Trois contes*. The theatrical conclusion of *Hérodias,* we might call it the last act of *Hérodias*, opens with an illumination, "A l'instant où se levait le soleil." The light which spills over in the concluding scene symbolizes the moment of revelation; the meaning of the prophet's message becomes clear. Its breadth overwhelms those who understand it. Christ's potential for the future is acknowledged. By the same token, the implication, here, is that the meaning of the *Trois contes* ought to be, by now, clear as well. Expansion and dilation are represented as enlightenment and dissemination. "Console-toi! Il est descendu chez les morts annoncer le Christ!" (203). Thus, Iaokanann continues his descent (and the narrative's topographic descent from the citadel of Machærous) below the surface to disseminate the message to the dead, while at the surface, his head, this head heavy with disseminating potential, spreads horizontally, to the living on earth, the message of the coming of Christ and of hope.

Not only does the conclusion of *Hérodias* serve as a conclusion to the *Trois contes*. The story as a whole represents a dramatic conclusion to the work. *Hérodias* completes the previous tales by repeating their main themes and, most dramatically, by making more explicit what had been only implicit in the two narratives. This last story is a revelation or an unraveling on the surface of the secrets which *Un Cœur simple* and *Saint Julien* keep hidden both from the power system they target and from the reader who keeps only to the straight text.

What is the "revealed" meaning of the *Trois contes* which the ending of *Hérodias* refers to? The *Trois contes* is distinguished from all of Flaubert's previous works, as I have claimed throughout this book, by the way each of the three stories dramatizes the victory of the individual over the system in power. The characters find ways of undermining this system and of triumphing over it by imposing their own interpretations, their own values, over those values and interpretations the system has imposed as law. Thus, Félicité finds a way of achieving salvation through a mis-reading and a mis-representation of the Holy Spirit. Julien, in turn, uses the text of sainthood (the hagiographic model) to act out his hostility toward society. In *Saint Julien*, much as in *Hérodias*, the parental couple, the king and the queen, represents the law, the root of civilization and of corruption. Julien's parricide is an attempt to reverse the process of civilization and return to a primitive and ideal state. Julien's repressed oedipal struggle is reflected and amplified in Iaokanann's voice decrying the incestuous relationship of Herod and Hérodias and calling upon the destruction of the civilization they celebrate.

Both Félicité's and Julien's subversive plans are personal and secretive. However, no one can doubt that Iaokanann is expressing, and loudly at that, the same hostility and the same subversive message that Félicité and Julien do privately and on the sly. Iaokanann, quite literally, gives voice to Félicité and Julien's grievances against civilization. When Félicité struggles against the oppressive and repressive male-dominated system, she is struggling against her gender-biased, bourgeois-dominated civilization. Julien may not be motivated by the same injustice; he is twice privileged by birth, being both male and rich. Yet, he is moved even more strongly than she is to undermine civilization. In a manner, Julien's answer to Félicité is that civilization itself is the cause of the individual's suffering and not the specific injustices (be it poverty or sexual domination) through which it might express itself; civilization is, by its very nature, repressive.

In *Saint Julien*, the repudiation of civilization and the violence against it are more total than in *Un Cœur simple*. We can note a progression; this repudiation and this violence become even more pronounced in *Hérodias*. In the *Trois contes*, men (or the father) are the signifiers of the "law" of civilization. In *Hérodias*, the father as the signifier of the law is impotent. He is in fact absent as person, as character. Conceptually, standing as he is in the oedipal scenario, as the representative of the primary social taboo that founds society, the interdiction of incest, his impotence and his failure to uphold the law are obvious in the incestuous relationship (incestuous in Iaokanann's eyes) between Herod and Hérodias. Furthermore, the fact that the father is absent from *Hérodias* and that thematically *Hérodias* underscores the end of a civilization dominated by the Father (the Judaic God) confirms the positive and optimistic ending of the *Trois contes* as a whole. In *Un Cœur simple*, Félicité finds a way to exclude men from her world; in *Saint Julien*, Julien tries to kill the father and, in an important sense, succeeds; *Hérodias* marks the end of his rule and the triumph of the son. Like Félicité and Julien, Iaokanann wins in the end; in winning, he confirms the successes of Félicité and Julien in subverting the system in power.

In *Bouvard et Pécuchet*, Flaubert carries through this theme of the oppressive nature of civilization and suggests that here, too, the characters will succeed in undermining Western myths and values. Peter Smith is right when he argues that Flaubert in *Bouvard et Pécuchet* has "won his freedom from irony," that the novel is about hope; the "novel's hope is that a wise man can still live a happy and a useful life in the midst of precisely the same incurable chaos that *L'Education sentimentale* had described."[4]

The *Trois contes* suggests that the way to triumph over the power structure is to work from within it. This is suggested, one would say, literally and graphically in *Hérodias* (Iaokanann is most literally or topographically inside the power structure). To understand is to be inside; similarly, to destroy one must also be inside, like a virus in an organism. Understanding the system is, then, a necessary first step in the process of subversion (Bouvard and Pécuchet are engaged in trying to understand the system and its values). This is the reason why the system in power tries to limit access to key texts by making these texts too abstract for the likes of Félicité. Those in power are in charge of administering and communicating these texts. Power slips from one group to another when the group in power can no longer control the meaning and the interpretations of these texts. Texts that are likely to slip the control of the dominant group and serve to encourage subversive behavior and thought are, Flaubert tells us, texts that appeal to the imagination and to sentiment (the Gospels for Félicité, hagiography for Julien). This is why literature, art, is feared by governments and by the moral bourgeois majority; it is "insurrectionnel aux gouvernements et immoral aux bourgeois"; "La littérature n'est pas une chose abstraite; elle s'adresse à l'homme tout entier."[5] Thus, in *Un Cœur simple*, the language of the dogma is too abstract and too obscure to be understood and used by Félicité. The Gospels, on the other hand, are more accessible. Though we would undoubtedly consider her understanding of the Gospels a faulty one, it remains true that Flaubert presents her as willfully, perhaps by some superior intuition, misunderstanding and misrepresenting these texts. The Gospels offer her the working model for subverting the system. Similarly, it is because Julien understands the workings of both the worldly and the religious ethics of his father and his mother that he is able to subvert both and define himself as a being apart. It is not important how Félicité and Julien receive this knowledge; what is important is that they use it *systematically* to plot against their oppressors. Both Julien and Félicité succeed because they are able to penetrate the system and, using its own values and its own language, undermine it and, ultimately, destroy it.

If Herod fails miserably, it is because, unlike Félicité, Julien, and Iaokanann, he is unable to understand (on any level) either the magical power of Hérodias (his oppressor) or the meaning of the prophet's message (his only chance to be saved). And he does not understand mainly because he seems to lack the desire to understand; he shows little desire to penetrate the mysteries which surround him. Thus, he is often presented gazing at the surface and from a distance. He is indifferent to everything save aesthetic and sensual pleasures. Of all the characters in the *Trois contes*, he is the most passive; even Madame Aubain responds more decisively to situations that concern her family. Herod's ignorance of the meaning of things which touch his life is shown as a factor of his unwillingness to be involved, his reluctance to make decisions and to take responsibilities for his choices. For this reason, he would postpone indefinitely the decision to kill Iaokanann. For this reason, too, he loses the only chance he has of escaping the tyranny of Hérodias. Herod is the most (anachronistically) Sartrian of Flaubert's characters. Before Iaokanann's decapitation, and throughout the story, Herod has a vague sense that the prophet's words carry an important message. Yet he fails to pierce the meaning of this message because, as Hérodias shows too well, he can be distracted by easy pleasures. In the end, Herod follows his nature and opts for aesthetic and sensual pleasures over meaning and hope—exemplified in Iaokanann's message. Meaning, on the contrary, is precisely what both Félicité and Julien vigorously and surreptitiously seek. Meaning (salvation and union with the idealized other) is what they find; to be more accurate, meaning is what they, by dint of effort and design, forge for themselves.

* * *

Réunir dans un même espace Achab et la baleine, les Sirènes et Ulysse, voilà le vœu secret qui fait d'Ulysse Homère, d'Achab Melville et du monde qui résulte de cette réunion le plus grand, le plus terrible et le plus beau des mondes possibles, hélas un livre, rien qu'un livre.
—Maurice Blanchot, *Le Livre à venir*

There is a temptation to identify Herod the aesthete with Flaubert; this position would not be wholly unjustified. But as I suggested in the last chapter, Flaubert is only partly reflected in the lame and troubled figure of Herod. He is more fully represented by the figure of Herod's alter ego, Iaokanann, who embodies the meaning and the message of Christ. Flaubert, in *Hérodias*, fantasizes sharing in the glory of the character who overcomes pessimism and sterility and brings hope to mankind. He identifies with that part of Iaokanann (whom I have read as a figure for the writer and the writing process) that holds that a work of art as a purely aesthetic object is doomed to the kind of sterility that Herod symbolizes. In Herod, Flaubert might indeed be seeing himself, but only a certain aspect of himself; namely, the aesthete, the one responsible for the dead end he had reached in *Bouvard et Pécuchet*.

To undermine the optimistic ending of both *Hérodias* and the *Trois contes* on the assumption that the conclusion of *Hérodias* is an ironical statement based on the similarities we can point to between Herod's decadent civilization and Flaubert's own—thus suggesting Christ's (the Son's) failure to bring about change—is both unfruitful and incorrect. Flaubert may not have been optimistic about the state of affairs of his time; and he may not have been optimistic about the turn his own life had taken, both professionally and personally. But in the *Trois contes*, Flaubert draws up a scenario in which he comes to terms with illusion (hence fiction) as the only way to confront reality and win. Forging new and creative strategies by which to negotiate with society, not on its own terms but on his own, seems to have offered Flaubert what he needed at this point in his career; namely, the sense that art was indeed supreme and redemptive both for the individual in his most private self and for the individual in his interaction with society.

Illusion in the *Trois contes* is not, as elsewhere in Flaubert, tested by circumstances and, in the process, found to fall short of fulfilling the character's desires. Rather, it is shown to be a legitimate form of action. The *Trois contes* represents an example, perhaps the sole example in Flaubert's work, which considers fiction as a productive way of dealing with the world. Just as the historical Christ changed Western culture through his visions, so might the artist change perceptions of the world and, ultimately, change the world itself. Flaubert inserted in the margins of the drafts of *Un Cœur simple* a phrase concerning Félicité: "il faut que l'on veuille l'imiter." This is a telling phrase. Though he did not say the same of Julien and Iaokanann, it is obvious that, despite their overbearing nature, the three characters are meant to strike the reader (of both the straight and the subversive interpretations) as exemplary, thus, as worthy of imitation. Here, Flaubert may have felt especially good about his faithfulness to the classical principle of "plaire et enseigner." Flaubert's fantasy about the potential of fiction may have been more than a fantasy; writing with a sense of optimism may have convinced Flaubert of the power of fiction to change the world.

In the *Trois contes*, Flaubert fantasizes, as I said, he might have even believed, as did his friend George Sand, that through literature one can empower those who have been estranged and silenced by the system. By giving them a voice, as Iaokanann gives voice to Félicité's and Julien's grievances, and by providing them with a space where their desires might be reflected, the writer can claim a community with whom to undermine and, eventually, reshape society in view of accommodating the singular and the disenfranchised. Rimbaud believed in the "verb," and perhaps to a certain extent so, too, did Flaubert. If illusion had the power to alter states of mind (Saint Antoine would be the most dramatic example of that), perhaps it had the power to alter the world. Indeed it may well be that one of the things Flaubert learned about writing fiction through writing the *Trois contes* is that in order to revitalize fiction and to revitalize himself as a writer, he had to convince himself that literature mattered, that it could offer hope to readers who felt alienated from the system.

Just as Flaubert reevaluates his relationship to the characters and uses them to express a fantasy of power over the dominant culture, Flaubert in the *Trois contes* rethinks the place and the role of the reader in his work.

> Quant à laisser voir mon opinion personnelle sur les gens que je mets en scène, non, non, mille fois non! Je ne m'en reconnais pas le droit. Si le lecteur ne tire pas d'un livre la moralité qui doit s'y trouver, c'est que le lecteur est un imbécile ou que le livre est *faux* au point de vue de l'exactitude. (7: 285)

By refraining from offering explicit indications about a work's meaning and by refusing to volunteer his views on the characters and the way the reader is meant to perceive them, Flaubert had opened the way for the reader to participate in the interpretation of the work to a larger and more significant extent than ever before in the novel. The reader in Flaubert holds a key role in the formulation of the work's meaning. This is due in large part to Flaubert's deliberate effort to keep out of the work explicit references concerning his intentions, references which might bias the interpretation of the work and discourage the reader from questioning the text and questioning his or her own values with regards to subjects treated in the text. It is also because Flaubert's aesthetic sense demanded that his style be allusive and that his meaning be suggested rather than stated. Fredric Jameson's remark that Flaubert's "laundering" of authorial presence, his depersonalization of the text, has led to the disinterest and disappearance of the novel's readership is an extreme view.[6] The reader does not "disappear" but the role is redefined. Reading does become more demanding and, therefore, the novel's readership is reduced. Flaubert's aesthetics of suggestion raises the status of the novel to that of an art form so that from that point on in the history of the novel, novels will be written for the general reader as well as for the smaller audience interested in the novel as an art form. When Jameson speaks of the disappearance of the novel, he is, presumably, referring to the latter; because, even today in the age of television, novels are still widely read by the general public.

Flaubert's reluctance to validate certain narrative facts, some trivial and some not so trivial (say, the color of Emma's eyes or the question of whether Julien's parricide is determined by his psychology or by supernatural causes), leaves the reader with the impression that he or she is alone with the work, that he or she alone is responsible for its meaning. To a certain extent, this is true. But to a much greater extent, it is not. Depersonalization of the narrative may give the impression that the author is absent; but Flaubert's presence in his narrative is, on a certain level, even more pervasive and insidious than Balzac's or Stendhal's presence in their works precisely because it is not as obvious. Flaubert's text offers the reader the sense of the autonomy of the narrative; what it does not offer is explicit guidance; the key word here being explicit. It is, therefore, inevitable that some readers will misread; and this is not at all undesirable, as Félicité's and Julien's examples suggest.

Thus by minimizing the explicit presence of the author in his work, Flaubert gives the reader an important function in the interpretation of the work. The reader is perceived in a special relationship to the writer; he or she is responsible for framing and formulating the work's meaning. The reader is, so to speak, an author-ity. But by the same token, and perhaps because the role has become so important, the reader becomes for Flaubert a source of ambivalent feelings. In Flaubert's mind, the reader is an accomplice, but an accomplice who cannot be trusted to share the same values as Flaubert himself. Though in the *Correspondance* Flaubert, at times, speaks of the "public" as intuitively enlightened, far more often he refers to it as severely handicapped in matters of art. Flaubert was convinced that only a few readers would understand the enormity of the task he had assigned himself in a given work. Only a few could be expected to follow the complexities of its designs, the "ruses" of style and the "profondes combinaisons" necessary for expressing his complex intentions. Thus, by opening the text to the reader's interpretation by his own reticence to explain, interpret, and judge character and event, Flaubert had also opened the way for an unreliable and an undesirable alliance. Flaubert's work as a whole, from *Madame Bovary* to *Bouvard et Pécuchet*, is built on his tacit acknowledgment that he is not alone in fathering his texts, but that they are likely to be fathered, mostly, by incompetent readers.

Why does Flaubert place the reader in this position? Why does he give the reader responsibility for formulating the meaning of the work when he was convinced that most readers are incapable of seeing its value, its artistic merit? There is in this gesture a form of masochism or, more specifically, an impulse toward self-sacrifice in the name of art. This attitude serves a special need. This complicity with the reader is, in point of fact, what redeems Flaubert's literary vocation; it is what helps him to distinguish himself from that despised yet important other, the "common" man, the utilitarian bourgeois. Because the alliance with a despised reader is so difficult to accept and because an aesthete like Flaubert could not imagine, and thus could only be obsessed by, such an alliance, Flaubert could experience literature as his ultimate suffering, his ultimate sacrifice, and, by the same token, his ultimate contribution to humanity. "Saint Flaubert," as Valéry rightly called him, must seek and must accept (or must imagine) the indifference and the abuse of those he serves, namely, the general reader, just as Saint Julien, assisting travelers to cross the dangerous river, accepts and, also, invites their abuse. Flaubert in his text, once again like Saint Julien ferrying travelers, does not conceal well his contempt and his desire for violence against the people he so clearly seeks out. These feelings of contempt and hostility toward the reader motivate Flaubert to make the reader's task of interpreting, of finding meaning, a frustrating and thankless task for most readers. Flaubert's strategies are not intended to undermine interpretation or meaning itself; after all, he expected that a "few" would understand, and he wrote for them. What appears to be a deliberate sabotage of this search for meaning is the result of trying to manage a complex and ambivalent attitude toward the reader as an active factor in the interpretation of the work. The result is a work whose meaning must not be easily seen. Rather, it must be uncovered by sheer effort, desire, by aesthetic sensibility. Thus, much in Flaubert's revisions are meant to make the work enigmatic. Psychologically, Flaubert needed to find a style and a structure that would raise the hostility of some of his readers while inviting others to read him differently from the way they had read novels before.

Even though in the *Trois contes* Flaubert works to make the meaning of his narratives more difficult to decipher, his attitude toward his reader becomes somewhat more accommodating and more tolerant than in previous works. In fact, more so than anywhere else in Flaubert, one cannot speak of reader and text in the singular. Flaubert no longer seems to be writing and counting on only the "few" to understand and appreciate his work. He writes a work that is accessible to them and to a more general readership—not necessarily the bourgeoisie, but not excluding them. What is especially striking in the *Trois contes*, what gives the work such power, is that Flaubert does not undermine the common reader's interpretation; in other words, he does not undermine the surface and literal reading of the three stories—as accounts of the lives of three exemplary individuals who can be related easily to a model, namely sainthood or the process of sacrificing worldly pleasures and happiness for a transcendent goal. Neither does he valorize, as he often does in his letters and elsewhere, the importance of reading in depth to understand the characters' psychology, as the reader does in the reading of the subversive text. In the *Trois contes*, Flaubert creates a narrative structure able to support what is, essentially, two contradictory readings with neither one standing as more legitimate than the other. In this lies the brilliance of Flaubert's conception. At all moments, we are presented with a surface and a depth which run concurrently and yet independently of one another. Alongside the techniques of multiple points of view and free indirect discourse, this narrative structure, which we also find in *Bouvard et Pécuchet*, must count as one of Flaubert's more successful strategies for expanding and enriching prose, Flaubert's ultimate design and ambition. By allowing form ("la plastique") to support more substance ("la matière"), Flaubert expands the space of representation.

* * *

Ah! comme on perd de trésors dans sa jeunesse! Et dire que le vent seul ramasse et emporte les plus beaux soupirs des âmes! Mais y a-t-il quelque chose de meilleur que le vent et de plus doux? Moi, aussi j'ai été d'une architecture pareille. J'étais comme les cathédrales du XVe siècle, lancéolé, fulgurant. Je buvais du cidre dans une coupe en vermeil. J'avais une tête de mort dans ma chambre, sur laquelle j'avais écrit: "Pauvre crâne vide, que veux-tu me dire avec ta grimace?" Entre le monde et moi existait je ne sais quel vitrail, peint en jaune, avec des raies de feu et des arabesques d'or, si bien que tout se réfléchissait sur mon âme comme les raies sur les dalles d'un sanctuaire, embelli, transfiguré et mélancolique cependant, et rien que de beau n'y marchait. C'étaient des rêves plus majestueux et plus vêtus que des cardinaux à manteaux de pourpre. Ah! quels frémissements d'orgue! quels hymnes! et quelle douce odeur d'encens qui s'exhalait de mille cassolettes toujours ouvertes! Quand je serai vieux, écrire tout cela me réchauffera. Je ferai comme ceux qui, avant de partir pour un long voyage, vont dire adieu à des tombeaux chers. Moi, avant de mourir, je revisiterai mes rêves.

—Flaubert, *Correspondance*

Nothing like the "wind" expresses the yearning of the soul. But the wind, sweet as it is, is not really adequate for the writer; it cannot record and preserve the memories and the yearnings that it sweeps up along its way. This passage, written in 1853, cannot help but bring to mind the *Trois contes*—indeed the work of old age. In this passage, Flaubert looks back with nostalgia at a fantasized past, adding to this perspective the vantage point of an equally fantasized future. Michel Foucault in *Les Mots et les choses* argues that in the early nineteenth century man found himself "emptied of history" and sought in different forms to recover his past; the importance of history as a field of investigation and the preoccupation in literature and in art with lifelike representation are attempts to come to terms with this overpowering sense of loss. I have suggested throughout this book that the stories in the *Trois contes* can be read as allegorical narratives of writing. In writing the three stories, Flaubert was trying to understand how he wrote and, even more basically, what is writing. I consider the *Trois contes*, in part, as Flaubert's attempt to recover his own past, both his personal past (in *Un Cœur simple*, for example) and his own literary past (in the way the three stories relate stylistically and thematically to the larger works). More importantly for me, I see the work as Flaubert's attempt to recover a lost sense of wonder and optimism about the capacity of language to express being and to transform the self, to reflect the world and to transfigure that world. In the passage quoted above, Flaubert compares himself to a cathedral whose stained-glass window reflects on his soul the beauty of the universe. The stained-glass window, however, does more than reflect; it transforms the universe. Similarly, the narrator/scribe at the end of *Saint Julien* has not simply recorded the life of the saint as it is represented in the stained-glass window; he has transfigured it. In the passage cited above, Flaubert expresses the fantasy of a language that would be (like the stained-glass window which is between himself and the world) transparent and yet, paradoxically, "transfiguring" (the stained-glass window, language, makes the world more beautiful).

What Flaubert sought to recover in the *Trois contes*, what he thought he once possessed—and which he, perhaps, never really possessed—was the sense that language is all powerful and magical. The dramatization of this ideal is especially striking in *Un Cœur simple* and *Hérodias*. *Saint Julien*, the first of the three stories to have been written, and written specifically, Flaubert tells us, to find out if he still knew how to write, is the story in which Flaubert acts out in most elemental terms the workings of language and the problems he encountered when writing. In writing this story, he discovered something important. It is only with the conclusion of *Saint Julien* that he finds, fantasizes, a solution; and this solution enables him to continue with the *Trois contes* and to return with enthusiasm and optimism to *Bouvard et Pécuchet*.

Flaubert's problems with language and the resolution of these problems are in *Saint Julien*, as in each of the stories, dramatized through the character's attempt to act out his desires on the world. I suggested in the chapter on

Saint Julien that hunting is a metaphor for writing, that Julien's arrows represent the writer's pen and that the animals stand for the world. At first, things seem relatively simple for the hunter. Julien aims at his prey and kills it. He succeeds at hunting because he does not realize the implication of his act. He does not realize that this violence touches not only the animals he kills but his own parents. His passion, in other words, becomes a crime. When Julien realizes the consequences of his passion for hunting, he stops hunting and suffers from melancholy and impotence. He is debilitated by the realization that to hunt is, in fact, to kill. In terms of the linguistic analogy, the writer becomes aware that language in the process of naming necessarily destroys the object the writer aims to represent; language, in other words, substitutes itself for the world. This act of substitution and appropriation makes the writer feel responsible for violating the integrity of the world he wants to represent. The dilemma is clear; on one hand, writing abolishes the world, on the other, not writing destroys the writer (Julien suffers when he cannot go hunting).

The writer's problem stems from having once believed, and expected, that words stood for things and from having discovered, subsequently, to his anguish, that they do not, really. The writer discovers that in the process of representing, language deforms and destroys the world. To put it another way, for Flaubert, language, through style, "ought" to reflect the world; it ought to be as simple as aiming your arrow and striking your prey. His experience as a writer, however, assures him that this is not the case; language is in a troubled relationship to the world. In his desire and expectation that words communicate in as direct a way as possible, Flaubert remains true to the classical ideal he defended throughout his career.

When he speaks about classical principles of representation, Flaubert nearly always speaks in a lofty tone which can only put us on guard against taking these remarks as anything more than fantasy, the fantasy of simplicity, of perfect word to world fit. But, for being a fantasy, this ideal is not less a preoccupation, a goal, and a problem to work out. In his *Hommage à Louis Bouilhet*, Flaubert praises his friend for a style where words reflect thought in a most direct way: "Voilà un style qui va droit au but, où l'on ne sent pas l'auteur; le mot disparaît dans la clarté même de l'idée, *ou plutôt, se collant dessus, ne l'embarasse dans aucun de ses mouvements, et se prête à l'action*"[7] (my italics). Indeed, Flaubert's fantasy is for the writer to disappear from his writing and for words to stick like glue to ideas and then to vanish. The fundamental problem facing Flaubert in the moment of writing is what degree of tolerance, or distortion, can he accept before he considers that the system has broken down—before the relationship between words and world becomes too tenuous for him to support? The question posed implicitly in *Saint Julien* is will the writer continue to seek a language that is transparent and reflecting or will he acknowledge the impossibility of this task and accept that the gap between sign and signifier is inevitable, that words do not "stick" to things because there is interference from the perceiving and desiring subject (the writer)? In other words, to what extent do point of view and desire distort the world and is this distortion (or violence) acceptable for a writer who insisted on impersonality and on the classical notion of word to world fit? Until he has answered this question, writing remains problematic.

I pointed out in *Saint Julien* that to write, for Flaubert, is to write against the father. This is a difficult task, since the father is the signifier of the law and of language. To write against the father would be, then, to write against language. How can one write with language and against it? This not only means that language as a theme will be undermined (as is the case in so many of Flaubert's novels—Flaubert has a way of undercutting characters who use language well). More seriously, it will mean that the writer cannot write. But Flaubert must write, just as Julien must hunt. In the chapter on Julien, I remarked that the answer lies in an alternate language, one which does not perceive a difference between the concepts and the metaphors of "reflection" and of "transformation." To continue writing, Flaubert will have to imagine a language that is not governed by the father, by difference and by violence, by interference and by distortion. Julien can only be the happy man his name implies and Flaubert can only be happy writing if a way can be found to kill the father (suppressing violence and difference) without, by the same stroke, giving up their passions, without giving up hunting and writing. Flaubert finds the answer when he realizes, through Julien's oedipal struggle for individuation at the end, that the son can be victorious over the father if he can appropriate for himself the father's authority (recall the fountain episode) and if he can take the mother as a model for a kind of writing against the father. This realization on the part of Flaubert regarding the mother's contribution in the formulation of the ideal language might explain why Flaubert comes to terms with his mother's death during the composition of the *Trois contes*. Four years after her death, he finds himself consoled. "Faut-il te dire mon opinion?" he writes Caroline. " Je crois que (sans le savoir) j'avais été malade profondément et secrètement depuis la mort de notre pauvre vieille. Si je me trompe, d'où vient cette espèce d'éclaircissement qui s'est fait en moi, depuis quelque temps! C'est comme si des brouillards se dissipaient. Physiquement, je me sens rajeuni" (7: 338-39).

The mother offers Julien a model for a language which, like the "dialogues" between Félicité and Loulou, has no recourse to violence and to difference. The mother is a figure of abjection, the figure of identity, of the dissolution of difference. She represents the ideal of a pre-oedipal paradise, a space where the son can rethink (re-write) himself anew without reference to the father. The language the mother suggests to the son is dramatized in all the scenes of fusion and union we find in the *Trois contes*. We find it first in the conclusion of *Saint Julien,* where Julien lying atop the leper merges with him and expands until he dissolves into the firmament, having been transfigured into Christ. The fusion of the bodies of the leper, of Julien, and of Christ recalls the passage quoted earlier from Flaubert's homage to Bouilhet, where he expresses the ideal style as one in which words stick to thought, become invisible, and follow thought to action. These images or metaphors for writing as the process by which the world is reflected and, at the same time, transfigured are expressed, as I have shown earlier, in the very last sentence of *Saint Julien,* where the narrator/scribe informs the reader that he (the narrator/scribe) had been the vehicle of this process, of this translation (reflection and transformation). It is also expressed in the drama of Julien's metamorphosis into Christ through the leper (a figure for the abject/mother). It is further expressed in the image of Loulou as one and the same as the Holy Spirit through Félicité's desire for this union. The example of Iaokanann is an even more dramatic expression of the process of reflection and transformation; Flaubert presents a character who is one with his words through his powerful voice. His words are, indeed, his body; Iaokanann is the message (and the message itself is about messages). But this message will have meaning only when it is embodied and transfigured in Christ; it will only have a meaning through his presence: "Pour qu'il [for Christ, for Christ's message] grandisse il faut que je [my voice, my body, my person] diminue." Iaokanann's example highlights Flaubert's desire for a perfect fit between words and their referents. It highlights, as well, the importance of the writer's voice (his point of view and his desires) in shaping (transfiguring) the message. Having shaped the message, the writer's voice must then be suppressed or buried in order to allow the message, the idea, the word to appear as the perfect reflection of the world.

Flaubert's ideal language is an erotic language, a language of sameness and identity that excludes difference and violence. It is a language that could only achieve its goal by gliding from one signifier to the other, by sliding from one domain ("reality") to the other ("dream/desire"). It does not proceed by difference and reason. Masculine discourse by its valuation of difference as a means of producing meaning cannot serve to reflect the world or to reflect being and makes way for the erotic feminine. Flaubert, in the *Trois contes*, conceives of discourse as a transparent and unresisting medium (less a "body" than a glass, a filter where the world/text is figured). It is a language which, at once, reflects and, magically, transfigures. It is in these terms that Flaubert describes poetic language, as we see, for example, in his description of the style of Leconte de Lisle: "La poésie n'est qu'une manière de percevoir les objets extérieurs, un organe spécial qui tamise la matière et qui, sans la changer, la transfigure. . . . Il faut pour bien faire une chose, que cette chose-là rentre dans votre constitution" (3: 149). Flaubert's fantasy of writing a language that is both reflecting and transfiguring finds expression in the *Trois contes* as a discourse and an aesthetics of pleasure, of eroticism, of the feminine. A style that is both reflecting and transfiguring might just be what Flaubert envisaged when he spoke of "poetic prose." This would be a style where suggestion, identity, union, and harmony would take the place of declaration, definition, difference, and violence.

Both *Un Cœur simple* and *Hérodias* are informed by the conclusion of *Saint Julien*. *Un Cœur simple* offers a striking example of continuity. The repudiation of the masculine, of the father, is carried through with a vengeance. *Un Cœur simple* is a feminine world, the reverse in many ways of *Saint Julien*. Instead of a male protagonist, Flaubert chooses a woman; Julien's violence is converted into tenderness and compassion in the character of Félicité. Julien had already, in Part 3 of the story, tried to substitute love for violence—and he succeeded in reaching his goal better through love than through violence. In *Un Cœur simple*, Félicité can be said to have benefited by the resolution of *Saint Julien*. Realizing that one cannot eliminate the masculine head-on, that to kill the father means to steal his authority, undermine it and make it slip to a more desirable order, Félicité uses (mis-uses) the male-dominated linguistic system to bring about the desired results. The Gospels' imaginative discourse furnishes her with the model. Flaubert's fantasy of a sign that is only minimally distanced from the signifier, already dramatized in the conclusion of *Saint Julien*, translates into the union of Loulou and the Holy Spirit. The distance between sign and signifier is made even closer, as I have indicated, in the case of Iaokanann. There is a certain pleasure expressed on the part of Flaubert in showing that imagination (Félicité) and eloquence (Iaokanann) can communicate desire and satisfy both the mind and sentiment. Flaubert in the *Trois contes* does not accept the linguistic fact that words are inevitable distortions of the world they represent and that the voice is not closer to truth than are words on a page. Instead, he fantasizes a kind of erotic feminine language that signifies (reflects and transfigures) by eliminating difference, by abolishing distances.

Thus, from *Saint Julien* to *Hérodias*, there is a consistent attempt to excise the masculine and the violent from issues that reflect Flaubert's attitude to language and signification. *Hérodias* with its strong dramatization of the evil character of Hérodias, a woman, is no exception. She may be, literally speaking, a woman. But, more importantly, she represents the power of masculine rule, civilization. Flaubert wrote: "La femme est un produit de l'homme. *Dieu a créé la femelle, et l'homme a fait la femme*; elle est le résultat de la civilisation, une œuvre factice. Dans les pays où toute culture intellectuelle est nulle, elle n'existe pas (car c'est une œuvre d'art, au sens humanitaire; est-ce pour cela que toutes les grandes idées générales se sont symbolisées au féminin?" (3: 149). Indeed, Hérodias is not a "femelle"; she is anything but "natural." Moreover, her relationship with Herod brings no offspring. This is a criticism that Iaokanann levels at her; and she is sensitive to it. True, she is a woman and a mother. But, as I pointed out in the last chapter, she has brought to the world a perversion of nature; Salomé, like herself, is a figure for artifice, for art and deception. Iaokanann, however, is the figure for the feminine, and his violent vituperations against Hérodias are meant to taunt her and make her envy him. Just as Loulou represents feminine discourse, and yet is for Félicité both a "son" and a "lover," so, too, is Iaokanann an androgynous figure for writing. As Charles Berheimer has argued in *Flaubert and Kafka*, Flaubert, as a writer, identifies with the feminine.

Flaubert, like the stained-glass window of a cathedral (he often compared himself to a cathedral), sees the artist as the medium through which reality is reflected but, also, through which it is transfigured and redefined. He wrote: "Une âme se mesure à la dimension de son désir, comme l'on juge d'avance des cathédrales à la hauteur de leurs clochers" (3: 201). Flaubert's desire to reconcile within himself the paradox of a language that he wanted so much to believe reflected being and yet that he suspected, desired, and tried so hard to make more magical, more responsive to desire, leads him in the *Trois contes* to imagine a wonderful structure whereby the text of the *Trois contes* opens itself and makes available a narrative that both reflects (the straight text) and magically transfigures (the suspect text) his and his characters' desires. This structure of optimism, doubly optimistic in that we find it so clearly in both the straight and the suspect readings, is the backbone of the *Trois contes*. The promise this work holds of a better future for illusion and for fiction makes the *Trois contes* unique in Flaubert. Flaubert's "swan song" is, ironically for a writer who has been so consistently characterized as a cynic and a hater of humanity, the most hopeful and, aesthetically, the most beautifully crafted of all his works.

Notes

¹   Gustave Flaubert, *Correspondance,* 9 vols. (Paris: Conard, 1926-33) 3: 240. All further references to this work will be included in the text.

²   Martin Turnell suggests that Madame Bovary, for example, has all the markings of "doctrinaire pessimism and immature cynicism masquerading as mature vision" (in Leo Bersani's edition of *Madame Bovary* [New York: Bantam, 1972] 401). Flaubert had a strong sense of purpose and ethical concern. Moreover, he was sensitive to the power and the mysteries of nature and of the universe. It was men, as social beings, that he rejected.

³   Charles Baudelaire, *Petits poèmes en prose* (Paris: Garnier–Flammarion, 1967) 31.

⁴   For a lively and intelligent discussion on this subject, see the exchange between Marcel Proust ("A propos du 'style' de Flaubert," *Chroniques* [Paris: Gallimard, 1927] 193-211) and Albert Thibaudet (*Gustave Flaubert 1821-1880* [Paris: Plon, 1922]). The discussion centers around the nonconnective *et,* the use of the present participle in place of the imperfect tense, the placing of the adverb at the end of the sentence, the deadening use of the verb *avoir* ("les maisons avaient des jardins en pente," "les quatres tours avaient des toits pointus," etc.), the odd use of the present tense in lieu of the past ("Ils habitaient le fond de la Bretagne . . . *C'était* une maison basse, avec un jardin montant jusqu'au haut de la colline, d'où l'on *découvre* la mer") (cited by Proust in "Ce que signifie le style de Flaubert," his preface to Flaubert's *L'Education sentimentale* [Paris: Gallimard et Librairie Générale Française, 1965] 16). Thibaudet cites an example from *L'Education sentimentale* of an adverb placed in an unexpected position ("Je commence à terriblement me repentir de m'être chargé de ta personne" [Thibaudet 261]) and examples of commas in unlikely places ("c'était pour lui un grand bonheur que de ramasser, quelquefois, ses ciseaux," and "car, je t'aime"

[Thibaudet 183]). In *Un Cœur simple*, we can point to an instance of odd or illogical grammar in the second paragraph. The subject of the second paragraph is Félicité yet, when reading the story for the first time, we take logically Madame Aubain as the subject. "Pour cent francs par an, elle faisait la cuisine et le ménage, cousait, lavait, repassait, savait brider un cheval . . . et resta fidèle à sa maîtresse." The *elle* at the start of the following paragraph should grammatically continue to refer to Félicité. It does not; "Elle avait épousé un beau garçon . . . " refers to Madame Aubain. These examples and others like them are not grammatically incorrect; they are simply awkward and disorienting. In *Hérodias* and *Saint Julien*, we have passages where important connections like *car, alors,* or *puis* are absent. The effect is to make the meaning less obvious, the grammar awkward (see the examples furnished by Raymonde Debray-Genette in *Métamorphoses du récit* [Paris: Seuil, 1988] 42-44 and 77).

⁵ Jonathan Culler, *Flaubert: The Uses of Uncertainty* (Ithaca: Cornell UP, 1974) 203.

⁶ Culler 206.

⁷ Cited in Claire-Lise Tondeur, *Gustave Flaubert, critique: Thèmes et structures,* Purdue University Monographs in Romance Languages (Amsterdam: Benjamins, 1984) 33.

⁸ Michel Butor, *Improvisations sur Flaubert* (Paris: Littérature–Editions de la Différence, 1984) 192.

⁹ Wolfgang Iser, *The Act of Reading: A Theory of Aesthetic Response* (Baltimore: Johns Hopkins UP, 1978).

Chapter 1: The *Trois Contes*

¹ It is likely, however, that Flaubert was thinking of a version of *Saint Julien*. He was working on a version of this story in 1845.

² George Sand, *Correspondance entre George Sand et Gustave Flaubert* (Paris: Calmann-Lévy, 1904) 428.

³ Barbara Beaumont, *Flaubert and Turgenev: A Friendship in Letters: The Complete Correspondence* (New York: Norton, 1985) 19.

⁴ Enid Starkie, *Flaubert The Master: A Critical Biographical Study (1856-1880)*, 2 vols. (New York: Atheneum, 1971) 2: 298.

⁵ Ferdinand Brunetière, *La Revue des Deux Mondes*, June 1877. Cited in Ernest Jackson, *The Critical Reception of Gustave Flaubert in the United States 1860-1960* (The Hague: Mouton, 1966) 166.

6   John Fletcher, *A Critical Commentary on Flaubert's "Trois contes"* (New York: Macmillan–St. Martin's, 1968) 38.

7   Marc Bertrand, "Parole et silence dans les *Trois contes* de Flaubert," *Stanford French Review* 1.2 (1977): 202-03.

8   Harry Levin, "Flaubert," *The Gates of Horn* (New York: Oxford UP, 1966) 286.

9   Thibaudet 229.

10   Margaret Tillet, *On Reading Flaubert* (London: Oxford UP, 1961) and Jacques Suffel, *Flaubert* (Paris: Editions Universitaires, 1958) 94.

11   Michael Issacharoff, *L'Espace et la nouvelle* (Paris: José Corti, 1976) 42.

12   Per Nykrog, "Les 'Trois contes' dans l'évolution de la structure thématique chez Flaubert," *Romantisme* 6 (1973): 55-66.

13   Bertrand, "Parole et silence."

14   Robert Chumbley, "An Enormity for Flaubert: Exercises in Semiotic Fore-play," *Sub-Stance* 20 (1978): 65.

15   John O'Connor, "Flaubert: *Trois contes* and the Figure of the Double Cone," *PMLA* 95.5 (Oct. 1980): 812-26.

16   Victor Brombert, *The Novels of Flaubert: A Study of Themes and Techniques* (Princeton: Princeton UP, 1966) 234.

17   Giovanni Bonaccorso, *Corpus Flaubertianum I, Un Cœur simple* (Paris: Société d'Editions "Les Belles Lettres," 1983).

18   Raymonde Debray-Genette, *La Production de sens chez Flaubert* (Colloque de Cerisy) (Paris: Union Générale d'Editions–10/18, 1975) 348, 363.

19   Fletcher 73.

20   Margaret Lowe, *Towards the Real Flaubert: A Study of Madame Bovary* (Oxford: Clarendon, 1984).

CHAPTER 2: THE WOMEN OF PONT L'EVEQUE: A SUBVERSIVE SORORITY

1   Writing about the *Trois contes*, in *Flaubert: The Uses of Uncertainty*, Culler defines irony as a mode which, on the one hand, strikes at views of a situation which it suggests are "foolish, deficient, or otherwise at odds with the 'facts,' " and, on the other hand, which "strikes indirectly at the general process of organizing the world in relation to oneself so as to make sense of it" (211). Culler suggests that in the *Trois contes*, as in *Salammbô*, Flaubert uses "a very special kind of irony, not directed against persons, nor even against any view of the world," but an irony which seems to display an instance of "the novel's own self-consciousness," "an instance of 'le plus haut dans l'art,' the ability to produce

contemplative reverie." One might argue, says Culler, that such ironies, in the process of interpretation, are "able to lead one beyond irony to a point where one can find the positive in the negative" (207). I agree with Culler that Félicité is not the target of Flaubert's irony and that Flaubert's handling of the character opens the door to a positive interpretation of her desires and fantasies. However, I do not accept Culler's view that irony is not directed "against any view of the world," since it is, as I will show, directed against the dominant bourgeois and masculine order.

   2 Ross Chambers, in his very insightful essay on *Un Cœur simple*, singles out and differentiates the positive from the negative attributes of Félicité's characterization and assigns to each position a mode of reading. He suggests that the negative aspect of Félicité's character is represented by the presence in the narrative of a "realist text" that focuses on Félicité's bourgeois cult of objects shared with her community. The positive reading is embedded in the "writerly text," the text which abandons this perception of the servant as a social being and focuses instead on how she differs from her community; this is the text which constitutes her as a unique individual. My reading fits Chambers's description of a reading susceptible to the text's "seduction," "its invitation to be loved," "an invitation to which the text itself teaches us to respond in an appropriate manner by its own exploration of the virtues of 'simpleness of heart'"(*Story and Situation: Narrative Seduction and the Power of Fiction* [Minneapolis: U of Minnesota P, 1984] 125).

   3 See Bonaccorso, *Corpus Flaubertianum I, Un Cœur simple,* and Rosa M. Di Stefano Palermo, *Le varianti di "Un Cœur simple"* (Messina: Ediziono A. Sfameni, 1984).

   4 Michal Peled Ginsburg, *Flaubert Writing* (Stanford: Stanford UP, 1986) 179.

   5 In her excellent analysis of the role of the narrator in *Un Cœur simple*, and in the *Trois contes* as a whole, Raymonde Debray-Genette ("Du mode narratif dans les *Trois contes*," *Littérature* 2 [May 1977]) points out that at times it is difficult to define the narrator's position, that it varies. There are cases where it is not clear to whom a certain description can be attributed, to the character or to the narrator. On the whole, however, she argues, "there is no hiatus between the character and the description" (51). I share Debray-Genette's view that narrative-descriptions are always, in the *Trois contes,* "focalised, that is to say, made from the point of view of a character" (46). On the same subject, Ross Chambers writes, "In 'Un cœur simple' the admirable simplicity of the narrative is pointed up by a contrast with the very discreet, but discernible, presence of a narratorial persona who displays attitudes of some sophistication" (128).

   6 As the study of the notes in the manuscripts of *Un Cœur simple* shows, Flaubert hesitated between presenting Félicité from the "inside," as she experiences herself, and presenting her from the "outside," as she is seen by others.

As for the narrator's sympathy with Félicité, many readers take the view expressed by Victor Brombert that "Félicité is decidedly not Flaubert's victim!" (242). Brombert suggests that "the meaning of the tale is in large part to be derived from this tone of tenderness and compassion. Any denial of the authenticity of this tone, on the assumption that goodness is here shown to be inept and that Flaubert could not possibly feel anything but contempt for as stupid a creature as Félicité, is most emphatically a misreading of the work" (237).

7 In the drafts, for example, Flaubert makes clear that we are meant to view Félicité as a saint. After Victor's ship leaves, she is "A genoux devant le Calvaire du bassin.—Clair de lune—en prières—immobile—comme on représente les Stes femm[es] au pied de la croix" (Bonaccorso 198). For more examples, see Di Stefano's work on the variants of *Un Cœur simple*, cited above in note 3.

8 Bonaccorso 17.

9 Victor Brombert has rightly said about *Un Cœur simple* that "Flaubert's tour de force is that he presents as a central character an individual devoid of any gift of articulation, and yet makes us participate in her vision of things" (239).

10 Debray-Genette, "Du mode narratif" 43.

11 Thibaudet 257. Erich Auerbach, "In the Hôtel De La Mole," *Mimesis* (Princeton: Princeton UP, 1953) 482-92.

12 For an excellent discussion of point of view and description in the *Trois contes*, see Debray-Genette, "Du mode narratif."

The status of description in Flaubert's work has undergone some changes since Thibaudet, Proust, Jean-Pierre Richard, and others. Post-structuralist discussions of its role are informed and eclipsed by the more general crisis of interpretation. Roland Barthes's celebrated remark that in Flaubert we are never quite certain who is speaking ("qui parle") has focused attention away from just how valuable descriptions are in communicating the characters' inner world to just how unreliable they are. Flaubert's descriptions are viewed as literary exercises which effectively dissociate fictional representations from the "real world." But although Flaubert's narratives do not spell out as clearly as do, for example, Balzac's or Zola's narratives what in a given description serves a diegetic function and what serves to represent a particular ideology, a particular character, or the author himself, we can generally tell what characters like Julien and Félicité think and feel because Flaubert has given the reader sufficient clues to reach this conclusion. "Who speaks" in a particular description is just as much a function of interpretation as is the more general question of the meaning of the work. Admittedly, in Flaubert, narrative voice is not always stable; we may not always be able to decide with "certainty" who is responsible for what is said. But I would like to suggest that the difficulty of identifying whose perspective is reflected in a particular description is the result of Flaubert's attempt to manage the principle of impersonality, that is, to reconcile the principle of impersonality with the more instinctive and repressed desire to comment on and to share in his characters' fictions.

Flaubert, both in the *Trois contes* and elsewhere, uses description to record or give weight to objects, phenomena, and structures that are part of the external world; these descriptions serve to give that world the illusion of "reality." They do not as a rule reflect the character's, any character's, inner feelings; for example, the descriptions of the ailing body of Old Colmiche, Julien's battles, Herod's guests, Herod's banquet, and, perhaps too, Salomé's dance. Though Salomé's dance is focalized from the point of view of Herod, it remains essentially the description of a spectacle described for its own sake, a scene that is described as it would be observed by all (as, indeed, Flaubert had observed it himself). This example is illuminating about Flaubert's problem with this function of description. Although, in a certain sense, he succeeds in giving the reader a relatively good ("realistic") picture of how Salomé's dance is performed, in a more serious sense, the description fails. It fails not because it is not exact but because it tries to be too exact, tries to record too much. There is a technical precision to it which, I think, works against it and renders the whole effect static, hence, so unlike dancing. Flaubert does not use this type of description frequently in his work for good reason. It is as if he could not bring himself, or he could not bring language, to simply represent or record reality; somehow, to use description in the very limited sense of building a case for the narrative as a faithful representation of reality could not inspire him as it did Balzac; and so Flaubert had difficulties simply informing his readers through his descriptions what the world he was describing might have looked like.

As a result, this function of description is, on the whole, less interesting for the way it represents the world than for the way it often, and inevitably, degenerates into something grotesque, unrealistic, un-imaginable (for example, Herod's banquet, Salomé's dance). It is as if in the process of composing these descriptions Flaubert became more interested in something else. Having started out as a reflection of reality, they often end up as reflections of Flaubert's fantasies. Some of the best-known examples outside the *Trois contes* are Charles's "casquette," Emma's wedding cake, and the description of Rouen in *Madame Bovary*. Though there are readers who tend to view these descriptions as reflections of the characters and their world, far more do these descriptions highlight Flaubert's own attitudes and views of the characters, the events, and the places he represents. They allow him to observe the principle of impersonality while, at the same time, allowing him to express his own attitudes and views. Moreover, these descriptions are to a certain extent, too, expressions of Flaubert's conscious or unconscious de-realization of reality; and it is because these descriptions are not focalized by a particular character and because they strike us, for the most part, as unrealistic, excessive, and hence the sign of an obsession, that we are justified in seeing them, I believe, as reflections of Flaubert's views on the work and on the world and not the views of his characters.

¹³ On the subject of the relationship between the drafts of *Un Cœur simple* and the final text, see Raymonde Debray-Genette, *Métamorphoses du récit*.

¹⁴ Culler 210.

¹⁵ The problem this widely held assumption creates is best illustrated by looking at one example which I have picked simply because at least three critics (Victor Brombert, Ross Chambers, and Raymonde Debray-Genette) have commented on it. It is the scene in which, after learning of Victor's death, Félicité goes to the river to wash the laundry: "Les prairies étaient vides, le vent agitait la rivière; au fond, de grandes herbes s'y penchaient, comme des chevelures de cadavres flottant dans l'eau" (39). Brombert calls this scene a metaphor, "a fusion of Flaubert's poetry and of Félicité's wild grief" (240). Similarly, Chambers remarks, "We are . . . invited to divide up the responsibilities, between the character's vision and the textual diction, so that the sympathy we achieve for the character in her grief is at least partly a function of the narrative vehicle, that is, of a certain understanding shared with the narratorial voice" (131). Though Brombert and Chambers both recognize correctly that Félicité's "grief" or "vision" is imparted by the description, they choose to articulate it in terms of a split between the narrator and the character, that is to say, they behold the narrator in a position of superiority to the character. Their conclusion is correct; one cannot read this scene differently. The mistake, however, is to assume that Félicité must not share in the intelligibility of her grief, which is to say, she is, in an important way, absent from herself, that she is nothing more than a throbbing, suffering heart. Brombert, Chambers, and Culler are guilty, to a degree, of representing what Luce Irigaray has identified as the masculine-dominated discourse of our culture, a discourse that does not recognize the value of a point of view which is not organized and made intelligible along the lines of linguistic competence, a point of view that is not theoretical. Speaking of the mother, more generally of the/a woman, in her typical tone of sarcasm and indignation, Irigaray remarks: "pour qu'on ne s'y trompe pas, elle n'aurait point d'yeux, serait privée du regard, de l'âme. De la conscience, de la mémoire. Du langage. Et si vers elle on se retourne, peut-être pour y r-entrer, ce n'est pas à son point de vue qu'on aurait à s'affronter. Le danger serait plutôt de perdre là tout re(-)père. Trou obscur où risque de sombrer la claire raison" (*Speculum de l'autre femme* [Paris: Minuit, 1974] 425).

Surely Félicité does not, cannot, express herself in the narrator's language; is this not generally the case in third person narratives? Yet in her narratological reading of the same wash scene at the river, Debray-Genette, not particularly sympathetic to feminism but looking at the text from a narratological (more "objective"?) perspective, places the accent *wholly* on Félicité's vision. She does not hesitate to identify this passage, as do Brombert and Chambers, as the narrator's way of letting us in on what Félicité herself is thinking at that moment. But in addition to *not* distinguishing narrator and character in her discussion of the scene, she points out further that Flaubert had written in an early draft "Le ciel avait une couleur toute blanche" and eliminated it because, in all likelihood, "he wanted the focalisation to be homogenous"("Du mode narratif" 57). In other words, Debray-Genette points out that Flaubert wanted the scene to be read as if derived exclusively—poetry and all—from the character herself. Debray-Genette's analysis legitimizes the character, acknowledges that she has consciousness, presence.

[16]   Gustave Flaubert, *Trois contes*, ed. Edouard Maynial (Paris: Garnier, 1969) 9. All further references to this work will appear in the text.

[17]   Debray-Genette, *Métamorphoses du récit* 249. For an interesting discussion of the way Flaubert constructed descriptions in *Un Cœur simple*, see Rosa M. Di Stefano Palermo, "La descrizione di paesaggio in 'Un Cœur simple,'" *Rivista di Letterature Moderne e Comparate* 32 (1979): 181-94.

[18]   For a reading of this passage as an example of "mise en abyme de l'énoncé," see Chambers 133-34.

[19]   There are several other examples of Flaubert's picturing of Félicité's mental states. Some are as subtle as those I have quoted. Others are strongly focalized and heavy-handed. An example of the latter is the scene after she has learned of Victor's death. In this scene Félicité goes to the river to wash her clothes, and the sounds that her bat makes can be heard in the neighboring gardens. Appropriately, Debray-Genette interprets these sounds as nothing less than "des cris." There is, too, the scene where, having missed seeing Victor off to America, Félicité stands with her face wet with tears. To dramatize her sadness and her tears, Flaubert writes: "La ville dormait, les douaniers se promenaient; et de l'eau tombait sans discontinuer par les trous de l'écluse, avec un bruit de torrent" (34).

[20]   Bonaccorso 52-53.

[21]   Bonaccorso lxx.

[22]   Lucette Czyba, *La Femme dans les romans de Flaubert: Mythes et idéologie* (Lyon: Presses Universitaires de Lyon, 1983) 287-88.

[23]   In the drafts, the house Félicité enters has many masculine objects that belong to Monsieur Aubain, like "une selle à cheval, une ligne à pêcher, une carnassière, des éperons, un fusil" (Bonaccorso 67). All that is left in the final text is his portrait and "une des redingottes de Monsieur," one of the many items that Félicité collects in her room.

[24] For an interesting view of the relationship between Flaubert's *Un Cœur simple* and Bernardin de Saint-Pierre's *Paul et Virginie,* as well as of the possible meaning of the characterization "simple heart," see English Showalter, Jr., *"Un Cœur simple* as an Ironic Reply to Bernardin de Saint-Pierre," *French Review* 40 (1966/67): 47-55.

[25] Bonaccorso 253.

[26] Flaubert wrote Caroline on 10 August 1876, when he was hard at work on *Un Cœur simple* : "Faut-il te dire mon opinion? Je crois que (sans le savoir) j'avais été malade profondément et secrètement depuis la mort de notre pauvre vieille [Flaubert's mother died on 6 April 1872]. Si je me trompe, d'où vient cette espèce d'éclaircissement qui s'est fait en moi, depuis quelque temps! C'est comme si des brouillards se dissipaient. Physiquement, je me sens rajeuni" (7: 338-39). It would be interesting to investigate how writing *Un Cœur simple* might have helped Flaubert come to terms with his mother and with her death.

[27] In "Illusion réaliste et répétition romanesque," *Change* 16-17 (1973): 286-97, Shoshana Felman points out that in *Un Cœur simple* Flaubert makes a critique of "realism"; and that, as illustrated in the episode with the atlas, Bourais, in particular, embodies the realistic gesture par excellence which " 'points purely and simply' to the objects in the world." Since the language of realism respects the "authority of words," Bourais's gesture, Felman argues, is inhabited by an ideology of domination and oppression. I agree with Felman's observation that Flaubert makes a critique of the language of authority. I disagree, however, that this critique targets "realism" as a genre. Rather, my contention is that Flaubert's critique is more general; it is directed against language as a whole, especially against language as the abstract and impersonal system which it fundamentally is.

[28] The gravures d'Audran which decorate the wall of the Aubain household represent battle scenes of Alexander. This is a detail Flaubert does not include in the final text.

[29] Bonaccorso 95.

[30] Bonaccorso 112.

[31] Bonaccorso 417.

[32] Bonaccorso 12.

[33] Gustave Flaubert, *Madame Bovary* (Paris: Texte Intégral–Livre de Poche, 1965) 53.

[34] Bonaccorso 157.

[35] Bonaccorso 159-60.

[36] Flaubert shares similar animistic tendencies. For instance, commenting on the "Théâtre des marionnettes" in *Italie et Suisse,* he writes: "Quand il y a quelque temps qu'on y est, on finit par prendre tout cela au sérieux et par croire que ce sont des hommes; un monde réel, d'une autre nature, surgit alors pour vous et, se

mêlant au vôtre, vous vous demandez si vous n'existez pas de la même vie ou s'ils n'existent pas de la vôtre. Même dans les moments de calme on a peine à se dire que tout cela n'est que du bois et que ces visages coloriés ne soient animés par des sentiments véritables; à voir l'habit, on ne peut s'imaginer qu'il n'y ait pas de cœur" (*Œuvres complètes* [Paris: Seuil–L'Intégrale, 1964] 2: 467). He writes again in *Par les champs*: "Les oiseaux se taisent ou sont absents; les feuilles sont épaisses, l'herbe étouffe le bruit des pas, et la contrée muette vous regarde comme un triste visage" (*Œuvres complètes* 2: 513). Visiting a church on a trip to Bordeaux, Flaubert writes in *Pyrénées et Corse*: "J'avoue que je me suis assez diverti à contempler les grimaces de tous ces cadavres de diverses grandeurs, dont les uns ont l'air de pleurer, les autres de sourire, tous d'être éveillés et de vous regarder comme vous les regardez. Qui sait? Ce sont peut-être eux qui vivent et qui s'amusent à nous voir venir les voir" (*Œuvres complètes* 2: 428).

37   Gérard Genette, "Métonymie chez Proust," *Figures III* (Paris: Seuil, 1972) 41-63; Paul de Man, *Allegories of Reading* (New Haven: Yale UP, 1979) 67-74; Jacques Derrida, "White Mythology: Metaphor in the Text of Philosophy," trans. F. C. T. Moore, *New Literary History* 6.1 (Autumn 1974): 5-74.

38   Czyba 281 and 285.

39   Luce Irigaray, *Ce sexe qui n'en est pas un* (Paris: Minuit, 1977) 85-93.

40   Irigaray, *Ce sexe* 88-93. Hélène Cixous, "The Laugh of the Medusa," trans. Keith Cohen and Paula Cohen, *Signs* 1.4 (Summer 1976): 875-93.

41   Irigarary, *Ce sexe* 132.

42   The fact that she helps a Pole, an enemy of France, can be interpreted both as a defiant gesture and as an act of charity. Both interpretations are valid within the parameters of the straight and suspect narratives.

43   In a draft, it is the women of the neighborhood who come to their windows and laugh as they watch Bourais harassed by the bird.

44   See Felman 291-94.

45   Julia Kristeva, *Desire in Language: A Semiotic Approach to Literature and Art* (New York: Columbia UP, 1980) 240.

46   I cannot agree with Czyba when she writes: "L'histoire de Félicité, sous la forme condensée du conte, met en relief ce que *Madame Bovary* et *L'Education sentimentale* donnent à lire de façon plus diffuse: la dislocation et la dégradation de ces valeurs religieuses qui se reportent dérisoirement sur les objets, le qualitatif et la multiplication des métonymies devenant le signe d'une absence irrémédiable" (327). I think it flies in the face not only of my own reading but of what seems to me and to others, like Brombert, to be the compassionate and tender way in which Flaubert presents the last days of Félicité's life. I do not share Czyba's view that "les objets qui représentent les affections les plus chères de Félicité,

véritables métonymies religieuses, sont les premiers à signifier le néant universel, comme le donne à entendre le rappel de la vermine qui mange à la fois le petit chapeau de Virginie et le perroquet de Loulou" (285).

[47]　*Œuvres complètes* 508.

[48]　Cited in Susan Rubin Suleiman, "(Re)Writing the Body: The Politics and Poetics of Female Eroticism," *Poetics Today* 6.1/2 (1985): 54.

[49]　Irigaray, *Ce sexe* 73-74. From a different perspective, and without singling out women or stressing the motivation which informs such a response to power, Michel Foucault notes much the same thing when he writes that "where there is power, there is resistance, and yet, or rather consequently, this resistance is never in a position of exteriority in relation to power." Those who resist power are also those who support it (*The History of Sexuality,* trans. Robert Hurley [New York: Vintage, 1980] 95).

[50]　Félicité's fetishism has been treated by Debray-Genette in "Les Figures du récit dans *Un Cœur simple,*" *Poétique* 3 (1970): 362, and by Chambers in *Story and Situation* 138. Both, however, treat Félicité's fetishism as a form of generalized object worship or attachment.

[51]　Sigmund Freud, "Fetishism," in "Three Essays on the Theory of Sexuality," *The Complete Psychological Works of Sigmund Freud,* standard ed., ed. and trans. James Strachey (London: Hogarth, 1953-74) 7: 152-57.

[52]　For an interesting case of female fetishism, see Naomi Schor's "Female Fetishism: The Case of George Sand," *Poetics Today* 6.1/2 (1985): 301-10. For Schor, the function of the fetish in Sand's case is that it allows Sand to identify with the masculine, with the father. Schor does not argue, as I do here in the case of Félicité, that the fetish serves to displace and undo the power of the masculine and establish the mother as unviolated and independent.

[53]　For Kristeva, the semiotic relation to the maternal body must undergo repression for the acquisition of language (*Desire in Language* 136).

[54]　See Naomi Schor, "For a Restricted Thematics: Writing, Speech, and Difference in *Madame Bovary,*" *Breaking the Chain: Women, Theory, and French Realist Fiction* (New York: Columbia UP, 1985).

[55]　Elizabeth Janeway, "On 'Female Sexuality,' " in Jean Strouse, ed., *Women and Analysis* (New York: Grossman, 1974) 58.

[56]　That the objects in Félicité's room have meaning is made more obvious in some of the drafts of *Un Cœur simple.* For example, Flaubert notes: "Les objets de sainteté—reliques des personnes—objets ayant appartenu à des personnes qu'elle avait aimées et qui par leur étrangeté-insignifiance et étrangeté avaient le caractère ou tout au moins la signification de reliques" (cited in Sylvia Douyère, *Un Cœur simple de Gustave Flaubert* [Paris: La Pensée Universelle, 1974] 55-56).

[57] Culler puts it well when he suggests that in the *Trois contes* the sacred is "the sentimental purified by irony, emptied of its content, so that it may come to represent in the allegory of interpretation the formal desire for connection and meaning which governs the activity of readers and characters" (226).

[58] Cixous 875-93.

[59] Irigaray, *Ce sexe* 141.

CHAPTER 3: MURDERING THE FATHER: RE-WRITING THE LEGEND OF SAINT JULIEN L'HOSPITALIER

[1] Ginsburg 2.

[2] Lecointre-Dupont writes: "Les exercices ascétiques, les pénitences et les macérations des saints, leur charité ardente, leur abnégation héroïque, n'auraient point captivé seuls un auditoire vain et léger, qui ne respirait que batailles, amour, blasons, tournois et aventures; aussi la vérité historique ne présidait pas toujours à ces contes dévots, et la pieuse fraude du narrateur, pour donner quelque attrait aux utiles vérités qu'il voulait faire entendre imaginait en l'honneur des saints. . . ." (cited in Benjamin Bart and Francis Cook, *The Legendary Sources of Flaubert's Saint Julien* [Toronto and Buffalo: U of Toronto P, 1977] 141; my translation).

[3] Gustave Flaubert, *Œuvres complètes* 2: 441.

[4] Jules and Edmond de Goncourt, *Journal*, 22 vols. (Monaco: Editions de l'Imprimerie Nationale de Monaco, 1956-58) 12: 29.

[5] See Pierre-Marc de Biasi's interesting discussion of the "meta-symbolic" value of the stained-glass window at the conclusion of *Saint Julien* ("L'élaboration du problématique dans *La Légende de Saint Julien l'Hospitalier*," *Flaubert à l'œuvre* [Paris: Flammarion, 1980] 99-102).

[6] De Biasi reminds us: "La légende, que Flaubert prétend écrire pour se reposer de l'énorme travail de *Bouvard et Pécuchet,* partage avec ce roman un certain usage de l'élément parodique" (82).

[7] Culler 23-24.

[8] Starkie 2: 256.

[9] Leo Bersani, *From Balzac to Beckett* (New York: Oxford UP, 1970) 147.

[10] Moskos, for example, writes that "Julian is curiously 'absent' from the story," that "the narrator insists on Julian's almost total ignorance of both his actions and their motivations" ("The Individuation Process in *Saint Julian*," William J. Berg et al., *Saint/Oedipus: Psychocritical Approaches to Flaubert's Art* [Ithaca: Cornell UP, 1982] 69). John R. O'Connor suggests that Julien is the

"emblem of a figure connecting two worlds, providing a link between them, a figure who has become an emblem of mediacy itself" (821).

[11] Bart and Cook 58.

[12] Sartre, Bart, and Cook, among others, have noted that the addition by Flaubert of Julien's violence, his obsession with hunting, has brought about a significant change to the meaning of the traditional legend, and they suggest that this addition avails the text to a psychological reading of Julien's motives. Eugène Vinaver, in *The Rise of Romance* (London: Oxford UP, 1971), points out that as early as Voragine's version and with each new step in the evolution of the story, the relative weight and interest of Julien's crime is increased and some attempt is made to supply if not the reasons for it, at least its antecedents. "Unlike the early writers of saints' lives," writes Vinaver, "Flaubert was primarily concerned not with the consequences but with the antecedents of Julien's crime; what he wanted to know was not how Julien became a saint, but how he became a sinner" (117). Curiously, however, Vinaver finds Julien's psychological motivation of little interest to Flaubert. Bart and Cook, on the other hand, in their fascinating pursuit of Flaubert's contributions and indebtedness to earlier versions of the legend, have made clear that unlike Flaubert's Julien, "the medieval French prose author's Julian has the mentality of his saintly class, i.e., no marked individual psychology at all: more specifically, he is *not* haunted by the *volupté* of killing. . . . He comes to realize he is doing penance for a crime he has not committed, a crime which does not exist, and which he does not find himself tempted to commit . . ." (91). Bart and Cook's study also reveals that even when we compare Flaubert's treatment to that of his principal sources, namely, the nineteenth-century romantic versions of E. H. Langlois (*Essai historique et descriptif sur la peinture sur verre ancienne et moderne . . .*) and G. F. G. Lecointre-Dupont's adaptation of the *Prose Life of Saint Julien* (the former plays a more important role), psychological motivation in Flaubert's version is by far the most clearly drawn.

[13] Victor Brombert, in his classic study of Flaubert, calls *Saint Julien* one of Flaubert's "most turbulent texts" (217). What motivates Julien to commit the crime? Is Julien's parricide the resolution of a family crisis or does it suggest a more generalized and even more radical desire? William Berg has argued that Julien suffers from a deep sense of inferiority vis à vis his parents, and that the parricide is the result of his attempts to prove his superiority ("Displacement and Reversal in *Saint Julian*," Berg et al., *Saint/Oedipus* 25-67). Georges Moskos, while differing in his approach, concludes similarly that Julien is struggling for individuation, that the parricide represents the birth of the ego ("The Individuation Process," Berg et al., *Saint/Oedipus* 68-128). In Michel Grimaud's view, the parricide corresponds to a paradoxical denial of the parents' sexuality; Grimaud suggests that the parricide is an expression of his repressed rage against them ("A

'Ferocious Heart': Love and Parricide in *Saint Julian*," Berg et al., *Saint/Oedipus* 129-75). Shoshana Felman sees Julien as living the paradox of his dual nature to the end, at once innocent and guilty ("Flaubert's Signature: *The Legend of Saint Julian the Hospitable*," Naomi Schor and Henry F. Majewski, *Flaubert and Postmodernism* [Lincoln and London: U of Nebraska P, 1984] 46-74). Jean-Paul Sartre's discussion of *Saint Julien* pinpoints just what strikes the reader as so peculiar and disturbing about Julien's character. According to Sartre, what attracted Flaubert to the legend in the first place is the portrayal of radical origi-nal Evil, Julien's cruelty, as "a necessary condition of Good." And when Evil is radical, says Sartre, "one cannot work one's way out of it" ("The Family Idiot," Berg et al., *Saint/Oedipus* 176-202). What interests and irks Sartre about Flaubert's character, however, is that Julien is never really good and yet "he achieves his salvation." He achieves it, moreover, not in spite of his parricide "but directly *because of it*." For Sartre, Julien is a criminal, not a saint; Julien is egotistical and cruel to the end, and he gives no sign of having really changed or of feeling remorse. Although Sartre's argument is full of insight, insights which the present study will acknowledge in the course of the discussion, Sartre remains indifferent to Flaubert's aesthetic concerns. His interest in Flaubert the man, the type of the nineteenth-century writer, makes him neglect the character's com-plexity and Flaubert's irony. My work shares Sartre's conclusion that Julien's conversion, indeed his saintliness, is a sham, yet gives more space than Sartre's work does to framing and grounding this suspicion in Flaubert's aesthetics. It is my view that Flaubert is conscious of writing a narrative that works equally well as a straight and subversive story of "sainthood."

[14]   Moskos does not interpret the scene in the chapel as an aggression directed against the parents but as a sign that the state of unity with the parents has been shattered, that Julien, metaphorically represented by the mouse, has eliminated himself from what was a "charmed experience." Grimaud suggests that to Julien, the mouse "symbolizes" all that he wishes to be but cannot be; the mouse is free where he is not. Based on the white coloring of the mouse and its association with the church, Shoshana Felman identifies it with the mother.

[15]   Michel Grimaud makes an interesting commentary on the wife's advice to Julien to go out hunting: "When Julian finally tells his wife his horrible secret . . . she reasons *very convincingly* ("en raisonnant très bien,") that he must be wrong. There is much obvious irony in this phrase, yet its impact should not be reduced to dramatic irony. It functions also as an explicit indicator of how not to read *Saint Julian* ; if we insist on reasoning and attributing chance events to chance rather than to meaningful poetic 'fate' (cf. the parricide) we are missing the literary aspect of the narrative, its inclusion in a world of meanings" (Berg et al., *Saint/Oedipus* 147).

16   John O'Connor suggests that the two passages are radically different. In the goat episode, Julien's fall and the figure of the cross that his body takes is a chance accident. However, in the scene in church, he consciously places his body in the form of a cross. "Here Julien himself has constructed the emblematic situation, and in perfect consciousness of what he is doing" (819).

17   The reference to partridge (*perdrix*) is Flaubert's invention; there is no reference to these birds in the medieval and Romantic versions of the story of Saint Julien or in the stained-glass window of the cathedral at Rouen. The fact that the word *perdrix* in French is a feminine noun and that the moneme *per* brings to mind the word for father (*père*) is suggestive. However, what this scene brings out most strikingly is that Julien, who has managed to catch only one of the partridges, finds it long dead, and this is associated with the episode where Julien kills the spotted fawn; both animals represent an image and a sign of his abject nature. "With a number of symbols," Freud reminds us, "the comparison which underlies them is obvious. But again there are symbols in regard to which we must ask ourselves where we are to look for the common element, the 'tertium comparationis,' of the supposed comparison." Not all apparent symbols can or need to be integrated to construct the story (Sigmund Freud, *Introductory Lectures on Psychoanalysis* [New York: Norton, 1966] 151).

18   Diana Knight, in *Flaubert's Characters* (Cambridge: Cambridge UP, 1985) and John R. O'Connor relate the stained-glass window of the room where the parricide takes place and the stained-glass window the narrator mentions at the end of the story. For Knight, it is an example of *mise en abyme,* of representation within a representation (70-71). O'Connor's discussion is interesting, complicated, and unfortunately, somewhat obscure. The thrust of his argument and his conclusion, as I see it, is that the light entering the window multiplies, transforms, and annihilates the particularities of the components of the room; in so doing suggesting that any connection with a context other than itself is impossible (821).

19   Jean-Pierre Richard writes that the *goutte* ("bead") "naît d'une détente intérieure, elle perle à la surface d'un affaissement d'être; elle appaise momentanément la mollesse en la résumant et la rejetant à l'extérieur . . . Aussi la voit-on couler dans toutes les scènes de désir, d'ennui, de mort, à tous les moments où l'être à moitié défait a besoin de se rasssembler en une unité ultime, fût-elle liquide ou éphémère, avant de s'abandonner au néant . . . elle exprime, à l'arrivée au sol, toute la lourdeur du plaisir" ("La Création de la forme chez Flaubert," *Littérature et sensation* [Paris: Seuil, 1954] 137-38). The *goutte* Richard refers to is specific to a particular kind of liquid, say, water, sweat. It is meant to suggest the elemental process of "permeability," the process by which the interior (feelings, sensations, or what have you) passes through a "compact façade" and becomes visible

on its surface. In Flaubert, Richard points out, "la goutte se forme non à la source, mais au comble de la vie" (137).

[20]   In this passage, Czyba is referring more specifically to two other instances where images of women appear, only to disappear; namely, "les 'blancheurs (qui) traversent l'air,' lors de la vente aux enchères de *l'Education*" and the " 'poudre' des bottines d'Emma que le petit Justin 'regardait monter doucement dans un rayon de soleil' " (*La Femme dans les romans de Flaubert: Mythes et idéologie* [Lyon: Presses Universitaires de Lyon, 1983] 328). About *Saint Julien*, Czyba adds: "La séquence de la mère poignardée par Julien, alors qu'elle est couchée, avec le père, dans le lit de l'épouse soupçonnée d'infidélité, fait écho au rêve de la mère noyée des *Mémoires d'un fou*, c'est-à-dire de la mère punie d'avoir préféré le père rival et consenti à se dégrader par l'acte (ignominieux) de la chair; de la mère châtiée à cause de la 'scène primitive' " (276). She summarizes the case of Flaubert's oedipal scenario and his mysogyny in the following words: "Roman familial de Flaubert: fixation à une figure féminine de type maternel, permanence de la structure triangulaire . . . voyeurisme jaloux nécessaire à son entretien, attirance-répulsion pour le père rival, ambivalence à l'égard de la mère coupable de s'être dégradée dans l'acte de la chair, adoration de la figure maternelle, idéalisée en madone, fondée sur l'effroi de l'inceste qui justifie le recours constant à la contemplation fétichiste, au rêve et à la mythification de l'amour; dans le même temps, conditionnés par la métamorphose possible de Marie à Vénus, le ressentiment à l'égard de la femme aimée, la tentation de transgresser violemment l'interdit et la jouissance érotique exclusivement associée à une image dégradée de la fémininité." "Sadisme et idéalisation de la femme ont la même origine dans l'inconscient du créateur" (320 and 321).

[21]   Sartre calls attention to the episode where Julien mistakes his mother's cap for a stork, throws his javelin, and barely misses her. He writes: "Not for a moment did he doubt that it was a bird: we take his word for it. But since he now knows that parricide is indisolubly linked to his condemned hunter's instincts, isn't killing an animal, even once, accepting the murder of his parents?" (Berg et al., *Saint/Oedipus* 185).

[22]   See De Biasi's discussion of the parents/animals relationship in the drafts of *Saint Julien* in "L'Elaboration du problématique."

[23]   Grimaud interprets this fantasy as a rejection of procreation, especially, of sexuality: "Love and reference to women are patently absent from Julian's dreams: Adam is present but not Eve; the animals are by twos, but no mention of their being couples is to be found" (Berg et al., *Saint/Oedipus* 148).

[24]   Sartre, in Berg et al., *Saint/Oedipus* 191.

[25]   This is a view held by Sartre, O'Connor, and Moskos. O'Connor writes: "Julien has not changed at all, at least not in a narrowly literal sense; the change

comes rather from his having discovered a way of conceiving of himself, what Sartre calls the 'irréalisation' " (818).

26   Jacques Lacan, "Le Stade du miroir comme formateur de la fonction du Je," *Ecrits I* (Paris: Seuil, 1966) 89-97. It is true that in the classic Lacanian description of the mirror stage, the primary other is the specular image of the subject; in other words, the subject identifies with itself as other first before it proceeds to identify with the other as self. But in Julien's case, the subject never has a chance, so to speak, to identify with its image. This is just how devastating the role of the parents is in his case.

27   Jean Laplanche and J. B. Pontalis, *The Language of Psychoanalysis* (New York: Norton, 1974).

28   Lacan 90.

29   Berg, in Berg et al., *Saint/Oedipus* 66.

30   Moskos, in Berg et al., *Saint/Oedipus* 127.

31   Felman, "Flaubert's Signature" 55.

32   Berg suggests that the leper "represents a 'condensation' for Julian and a crystalization of the main currents of the story for the reader" (Berg et al., *Saint/Oedipus* 56).

33   Julia Kristeva, *Pouvoirs de l'horreur: Essai sur l'abjection* (Paris: Seuil, 1980).

34   Grimaud, in Berg et al., *Saint/Oedipus* 130.

35   Sartre, in Berg et al., *Saint/Oedipus* 196.

36   Sigmund Freud, *Moses and Monotheism* (New York: Vintage, 1939) lll.

37   The obvious parallel between Julien and Flaubert is biographical. Julien's parents recall Flaubert's own parents. Flaubert's father was a respected member of his community and of his profession. Like Julien's father, he was a worldly man. To the degree that Flaubert's parents strongly opposed his decision to undertake a literary career, and to the extent that Flaubert always sensed that his father was deeply disappointed in him, Julien's vocation and his triumph can be interpreted as Flaubert's assertion of the superiority of his craft over that of his father and as the expression of his liberation from his father's gaze.

38   Richard, "La création de la forme."

39   Flaubert, *Madame Bovary* 270.

40   For an analysis of Flaubert's relationship to classical aesthetics, both in theory and in practice, refer to Claire-Lise Tondeur, *Gustave Flaubert, critique: Thèmes et structures*.

41   Tondeur, 14-21 in particular.

42   Mitchell Greenburg, *Detours of Desire: Readings in the French Baroque* (Columbus: Ohio State UP, 1984) 9.

43   Greenburg 9-10.

44   Tondeur 15.

45   Richard 217.

CHAPTER 4: READING THE LANDSCAPE OF DESIRE AND WRITING

[1]   The following views were typical. For instance, Francisque Sarcey of the *Moniteur Universel* admitted to not understanding the "but," "l'utilité," and "la raison" for *Hérodias*. Georges de Saint Valry in *La Patrie* and Charles Bigot in *Le XIX siècle* admired both *Un Cœur simple* and *Saint Julien* but thought *Hérodias* confusing. Others found the story interesting. For instance, Hippolyte Taine was impressed by the historical accuracy of the story, and Karl Steen in the *Journal Officiel,* praised its suggestive rendition of local color.

[2]   Jeanne Bem points out that Iaokanann represents Flaubert himself and the "Word of Truth." "Le prophète est Parole de Vérité," she writes, in *Désir et savoir dans l'œuvre de Flaubert* (Neuchâtel, Switz.: Baconnière, 1979) 191.

[3]   Margaret G. Tillett has rightly suggested that the white horses "may be linked in the artist's mind with his conception of style" and that at this level they are "set in contrast with the no less violent impulse towards responsibility and repentance represented by the captive herald of Christianity in the next prison" ("An Approach to *Hérodias*," *French Studies* 21[1967]: 28).

[4]   Flaubert wrote Louise Colet: "Pourquoi dis-tu sans cesse . . . 'Poète de la forme!' c'est là le grand mot à outrage que les utilitaires jettent aux vrais artistes. Pour moi, tant qu'on ne m'aura pas, d'une phrase donnée, séparé la forme du fond, je soutiendrai que ce sont là deux mots vides de sens. Il n'y a pas de belles pensées sans belles formes, et réciproquement. La Beauté transsude de la forme dans le monde de l'Art, comme dans notre monde à nous [la littérature] il en sort la tentation, l'amour. De même que tu ne peux extraire d'un corps physique les qualités qui le constituent, c'est-à-dire couleur, étendue, solidité, sans le réduire à une abstraction creuse, sans le détruire en un mot, de même tu n'ôteras pas la forme de l'Idée, car l'Idée n'existe qu'en vertu de sa forme. Suppose une idée qui n'ait pas de forme, c'est impossible; de même qu'une forme qui n'exprime pas une idée. Voilà un tas de sottises sur lesquelles la critique vit" (1: 321). Thirty years later, while he was working on the *Trois contes,* Flaubert expressed the same thoughts to George Sand. She described him as interested only in the "surface" of art and not in its "content." He answered her in two long letters. I will quote from one of them: "Vous m'attristez un peu, chère maître, en m'attribuant des opinions esthétiques qui ne sont pas les miennes. Je crois que l'arrondissement de la phrase n'est rien. Mais que bien écrire est tout, parce que 'bien écrire c'est à la fois bien sentir, bien penser et bien dire' (Buffon). Le dernier terme est donc dépendant des deux autres puisqu'il faut sentir fortement afin de penser et penser pour exprimer . . . Ce souci de la beauté extérieure que vous me reprochez est pour moi *une méthode*. Quand je découvre une mauvaise assonance ou une répétition dans une de mes phrases, je suis sûr que je patauge dans le faux; à force

de chercher, je trouve l'expression juste qui était la seule et qui est, en même temps, l'harmonieuse. Le mot ne manque pas quand on possède l'idée" (7: 290).

⁵ Robert Chumbley points out that in the *Trois contes* "there is a clear growth in abstraction from the quasi-realistic setting of nineteenth-century France in *Un Cœur simple* through the medieval resurrection of *Saint Julien* to the pure archeology of form in *Hérodias*" ("An Enormity for Flaubert" 59). Victor Brombert refers to the "geometry" and "choreography" of form in *Hérodias* and suggests that "geometric figures," in spite of their "plastic and terrifying fixity," convey a disquieting psychological struggle" (*Novels of Flaubert* 256). Margaret Tillett compares the structure of the tale to an "architectural" structure and suggests that "*Hérodias* might be considered as an extreme example of the power of form to convey sense," that "certain points of Flaubert's structure take a weight of meaning" ("An Approach" 25).

See also my "Desire and Writing: An Allegorical Reading of Flaubert's *Hérodias,*" *Selected Proceedings 32nd Mountain Interstate Foreign Language Conference*, ed. Gregorio C. Martin (Winston-Salem: Wake Forest U, 1984) 153-58.

⁶ Richard 211-12.

⁷ Luce Irigaray, "The Politics of Difference," *French Feminist Thought* (Oxford: Basil Blackwell, 1987) 122.

⁸ Cited in Naomi Schor, *Breaking the Chain* 155.

⁹ See Charles Bernheimer's discussion of the *gueuloir* as Flaubert's identification with the female. Bernheimer writes: "Oral declamation integrates written language into the rhythms of being. Written marks are removed from their alien inscription on the page and made to live in their vocal rendition. Bellowing his words, identifying with a submissive woman, Flaubert seems to feel himself nourished by language, as if its constitutive possibilities were also his" (*Flaubert and Kafka* [New Haven: Yale UP, 1982] 58).

¹⁰ Cited in Paul Bourget, *Essais de psychologie contemporaine* (Paris: Plon, 1924) 129.

CONCLUSION: STRAIGHT AND SUSPECT TEXTS: A POETICS OF TRANSGRESSION

¹ On this subject, see Raymonde Debray-Genette's discussion in *Métamorphoses du récit* 160.

² René Girard, *Deceit, Desire, and the Novel; Self and Other in Literary Structure* (Baltimore: Johns Hopkins UP, 1976) 307.

³ On this subject, see Raymonde Debray-Genette's discussion in *Métamorphoses du récit* 87.

⁴ Peter Smith, *Public and Private Values: Studies in the Nineteenth-Century Novel* (Cambridge: Cambridge UP, 1984) 96.

⁵ Flaubert, "Notes de voyages," *Œuvres complètes* 2: 538.

⁶ Fredric Jameson, *The Political Unconscious: Narrative as a Socially Symbolic Act* (Ithaca: Cornell UP, 1981) 221.

⁷ Flaubert, "Hommage à Louis Bouilhet," *Œuvres complètes* 2: 763.

Bibliography and
Selected Works on *Trois contes*

Abel, Elizabeth. "Editor's Introduction." Special Issue: "Writing and Sexual Difference." *Critical Inquiry* 8 (Winter 1981): 173-78.

Bart, Benjamin. "D'où vient *Saint Julien*?" *Langages de Flaubert* (Actes du Colloque de London, Canada) Paris: Minard, 1976.

—————. *Flaubert*. Syracuse: Syracuse UP, 1967.

—————. "Flaubert and Hunting: 'La Légende de Saint Julien l'Hospitalier.'" *Nineteenth-Century French Studies* 4.1-2 (1975/76): 31-52.

—————. "The Moral of Flaubert's *Saint Julien*." *Romanic Review* 38 (Feb. 1947): 23-33.

—————. "Psyche into Myth: Humanity and Animality in Flaubert's *Saint Julien*." *Kentucky Romance Quarterly* 20 (1973): 317-42.

Bart, Benjamin, and Heidi Bart. "Space, Time, and Reality in Flaubert's 'Saint Julien.'" *Romanic Review* 59 (1968) 30-39.

Bart, Benjamin, and Robert F. Cook. *The Legendary Sources of Flaubert's Saint Julien*. Toronto and Buffalo: U of Toronto P, 1977.

Barthes, Roland. "L'Effet de réel." *Communications* 11 (1968): 88.

—————. "Flaubert et la phrase." *Le Degré zéro de l'écriture suivi de Nouveaux essais critiques*. Paris: Seuil, 1972.

—————. *Roland Barthes par Roland Barthes*. Paris: Seuil, 1986.

—————. *S/Z*. Paris: Seuil–Points, 1970.

Baudelaire, Charles. *Petits poèmes en prose*. Paris: Garnier–Flammarion, 1967.

Beaumont, Barbara. *Flaubert and Turgenev: A Friendship in Letters: The Complete Correspondence*. New York: Norton, 1985.

Bem, Jeanne. *Désir et savoir dans l'œuvre de Flaubert: Etudes de la Tentation de Saint Antoine*. Neuchâtel, Switz.: Baconière, 1979.

Berg, Elizabeth. "The Third Woman." Special Issue: "Cherchez la femme." *Diacritics* 12 (1982): 11- 20.

Berg, William, et al. *Saint/Oedipus: Psychocritical Approaches to Flaubert's Art.* Ithaca: Cornell UP, 1982.

Bernheimer, Charles. *Flaubert and Kafka: Studies in Psychopoetic Structure.* New Haven: Yale UP, 1982.

Bersani, Leo. *Baudelaire and Freud.* Berkeley: U of California P, 1977.

—————. "Flaubert and the Threats of the Imagination." *From Balzac to Beckett.* New York: Oxford UP, 1970. 140-91.

Bertrand, Marc. "Parole et silence dans les *Trois contes* de Flaubert." *Stanford French Review* 1.2 (1977): 191-203.

Bidney, Martin. "Parrots, Pictures, Rays, Perfumes: Epiphanies in George Sand and Flaubert." *Studies in Short Fiction* 22 (1985): 209-17.

Blanchot, Maurice. *Le Livre à venir.* Paris: Gallimard, 1959.

Blüher, Karl Alfred. "Ironie textuelle et intertextuelle dans les *Trois contes* de Flaubert." *Gustave Flaubert. Procédés narratifs et fondements épistémologiques.* Présenté par Alfonso de Toro. Tübingen, Ger.: Gunter Narr, 1987.

Bonaccorso, Giovanni. *Corpus Flaubertianum I, Un Cœur simple.* Paris: Société d'Edition "Les Belles Lettres," 1983.

—————. "L'Edition des manuscrits d'‘Un Cœur simple.’" *Cahiers de L'Association Internationale des Etudes Françaises* [Paris] 33 (May 1981): 171-86.

—————. "Elle chancela, et fut obligée de s'asseoir." *Rivista di Letterature Moderne e Comparate* 36 (1983): 133-56.

—————. "L'Influence de l'Orient dans les *Trois contes.*" *Amis de Flaubert* 50 (May 1977): 9-21.

—————. "Science et fiction: Le Traitement des notes d'*Hérodias.*" *Flaubert, L'Autre: Pour Jean Bruneau.* Textes réunis par F. Lecercle et S. Messina. Lyon: Presses Universitaires de Lyon. 85-94.

Bonnefis, Philippe. "Exposition d'un perroquet." *Revue des Sciences Humaines* 181 (1981): 59-78.

Bonnet, G. "Fétichisme et exhibitionnisme chez un sujet féminin." *Psychanalyse à l'université* 2 (1977): 231- 57.

Bourget, Paul. "Gustave Flaubert." *Essais de psychologie contemporaine.* Paris: Plon, 1924.

Brombert, Victor. "Flaubert and the Temptation of the Subject." *Nineteenth-Century French Studies* 12.3 (Spring 1984): 280-96.

—————. *The Hidden Reader: Stendhal, Balzac, Hugo, Baudelaire, Flaubert.* Cambridge: Harvard UP, 1987.

—————. *The Novels of Flaubert: A Study of Themes and Techniques.* Princeton: Princeton UP, 1966.

Bureau, J. "A propos d'un 'Cœur simple.'" *Les Amis de Flaubert* 25 (Dec. 1964): 11-12.

―――――. "En marge du centennaire 'Un Cœur simple.'" *Les Amis de Flaubert* 48 (1976): 29-32; and *Les Amis de Flaubert* 49 (1976): 5-10.

Burke, Carolyn. "Rethinking the Maternal." *The Future of Difference.* Ed. Hester Eisenstein and Alice Jardine. Boston: Hall, 1980. 107-13.

Burns, C. A. "The Manuscript of Flaubert's *Trois contes.*" *French Studies* 8.4 (Oct. 1954): 297-325.

Butor, Michel. "A propos des 'Trois contes' et des trois pièces." *Improvisations sur Flaubert.* Paris: Littérature–Editions de la Différence, 1984. 171-90.

Cannon, J. H. "Flaubert's Documentation for 'Hérodias.'" *French Studies* 14 (1960): 325-39.

―――――. "Flaubert's Search for a Form in 'Hérodias.'" *Modern Language Review* 57 (1962): 195-203.

Carlut, Charles. *Concordance to Flaubert's "Trois contes."* New York: Garland, 1980.

Cento, A. "Il 'plan' primitivo di 'Un Cœur simple.'" *Studi Francesi* 5 (1961): 101-03.

Chambers, Ross. *Story and Situation: Narrative Seduction and the Power of Fiction.* Minneapolis: U of Minnesota P, 1984.

Chodorow, Nancy. *The Reproduction of Mothering.* Berkeley: U of California P, 1978.

Chumbley, Robert. "An Enormity for Flaubert: Exercises in Semiotic Foreplay." *Sub-Stance* 20 (1978): 59-67.

Cigada, S. "L'episodo del lebbroso in 'Saint Julien l'hospitalier' di Flaubert." *Aevum* 31 (1957): 465-91.

―――――. "I 'trois contes' nella storia dell'arte flaubertiana." *Contributi del Seminario di Filologia Moderna, Serie Francese* 2 (1961): 252-69.

Cixous, Hélène. "The Laugh of the Medusa." Trans. Keith Cohen and Paula Cohen. *Signs* 1.4 (Summer 1976): 875-93.

Culler, Jonathan. *Flaubert: The Uses of Uncertainty.* Ithaca: Cornell UP, 1974.

Czyba, Lucette. *La Femme dans les romans de Flaubert: Mythes et idéologie.* Lyon: Presses Universitaires de Lyon, 1983.

Dariosecq, L. "A propos de Loulou." *French Review* 31 (1957-58): 322-24.

De Biasi, Pierre-Marc. *Edition critique et génétique de "La Légende de Saint Julien l'Hospitalier."* Thèse de troisième cycle. Paris: Université de Paris VII, 1982. 947 ff.

―――――. "L'Elaboration du problématique dans *La Légende de Saint Julien l'Hospitalier.*" *Flaubert à l'œuvre.* Paris: Flammarion, 1980. 69-102.

De Biasi, Pierre-Marc. *Gustave Flaubert: Carnets de travail.* Edition critique et génétique établie par Pierre-Marc de Biasi. Paris: Balland, 1988.

Debray-Genette, Raymonde. "Du mode narratif dans les *Trois contes.*" *Littérature* 2 (May 1977): 39-62.

————. "Les Figures du récit dans *Un Cœur simple.*" *Poétique* 3 (1970): 348-64.

————. *Métamorphoses du récit: Autour de Flaubert.* Paris: Seuil, 1988.

————. "Profane and Sacred: Disorder of Utterance in *Trois contes.*" In Naomi Schor and Henry F. Majewski. *Flaubert and Postmodernism.* Lincoln and London: U of Nebraska P, 1984. 13-29.

————. "Re-présentation d'*Hérodias.*" *La Production de sens chez Flaubert* (Colloque de Cerisy). Paris: Union Générale d'Edition–10/18, 1975.

————. "La Technique romanesque de Flaubert dans *Un Cœur simple:* Etude de genèse." *Langages de Flaubert* (Actes du Colloque de London, Canada). Paris: Minard, 1976.

————. " 'Un Cœur simple' ou comment faire une fin: Etude des manuscrits." *Revue des Lettres Modernes* 703-06 (1984): 105-33.

De Man, Paul. *Allegories of Reading.* New Haven: Yale UP, 1979.

Denommé, Robert. "Félicité's View of Reality and the Nature of Flaubert's Irony in 'Un Cœur simple.' " *Studies in Short Fiction* 7 (1970): 573-81.

Derrida, Jacques. "La Mythologie blanche." *Poétique* 5 (1971): 1-52. Rpt. as "White Mythology: Metaphor in the Text of Philosophy." Trans. F. C. T. Moore. *New Literary History* 6.1 (Autumn 1974): 5-74.

Descharmes, René. " 'Saint Julien l'Hospitalier' et 'Pécopin.' " *Revue Biblio-Iconographique* (1905): 1-7, 67-75.

Di Stefano Palermo, Rosa M. "La descrizione di paesaggio in 'Un Cœur simple.' *Rivista di Letterature Moderne e Comparate* 32 (3 Sept. 1979): 181-94.

————. *Le varianti di "Un Cœur simple."* Messina: Ediziono A. Sfameni, 1984.

Donato, Eugenio. " 'A Mere Labyrinth of Letters' / Flaubert and the Quest for Fiction / A Montage." *MLN* 89.6 (1974): 885-910.

————. "The Ruins of Memory: Archeological Fragments and Textual Artifacts." *MLN* 93.4 (1978): 575-96.

Douyère, Sylvia. *Un Cœur simple de Gustave Flaubert.* Paris: La Pensée Universelle, 1974.

Dubuc, André. "La Critique rouennaise des 'Trois contes.' " *Les Amis de Flaubert* 48 (May 1976): 29-32.

Duckworth, Colin. "Flaubert and the Legend of Saint Julian: A Non-exclusive View of Sources." *French Studies* 22 (1968): 107-13.

Felman, Shoshana. "Flaubert's Signature: 'The Legend of Saint Julian the Hospitable.'" In Naomi Schor and Henry F. Majewski. *Flaubert and Postmodernism*. Lincoln and London: U of Nebraska P, 1984. 46-75.

————. "Illusion réaliste et répétition romanesque." *Change* 16/17 (1973): 286-97.

Flaubert, Gustave. *Correspondance*. 9 vols. Paris: Conard, 1926-33.

————. *Œuvres complètes*. 2 vols. Paris: Seuil–L'Intégrale, 1964.

————. *Le Second Volume de Bouvard et Pécuchet*. Paris: Denoël, 1966.

————. *Trois contes*. Ed. Edouard Maynial. Paris: Garnier, 1969.

Flaubert à l'œuvre. Paris: Flammarion, 1980.

Fletcher, John. *A Critical Commentary on Flaubert's "Trois contes."* New York: Macmillan–St. Martin's, 1968.

Foucault, Michel. *The History of Sexuality*. Trans. Robert Hurley. New York: Vintage, 1980.

————. *Les Mots et les choses*. Paris: Gallimard, 1966.

Fournier, L. "Flaubert et le 'nouveau roman': Un Cas de paternité douteuse." *Les Amis de Flaubert* 52 (May 1978): 13-18.

Freud, Sigmund. *The Complete Psychological Works*. Standard ed. Ed. and trans. James Strachey. 24 vols. London: Hogarth, 1953-74.

————. *Moses and Monotheism*. New York: Vintage, 1939.

Frølich, Juliette. "Battements d'un simple cœur: Stéréographie et sonorisation dans 'Un Cœur simple' de Flaubert." *Littérature* 12.46 (May 1982): 28-40.

Genette, Gérard. "Démotivation in 'Hérodias.'" In Naomi Schor and Henry F. Majewski. *Flaubert and Postmodernism*. Lincoln and London: U of Nebraska P, 1984. 192-201.

————. "Métonymie chez Proust." *Figures III*. Paris: Seuil, 1972.

————. "Silences de Flaubert." *Figures*. Paris: Seuil, 1966. 223-43.

Ginsburg, Michal Peled. *Flaubert Writing: A Study in Narrative Strategies*. Stanford: Stanford UP, 1986.

Goncourt, Edmond and Jules de. *Journal*. 22 vols. Monaco: Editions de l'Imprimerie Nationale de Monaco, 1956-58.

Greenburg, Mitchell. *Detours of Desire: Readings in the French Baroque*. Columbus: Ohio State UP, 1984.

Haig, Stirling. *Flaubert and the Gift of Speech*. Cambridge: Cambridge UP, 1986.

————. *The Madame Bovary Blues: The Pursuit of Illusion in Nineteenth-Century French Fiction*. Baton Rouge: Louisiana State UP, 1987.

————. "The Substance of Illusion in Flaubert's 'Un Cœur simple.'" *Stanford French Review* 7 (1983): 301-15.

Hanoulle, Marie-Julie. "Quelques manifestations du discours dans les *Trois contes*." *Poétique* 10 (1972): 41-49.

Hansen, Kristen Lund. "*St. Julien l'Hospitalier* ou l'Œdipe de Flaubert, ou encore: Le Bestiaire de 'Trois contes.'" *(Pré) Publications* [Aarhus] No. 1 (1973): 7-18.

Hausmann, Frank-Rutger. " 'Trois contes'—drei Epochen, drei Gattungen, drei Stile—oder Flaubert und die 'Trinität.'" *Romantische Zeitschrift für Literatur-geschichte* 8 (1984): 163-76.

Herrmann, Claudine. *Les Voleuses de langue*. Paris: Edition des Femmes, 1976.

Herschberg-Pierrot, Anne. "Le Cliché dans Bouvard et Pécuchet." *Flaubert et le comble de l'art: Nouvelles recherches sur Bouvard et Pécuchet*. Paris: Société d'Edition d'Enseignement Supérieur, 1981.

Humphries, Jefferson. "Flaubert's Parrot and Huysmans's Cricket: The Decadence of Realism and the Realism of Decadence." *Stanford French Studies* 11 (Fall 1987): 323-30.

Irigaray, Luce. *Ce sexe qui n'en est pas un*. Paris: Minuit, 1977.

——. *Speculum de l'autre femme*. Paris: Minuit, 1974.

Issacharoff, Michael. *L'Espace et la nouvelle*. Paris: José Corti, 1976.

Jackson, Ernest. *The Critical Reception of Gustave Flaubert in the United States 1860-1960*. The Hague: Mouton, 1966.

Jameson, Fredric. "Flaubert's Libidinal Historicism: 'Trois contes.'" In Naomi Schor and Henry F. Majewski. *Flaubert and Postmodernism*. Lincoln and London: U of Nebraska P, 1984. 76-83.

——. *The Political Unconscious: Narrative as a Socially Symbolic Act*. Ithaca: Cornell UP, 1981.

Janeway, Elizabeth. "On 'Female Sexuality.'" In Jean Strouse, ed. *Women and Analysis*. New York: Grossman, 1974.

Jasinski, René. "Le Sens des *Trois contes*." In R. J. Cormier and V. T. Holmes. *Essays in Honor of Louis Francis Solano*. Chapel Hill: U of North Carolina P, 1970. 117-28.

——. "Sur le 'Saint Julien l'Hospitalier' de Flaubert." *Revue d'Histoire de la Philosophie* 15 Apr. 1935: 156-72.

Johansen, Svend. "Ecriture d' 'Un Cœur simple.'" *Revue Romane* 2 (1967): 108-20.

——. "Ecriture et fiction dans 'Saint Julien l'Hospitalier.'" *Revue Romane* 3 (1968): 30-51.

Knight, Diana. *Flaubert's Characters: The Language of Illusion*. Cambridge: Cambridge UP, 1985.

Kofman, Sarah. *L'Enigme de la femme: La Femme dans les textes de Freud*. Paris: Galilée, 1980.

Kristeva, Julia. *Desire in Language: A Semiotic Approach to Literature and Art.* New York: Columbia UP, 1980.

——. *Histoires d'amour.* Paris: Denoël–Folio, 1983.

——. *Pouvoirs de l'horreur: Essai sur l'abjection.* Paris: Seuil, 1980.

Lacan, Jacques. *Ecrits I.* 2 vols. Paris: Seuil, 1966.

Langages de Flaubert (Actes du Colloque de London, Canada). Paris: Minard, 1976.

Laplanche, Jean, and J. B. Pontalis. *The Language of Psychoanalysis.* New York: Norton, 1974.

Laubenthal, Wilhelm. "Flaubert: 'Un Cœur simple': La Structure de l'œuvre." *Die Neueren Sprachen* 17 (1968): 438-43.

Leal, R. B. "Spatiality and Structure in Flaubert's 'Hérodias.'" *Modern Language Review* 80 (1985): 810-16.

Lecointre-Dupont, G. F. G. *"La Légende de Saint Julien le Pauvre, d'après un manuscrit de la Bibliothèque d'Alençon."* *Mémoire de la Société des Antiquaires de l'Ouest,* 1838. (Published at Poitiers, 1839.)

Lemoine-Luccioni, Eugénie. *Partage des femmes.* Paris: Seuil–Points, 1976.

Léon, Yvonne. "Flaubert: 'Un Cœur simple.'" *L'Ecole des Lettres* 15 Mar. 1982: 33-50.

Levin, Harry. "Flaubert." *The Gates of Horn.* New York: Oxford UP, 1966. 214-304.

Lottman, Herbert. *Flaubert: A Biography.* Boston: Little, 1989.

Lowe, Margaret. "'Hérodias,' the Second Empire and 'La Tête d'Orphée.'" *French Studies Bulletin* 3 (Summer 1982): 6-8.

——. "'Rendre plastique . . .': Flaubert's Treatment of the Female Principle in 'Hérodias.'" *Modern Language Review* 78 (1983): 551-58.

——. *Towards the Real Flaubert.* Oxford: Clarendon, 1984.

Lytle, Andrew. "Three Ways of Making a Saint: A Reading of 'Three Tales' by Flaubert." *The Southern Review* 20 (1984): 495-527.

Madse, Börge Gedsö. "Realism, Irony, and Compassion in Flaubert's *Un Cœur simple.*" *French Review* 27 (1954): 253-58.

Malinowski, Wieslaw. "'Hérodias' de Flaubert et 'Thaïs' de France: Quelques affinités artistiques et intellectuelles." *Studia Romanica Posnaniensia* 7 (1981): 29-38.

Mankin, P. A. "Additional Irony in 'Un Cœur simple.'" *French Review* 35 (1961/ 62): 411.

Maranini, Lorenza. *"La Légende de Saint-Julien."* *Les Amis de Flaubert* 6 (1955): 2-15.

Marsh, Leonard. "Visual Perception in Flaubert's 'Un Cœur simple.'" *Studies in Short Fiction* 23 (1986): 185-89.

Marotin, François. "'Les Trois contes': Un Carrefour dans l'œuvre de Flaubert." *Frontières du conte.* Ed. François Marotin. Paris: Etudes du CNRS, 1982. 111-18.

Marston, Jane E. "Narration as Subject in Flaubert's *La Légende de Saint Julien l'Hospitalier.*" *Nineteenth-Century French Studies* 14.3&4 (Spring-Summer 1986): 341-45.

Massey, Irving. "Flaubert and 'La Légende de Saint-Julien l'Hospitalier.' " *The Gaping Pig: Literature and Metamorphosis.* Berkeley: U of California P, 1976. 156-84.

Miller, Nancy K., ed. *The Politics of Gender.* New York: Columbia UP, 1986.

Moi, Toril, ed. *French Feminist Thought: A Reader.* Oxford: Basil Blackwell, 1987.

Neefs, Jacques. "Le Récit de l'édifice des croyances: 'Trois contes.' " *Flaubert: La Dimension du texte: Communications du Congrès présenté par P. M. Wetherill.* Manchester, Eng.: Manchester UP, 1982. 121-40.

Nykrog, Per. "Les 'Trois contes' dans l'évolution de la structure thématique chez Flaubert." *Romantisme* 6 (1973): 55-66.

O'Connor, John. "Flaubert: *Trois contes* and the Figure of the Double Cone." *PMLA* 95.5 (Oct. 1980): 812-26.

Pendergast, Christopher. "Flaubert: The Stupidity of Mimesis." *The Order of Mimesis: Balzac, Stendhal, Nerval, Flaubert.* Cambridge: Cambridge UP, 1986.

————. "Madame Aubain's Barometer: Or, The Referential Illusion." *Paragraph* 5 (Mar. 1985): 27-55.

Peterson, Carla. " 'The Trinity' in Flaubert's *Trois contes*: Deconstructing History." *French Forum* 8 (1983): 243-58.

Pilkington, A. E. "Point of View in Flaubert's 'La Légende de St. Julien.' " *French Studies* 29 (1975): 266-79.

Planque, Joël. "La Poésie des 'Trois contes.' " *Etudes Normandes* (1981): fasc. 3, pp. 57-64.

Porter, Laurence. *Critical Essays on Gustave Flaubert.* Boston: Hall, 1986.

La Production de sens chez Flaubert. Paris: Union Générale d'Editions, 1975.

Proust, Marcel. "A propos du 'style' de Flaubert." *Chroniques.* Paris: Gallimard, 1927. 193-211.

Raitt, A. W. "The Composition of Flaubert's 'Saint Julien l'Hospitalier.' " *French Studies* 19.4 (1965): 358-69.

————. "Flaubert and the Art of the Short Story." *Essay by Divers Hands* 38 (1975): 112-26.

Rand, Nicholas. "Texte passeur: Dialogues intratextuels dans 'La Légende de Saint Julien l'Hospitalier' de Flaubert." *Romance Notes* 77 (1986): 42 -55.

Reish, Joseph G. " 'Those Who See Good' in Flaubert's 'Trois contes.' " *Renascence* 36 (1983-84): 219-29.

Ricardou, Jean. *Le Nouveau Roman.* Paris: Seuil, 1973.

————. *Pour une théorie du Nouveau Roman.* Paris: Seuil, 1971.

Richard, Jean-Pierre. "La Création de la forme chez Flaubert." *Littérature et sensation.* Paris: Seuil, 1954. 119-219.

Robertson, Jane. "The Structure of 'Hérodias.'" *French Studies* 36 (1982): 171-82.

Sachs, Murray. "Flaubert's *Trois contes:* The Reconquest of Art." *L'Esprit Créateur* 10 (1970): 62-74.

Sartre, Jean-Paul. *L'Idiot de la famille: Gustave Flaubert de 1821 à 1857.* 3 vols. Paris: Gallimard, 1971.

Schapira, Charlotte. "La Relative introduite par et dans les *Trois Contes* de Flaubert." *Romance Notes* 26.1 (Fall 1985): 22-26.

Schor, Naomi. *Breaking the Chain: Women, Theory and French Realist Fiction.* New York: Columbia UP, 1985.

——————. "Female Fetishism: The Case of George Sand." *Poetics Today* 6.1/2 (1985): 301-10.

——————. *Reading in Detail: Aesthetics and the Feminine.* New York: Methuen, 1987.

Schor, Naomi, and Henry F. Majewski. *Flaubert and Postmodernism.* Lincoln and London: U of Nebraska P, 1984.

Schwob, Marcel. "Saint Julien l'Hospitalier." *Spicilège.* Paris: Au sans Pareil, 1920.

Selvin, Susan Cauley. "Spatial Form in Flaubert's 'Trois contes.'" *Romanic Review* 74 (1983): 202-20.

Shepler, Frederic. "La Mort et la rédemption dans les *Trois contes* de Flaubert." *Neophilologus* 56 (1972): 407-16.

Sherzer, Dina. "Narrative Figures in *La Légende de Saint Julien l'Hospitalier.*" *Genre* 7 (1974): 54-70.

Showalter, English, Jr. "*Un Cœur simple* as an Ironic Reply to Bernardin de Saint-Pierre." *French Review* 40 (1966/67): 47-55.

Smith, H. L. "Echec et illusion dans 'Un Cœur simple.'" *French Review* 39 (1965): 36-48.

Smith, Peter. *Public and Private Values: Studies in the Nineteenth-Century Novel.* Cambridge: Cambridge UP, 1984.

Stanton, Domna C. "Difference on Trial: A Critique of the Maternal Metaphor in Cixous, Irigaray, and Kristeva." *The Poetics of Gender.* Ed. Nancy K. Miller. New York: Columbia UP, 1986. 157-82.

Starkie, Enid. *Flaubert the Master: A Critical Biographical Study (1856-1880).* 2 vols. New York: Antheneum, 1971.

Steele, Meili H. *Realism and the Drama of Reference: Strategies of Representation in Balzac, Flaubert, and James.* University Park and London: Pennsylvania State UP, 1988.

Strike, W. N. "Art et poésie dans 'Saint Julien.'" *French Studies in Southern Africa* 5 (1976): 52-63.

Suffel, Jacques. *Flaubert*. Paris: Editions Universitaires, 1958.

Suleiman, Susan Rubin. "(Re)Writing the Body: The Politics and Poetics of Female Eroticism." Special Issue: "The Female Body in Western Culture: Semiotic Perspectives." *Poetics Today* 6.1-2 (1985): 43-65.

Terdiman, Richard. *Discourse/Counter-Discourse: The Theory and Practice of Symbolic Resistance in Nineteenth-Century France*. Ithaca: Cornell UP, 1985.

Thibaudet, Albert. *Gustave Flaubert 1821-1880*. Paris: Plon, 1922.

Thompson, Patrice. "La Méthode de composition de Flaubert dans 'Hérodias.' " *Les Actes de la Journée Flaubert, Université de Fribourg, 1980*. Fribourg: Editions Universitaires, 1981. 49-63.

Tillet, Margaret. "An Approach to *Hérodias*." *French Studies* 21 (1967): 24-31.

Tondeur, Claire-Lise. *Gustave Flaubert, critique: Thèmes et structures*. Purdue University Monographs in Romance Languages. Amsterdam: Benjamins, 1984.

Toro, Alfonso de. *Gustave Flaubert: Procédés narratifs et fondements épistémologiques*. Tübingen, Ger.: Gunter Narr, 1987.

Travail de Flaubert. Réalisé sous la direction de Gérard Genette et Tzvetan Todorov. Paris: Seuil, 1983.

Turnell, Martin. "The Weaknesses of *Madame Bovary*." In *Madame Bovary*. By Gustave Flaubert. Ed. Leo Bersani. New York: Bantam, 1972.

Uitti, Karl. "Figures and Fiction: Linguistic Deformation and the Novel 'Un Cœur simple.' " *Kentucky Romance Quarterly* 17 (1970): 149-69.

Unwin, T. A. "La Présence de Flaubert dans les *Trois contes*." *Les Amis de Flaubert* 53 (1978): 12-20.

Valéry, Paul. "La Tentation de (saint) Flaubert." *Variété V*. Paris: Gallimard, 1944.

Vinaver, Eugène. "La Légende de Saint Julien l'Hospitalier." *Bulletin de l'Académie Royale de Langue et de Littérature* 48 (1970): 107-22.

————. *The Rise of Romance*. London: Oxford UP, 1971.

Wake, C. H. "Symbolism in Flaubert's 'Hérodias': An Interpretation." *Forum for Modern Language Studies* 4 (1968): 322-29.

Whitaker, Jeanne T., and Carlota Smith. "Some Significant Omissions: Ellipses in Flaubert's 'Un Cœur simple.' " *Language and Style* 17 (1984): 251-72.

Willemart, Philippe. "Le Désir du narrateur et l'apparition de Jean-Baptiste dans le manuscrit d' 'Hérodias.' " *Littérature* 13.52 (Dec. 1983): 112-22.

Willenbrink, G. *The Dossiers of Flaubert's Un Cœur simple*. Amsterdam: Rodopi, 1976.

Wing, Nathaniel. *The Limits of Narrative: Essays on Baudelaire, Flaubert, Rimbaud*. New York: Cambridge UP, 1986.

Winner, Anthony. "Flaubert's Félicité." *Mosaïc* 10.1 (1976): 57-68.

Zavitzianos, G. "Fetishism and Exhibitionism in the Female and Their Relationship to Psychopathology and Kleptomania." *International Journal of Psycho-Analysis* 52 (1971): 97-305.

Index

*References to the principal treatment of a subject
follow the entry word in boldface type.*

Animism, 41, 44
Auerbach, Erich, 29

Balzac, Honoré de, 7, 83, 112, 121
Barthes, Roland, 4
Baudelaire, Charles, 3, 8
Beckett, Samuel, 4
Berg, William, 78
Bersani, Leo, 64
Bertrand, Marc, 21
Bouilhet, Louis, 8, 83; *Hommage à Louis Bouilhet,* 109, 125, 127
Bouvard et Pécuchet, 3, 14, 15, 17-20, 23-24, 61, 81, 82, 116, 118, 121, 123, 124
Brombert, Victor, 21-22
Bruézière, Maurice, 20-21
Brunetière, Ferdinand, 20-21
Butor, Michel, 4, 11

Charpentier, Georges, 60-61
Chateaubriand, François-René de, 83

Chumbley, Robert, 21
Cixous, Hélène, 43-44, 47, 49, 56-57
Classicism, 6-8, 14-15, 85, 87, 100, 107, 111, 119
Cœur simple, Un , **25-58;** 1-2, 11, 14, 18-19, 21-22, 27, 59, 62-63, 65, 69, 70, 79, 81, 89, 90, 100, 107, 112, 113, 114-17, 119, 124, 128
Colet, Louise, 8, 10, 25, 29, 61, 83-84
Culler, Jonathan, 4, 5, 9, 30
Czyba, Lucette, 34, 42, 73

Daudet, Alphonse, 3
Debray-Genette, Raymonde, 22, 29
De Commanville, Caroline, 13, 20, 41
De Man, Paul, 42
Derrida, Jacques, 42
Description, 29, 32-33
Dictionnaire des idées reçues, 24, 61
Du Camp, Maxime, 60, 83

Education sentimentale, L' , 3, 82, 116

Felman, Shoshana, 47, 78
Fetish, 47, 50-54, 56, 79
Fish, Stanley, 10
Fletcher, John, 21-22
Foucault, Michel, 124
Freud, Sigmund, 50-53, 77, 80

Genette, Gérard, 4,5, 42
Genettes, Madame Roger des, 20, 48, 94
Gide, André, 109
Ginsberg, Michal Peled, 27, 59
Girard, René, 113
Greenberg, Mitchell, 85
Grimaud, Michel, 79
Gueuloir, 15, 104, 105; voice, 104, 105

Hérodias, **89-107**; 1, 12, 15, 18-19, 21-22, 81, 111, 113, 116, 118, 128-29
Hugo, Victor, 7

Impressionism, 7
Irigaray, Luce, 43, 44, 47, 49-50, 56-57, 103
Iser, Wolfgang, 12
Issacharoff, Michael, 21

Jameson, Fredric, 120
Janeway, Elizabeth, 53

Kristeva, Julia, 43, 47, 78, 79, 88, 104

La Bruyère, Jean de, 8, 110
Lacan, Jacques, 71, 76-77
Language, 4-7, 10, 15; in *Un Cœur simple,* 39, 43-44, 49, 52; in *Saint Julien,* 84, 86-88, 124-25; in *Hérodias,* 89, 91, 95, 98, 101, 103, 105, 107
Lecointre-Dupont, G. F. G., 59, 60, 65
Leconte de Lisle, Charles-Marie-René, 128
Levin, Harry, 21
Lowe, Margaret, 23

Madame Bovary, 1-3, 13, 22, 38, 40, 55, 82, 83, 84, 113, 121; Emma, 1,2, 40, 53, 62, 63, 120
Mallarmé, Stéphane, 4, 7, 8, 47
Maupassant, Guy de, 104
Michelet, Jules, 9
Mimetism, 50
Moskos, George, 76, 78

Nature, 20, 31-32, 54, 66, 92-93, 96, 101, 103
Nykrog, Per, 21

O'Connor, John, 21,

Par les champs et par les grèves, 32
Poetry, 6-10, 55, 82, 88, 107
Prose, 6-8, 10, 82, 88, 107
Proust, Marcel, 6, 8-9, 42

Racine, Jean, 100
Reader, 12-13

Ricardou, Jean, 4
Richard, Jean-Pierre, 101
Rimbaud, Arthur, 7, 8, 107, 119
Robbe-Grillet, Alain, 4

Saint Julien l'Hospitalier, **59-88**; 1,
    12, 14, 17-18, 21, 27, 89, 90, 100,
    107, 112, 114-16, 124-27, 129
Saint-Pierre, Bernardin de, 37
Salammbô, 1, 21, 82
Sand, George [*pseud. of* Aurore Dupin],
    3, 8, 18-19, 26, 119
Sarraute, Nathalie, 6
Sartre, Jean-Paul, 74, 80, 83
Smith, Peter, 116
Starkie, Enid, 64
Style, 8, 9, 11, 13; feminin, 56-57,
    81-84, 99-100, 102, 107, 111, 125
Suffel, Jacques, 21

Tentation de Saint Antoine, La, 1-3,
    18, 82-83
Thibaudet, Albert, 8, 21, 29
Tillet, Margaret, 21
Tondeur, Claire-Lise, 85, 86
Turgenev, Ivan, 8, 18, 104

Unity, 1, 9, 12-15, 21-22, 43, 83, 85,
    110

Valéry, Paul, 122
Violence, 39
Voyages aux Pyrénées et en Corse,
    32, 60

Writing process, 3, 6, 14-15, 83, 87-
    88, 98, 100, 103, 105-06, 125

Zola, Emile, 3, 7, 20

Since its inception in 1980, PURDUE UNIVERSITY MONOGRAPHS IN ROMANCE LANGUAGES has acquired a distinguished reputation for its exacting standards and valuable contributions to Romance scholarship. The collection contains critical studies of literary or philological importance in the areas of Peninsular, Latin American, or French literature or language. Also included are occasional critical editions of important texts from these literatures. Among the authors are some of the finest of today's writers from both the new generation of scholars and the ranks of more established members of the profession. Writing in English, French, or Spanish, the authors address their subjects with insight and originality in books of approximately 200 pages. All volumes are printed on acid-free paper.

INQUIRIES CONCERNING THE SUBMISSION OF MANUSCRIPTS should be directed to the General Editor, Howard Mancing, Stanley Coulter Hall, Purdue University, West Lafayette, Indiana 47907 USA.

Available from

1. John R. Beverley: *Aspects of Góngora's "Soledades."* Amsterdam, 1980. xiv, 139 pp. Cloth.
2. Robert Francis Cook: *"Chanson d'Antioche," chanson de geste: Le Cycle de la Croisade est-il épique?* Amsterdam, 1980. viii, 107 pp. Cloth.
3. Sandy Petrey: *History in the Text: "Quatrevingt-Treize" and the French Revolution.* Amsterdam, 1980. viii, 129 pp. Cloth.
4. Walter Kasell: *Marcel Proust and the Strategy of Reading.* Amsterdam, 1980. x, 125 pp. Cloth.
5. Inés Azar: *Discurso retórico y mundo pastoral en la "Egloga segunda" de Garcilaso.* Amsterdam, 1981. x, 171 pp. Cloth.
6. Roy Armes: *The Films of Alain Robbe-Grillet.* Amsterdam, 1981. x, 216 pp. Cloth.
7. David M. Dougherty and Eugene B. Barnes, eds.: *Le "Galien" de Cheltenham.* Amsterdam, 1981. xxxvi, 203 pp. Cloth.
8. Ana Hernández del Castillo: *Keats, Poe, and the Shaping of Cortázar's Mythopoesis.* Amsterdam, 1981. xii, 135 pp. Cloth.
9. Carlos Albarracín-Sarmiento: *Estructura del "Martín Fierro."* Amsterdam, 1981. xx, 336 pp. Cloth.
10. C. George Peale et al., eds.: *Antigüedad y actualidad de Luis Vélez de Guevara: Estudios críticos.* Amsterdam, 1983. xii, 298 pp. Cloth.
11. David Jonathan Hildner: *Reason and the Passions in the "Comedias" of Calderón.* Amsterdam, 1982. xii, 119 pp. Cloth.
12. Floyd Merrell: *Pararealities: The Nature of Our Fictions and How We Know Them.* Amsterdam, 1983. xii, 170 pp. Cloth.
13. Richard E. Goodkin: *The Symbolist Home and the Tragic Home: Mallarmé and Oedipus.* Amsterdam, 1984. xvi, 203 pp. Paper.
14. Philip Walker: *"Germinal" and Zola's Philosophical and Religious Thought.* Amsterdam, 1984. xii, 157 pp. Paper.
15. Claire-Lise Tondeur: *Gustave Flaubert, critique: Thèmes et structures.* Amsterdam, 1984. xiv, 119 pp. Paper.
16. Carlos Feal: *En nombre de don Juan (Estructura de un mito literario).* Amsterdam, 1984. x, 175 pp. Paper.
17. Robert Archer: *The Pervasive Image: The Role of Analogy in the Poetry of Ausiàs March.* Amsterdam, 1985. xii, 220 pp. Paper.
18. Diana Sorensen Goodrich: *The Reader and the Text: Interpretative Strategies for Latin American Literatures.* Amsterdam, 1986. xii, 150 pp. Paper.

19. Lida Aronne-Amestoy: *Utopía, paraíso e historia: inscripciones del mito en García Márquez, Rulfo y Cortázar.* Amsterdam, 1986. xii, 167 pp. Paper.
20. Louise Mirrer-Singer: *The Language of Evaluation: A Sociolinguistic Approach to the Story of Pedro el Cruel in Ballad and Chronicle.* Amsterdam, 1986. xii, 128 pp. Paper.
21. Jo Ann Marie Recker: *"Appelle-moi 'Pierrot'": Wit and Irony in the "Lettres" of Madame de Sévigné.* Amsterdam, 1986. x, 128 pp. Paper.
22. J. H. Matthews: *André Breton: Sketch for an Early Portrait.* Amsterdam, 1986. xii, 176 pp. Paper.
23. Peter V. Conroy, Jr.: *Intimate, Intrusive, and Triumphant: Readers in the "Liaisons dangereuses."* Amsterdam, 1987. xii, 139 pp. Paper.
24. Mary Jane Stearns Schenck: *The Fabliaux: Tales of Wit and Deception.* Amsterdam, 1987. xiv, 168 pp. Paper.
25. Joan Tasker Grimbert: *"Yvain" dans le miroir: Une Poétique de la réflexion dans le "Chevalier au lion" de Chrétien de Troyes.* Amsterdam, 1988. xii, 226 pp. Cloth and paper.
26. Anne J. Cruz: *Imitación y transformación: el petrarquismo en la poesía de Boscán y Garcilaso de la Vega.* Amsterdam, 1988. x, 156 pp. Cloth and paper.
27. Alicia G. Andreu: *Modelos dialógicos en la narrativa de Benito Pérez Galdós.* Amsterdam, 1989. xvi, 126 pp. Cloth and paper.
28. Milorad R. Margitić, ed.: *Le Cid: Tragi-comédie.* By Pierre Corneille. A critical edition. Amsterdam, 1989. lxxxvi, 302 pp. Cloth and paper.
29. Stephanie A. Sieburth: *Reading "La Regenta": Duplicitous Discourse and the Entropy of Structure.* Amsterdam, 1990. viii, 127 pp. Cloth and paper.
30. Malcolm K. Read: *Visions in Exile: The Body in Spanish Literature and Linguistics: 1500-1800.* Amsterdam, 1990. xii, 211 pp. Cloth and paper.
31. María Alicia Amadei-Pulice: *Calderón y el Barroco: exaltación y engaño de los sentidos.* Amsterdam, 1990. xii, 258 pp., 33 ills. Cloth and paper.
32. Lou Charnon-Deutsch: *Gender and Representation: Women in Spanish Realist Fiction.* Amsterdam, 1990. xiv, 205 pp., 6 ills. Cloth and paper.
33. Thierry Boucquey: *Mirages de la farce: Fête des fous, Bruegel et Molière.* Amsterdam, 1991. xviii, 145 pp., 9 ills. Cloth.
34. Elżbieta Skłodowska: *La parodia en la nueva novela hispanoamericana (1960-1985).* Amsterdam, 1991. xx, 219 pp. Cloth.
35. Julie Candler Hayes: *Identity and Ideology: Diderot, Sade, and the Serious Genre.* Amsterdam, 1991. xiv, 186 pp. Cloth.
36. Aimée Israel-Pelletier: *Flaubert's Straight and Suspect Saints: The Unity of "Trois contes."* Amsterdam, 1991. xii, 165 pp. Cloth.